THE
MILDENHALL BRANCH

'E4' No. 7504 at Mildenhall with a train for Cambridge c.1932.

Dr. I. C. Allen

THE
MILDENHALL BRANCH

PETER PAYE

WILD SWAN PUBLICATIONS LTD.

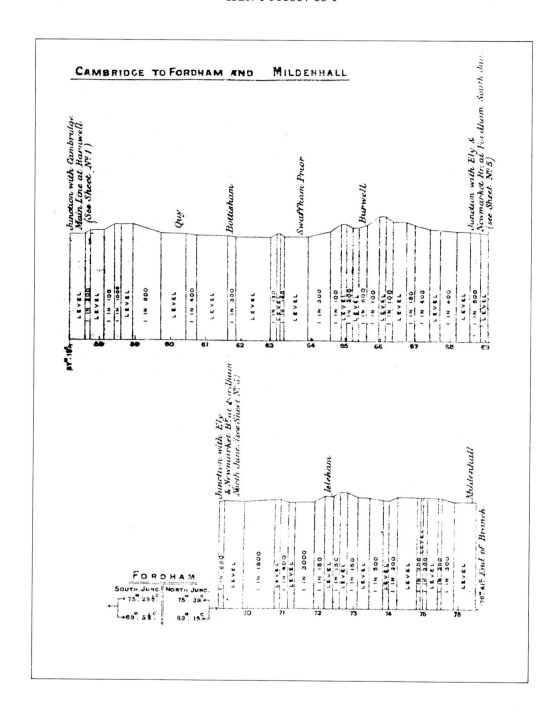

Designed by Paul Karau
Typesetting by Berkshire Publishing Services
Printed and bound by Butler & Tanner Ltd., Frome

Published by
WILD SWAN PUBLICATIONS LIMITED
1-3 Hagbourne Road, Didcot, Oxon OX11 8DP

CONTENTS

All track plans reproduced to approximately 2mm to 1 foot.

MAP OF THE LINE

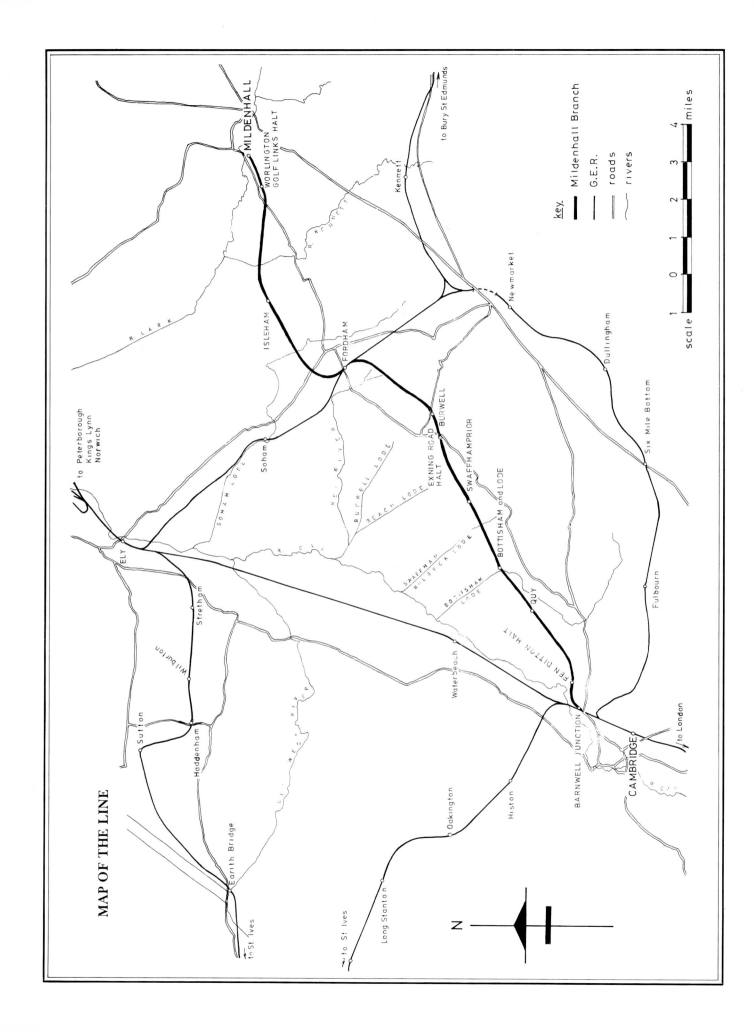

key
- Mildenhall Branch
- G.E.R.
- roads
- rivers

scale — miles

MILDENHALL
WORLINGTON
GOLF LINKS HALT
ISLEHAM
FORDHAM
Kennett
to Bury St Edmunds
Newmarket
Dullingham
Six Mile Bottom
BURWELL
EXNING ROAD HALT
SWAFFHAMPRIOR
BOTTISHAM and LODE
QUY
Soham
R. KENNETT
R. LARK
NEW RIVER
BURWELL LODE
REACH LODE
SWAFFHAM BULBECK LODE
BOTTISHAM LODE
R. CAM
SOHAM LODE
ELY
to Peterborough
Kings Lynn
Norwich
Stretham
Wilburton
Sutton
Haddenham
Earith Bridge
to St Ives
OLD WEST RIVER
Fulbourn
FEN DITTON HALT
Waterbeach
Oakington
Long Stanton
to St Ives
Histon
BARNWELL JUNCTION
CAMBRIDGE
R. CAM
to London

N

INTRODUCTION

'J15' class 0–6–0 No. 65391, fitted with side window cab, trundling a Mildenhall-Cambridge train along a straight section of line near Swaffhamprior.   *Dr. I. C. Allen*

The Mildenhall branch was a latecomer to the East Anglian railway network. The line was essentially the brainchild of Charles Allix of Swaffham Prior who had advocated a railway to serve the fen shore villages to the north-east of Cambridge. With other local landowners and farmers, he was dismayed to find the Eastern Counties, Newmarket and other railway routes bypassing the area to seek more lucrative pastures. With the advent of the Great Eastern Railway Allix hoped for greater success. Unable to raise enough capital locally to finance a line, he repeatedly approached the authorities at Bishopsgate for backing and support, but his proposals fell on deaf ears. Even an invitation to the London and North Western Railway to use his proposed line as a route from Cambridge into Norfolk was politely refused by the directors at Euston.

Salvation and the easing of the problems of the earlier agricultural depression came after the GER encountered serious flooding and the erosion of the track bed on the Ely to Norwich main line at Lakenheath. The main line company suffered traffic losses and, with no ready solution to hand to improve the situation, were once again confronted with Allix's proposal. Realising the mooted railway could provide a direct route from Cambridge via Mildenhall to Thetford, thus avoiding the troublesome area at Lakenheath and at the same time giving passengers a quicker journey from London to Norwich via Cambridge, the plans quickly came to fruition. The GER directors

were reluctant to finance the total scheme all at once and, before work was completed on the new line, effective repairs had been carried out to the main line. The alternative route was thus abandoned and the railway terminated at Mildenhall.

As with many GER branches, the new railway was a 'farmers line' conveying agricultural traffic to and from market and relying on freight for the majority of its receipts. The population of the area was sparse and passenger takings minimal, with the greatest amount of travel on local market days. As roads and motor vehicles improved so passenger traffic declined, attracted to the local bus services which offered an almost door to door service. The branch survived World War II but then declined rapidly so that services were withdrawn a year before the Beeching Report.

Freight traffic survived but a further two years, and the main portion of the line closed, leaving only a short section from Fordham to Burwell open to serve a local factory. Traffic failed to reach expectations and even this final section closed in 1965.

Now all is silent, many fixed assets are gone and the track formation in many places has reverted to farmland.

I have attempted to trace the history of the branch and details have been checked with available documents, but apologies are offered for any errors which may have occurred.

P. PAYE

Cambridge station, facing south, on 13th August 1911. Mildenhall trains usually departed from the north end bay platforms partially hidden in this view by the former Cambridge station north end signalbox. A 'Claud' 4—4—0 is featured here awaiting departure from the north end of the long single platform No. 4 with an express. The former direct Newmarket line can be seen curving away from under the third coach.

Collection M. Brooks

CHAPTER ONE

AUTHORISATION
AND CONSTRUCTION

FOR 156 miles from its source in Bedfordshire, the Great Ouse flows via Huntingdon, Ely and the fens to Kings Lynn. From Roman times this great meandering river and many of its tributaries were utilised as trading routes between settlements. By the 17th century the value of the fens for cultivation was realised and the Earl of Bedford and others contracted Sir Cornelius Vermuyden, a Dutch engineer, to drain the land. Despite vehement opposition to the scheme, Vermuyden subsequently diverted the waters of the River Ouse from its original winding course into a cut or drain 21 miles long from Earith to Denver. Unfortunately, further flooding occurred and later a second channel was constructed half a mile to the east and parallel to the former cut. The new channel became the Hundred Foot Drain or New Bedford River whilst the old channel became the Old Bedford River.

Further drainage of the fens followed as small dykes and cuts were made. The land was drained utilizing both wind and steam power and subsequently small-holdings and farms were quickly established on the newly acquired soil.

One of the tributaries of the Old Ouse or West River which continued to meander across the flat farming land via Ely, was the River Cam. Rising in neighbouring Essex and passing by way of Cambridge (where it is known as the Granta), the Cam flowed north across the fens to join the Ouse south of Ely. Between the University centre and the cathedral city artificial navigational cuts or 'lodes' were established from the existing river to serve shore villages including Bottisham, Swaffham Bulbeck and Fordham. These settlements, situated on the firmer chalk uplands of the East Anglian Heights on the southern edge of the black peat fens, were connected to their respective 'lode' ports by narrow access roads.

Another tributary of the Ouse, the River Lark, which joined the main waterway north of Ely, was navigable as far as Bury St. Edmunds. As late as 1856 the navigation was earning £30,000 per annum as fen lighters conveyed over 10,000 tons of merchandise, wines and coal from Kings Lynn to the Suffolk cathedral town. The intermediate town on the Lark, Mildenhall, soon became established as a river port with adjacent mills and warehouses. Regular imports and exports of merchandise and farm produce were conveyed to and from the Norfolk port.

Unfortunately, as trade expanded, water transport proved far too slow for the perishable crops grown in the fens, and goods often rotted before arrival at markets. In winter months almost eight days could be spent on the river journey from either Mildenhall, Fordham, Bottisham or Swaffham Bulbeck to King's Lynn or return and two days more to Bury St. Edmunds. Despite such problems the river remained in the early 19th century the major form of communication for villages and townships. Reliance on water transport meant that road improvements in the area were minimal. The arrival of the turnpike roads

made little difference and it was not until the advent of the railway that the communities of the area benefited.

As early as 1835 Cambridge was the intermediate goal for a railway route from London to York when Joseph Gibbs surveyed the route of a line via Dunmow and Saffron Walden. Presented to Parliament as the Great Northern Railway, the Bill was defeated at the second reading in 1836. When the GNR was again mooted ten years later, it followed a course far to the west through Hitchin and Huntingdon. Gibbs' survey was not the only one to be carried out, for James Walker surveyed a route for the proposed Northern and Eastern Railway from London to Cambridge. Walker's route followed the gradual rise of the Lea and Stort valleys to Bishops Stortford and thence over the watershed at Elsenham to Newport and Great Chesterford. Although opened from a junction with the Eastern Counties Railway at Stratford to Broxbourne on 15th September 1840, the line had only progressed a further 13 miles to Bishops Stortford by 16th May 1842. The N & E subsequently obtained powers the following year to extend their line to Newport whilst the Eastern Counties, which in the same year assumed responsibilities for N & E affairs, obtained the Royal Assent on 4th July 1844 to build a railway from Newport via Cambridge and Ely, to connect with the Norfolk Railway at Brandon. The section from Bishops Stortford to Brandon was opened throughout on 30th July 1845 allowing direct rail access from London to Norwich.

Anticipation of the Northern and Eastern reaching Cambridge brought a spate of schemes for other railways serving the university city including in 1836 the Cambridge Transverse Railway linking Bury St. Edmunds and Market Harborough. In 1844 a further plan was mooted to link Cambridge with Bury St. Edmunds but both schemes were unsuccessful. The area to the east of Cambridge was subsequently exploited by the Newmarket and Chesterford Railway incorporated in 1846 at a cost of £350,000. The Act authorised the construction of a main line, 16¼ miles in length from a junction with the ECR north of Chesterford station, to Newmarket, with an 8¼ mile branch from a junction at Six Mile Bottom to Cambridge. In 1847 further powers were obtained for an extension to the Norfolk Railway at Thetford with branches from Newmarket to Bury St. Edmunds and Ely. The civic authorities at Cambridge strongly opposed the scheme as through traffic from London to Norwich would bypass the city. The ECR also opposed the plans but the objections were outweighed by the enthusiastic support of the residents of Newmarket and the all powerful Jockey Club.

Legal and financial problems delayed the work on the Cambridge branch and no start was made to the extension or branches authorised in 1847. The main line was duly opened to traffic for goods on 3rd January 1848 and passengers on 4th April worked by the Newmarket Company. Fearing danger from the Royston and Hitchin Railway then approaching from the west, joining up with

1

the Newmarket at Chesterford, the ECR took over the Newmarket Company on lease on 2nd October 1848. After further arguments with the ECR, relationships between the two companies deteriorated. The Newmarket turned to the still legally independent Norfolk Railway for support, and arranged a joint committee, offering the future diversion of all through traffic to the Newmarket line from Thetford when construction of their line was completed. The ECR retaliated by offering the Newmarket proprietors terms equal to those enjoyed by its own proprietors on condition the 1847 extensions were abandoned. In the meantime the ECR takeover of the Norfolk Railway was completed although both the Newmarket and East Anglian Railways objected. Exhausted both physically and financially with proposals and counter proposals, the Newmarket situation was hopeless. Despite the verbal backing of the rich and wealthy, race traffic was not enough to support the line on which the ECR provided a poor service for exorbitant rates. Work on the branches remained unfinished and, because of its financial embarrassment, all services on the Newmarket Railway were suspended from 30th June to 9th September 1850. After the election of a new board of directors and re-negotiating working arrangements with the ECR, the line reopened. The Newmarket Company finally reached agreement with the ECR whereby, on completion of the Cambridge branch, the whole undertaking, except the Bury St. Edmunds extension, would be taken by the larger company at a guaranteed 3 per cent rental on the £350,000 capital, subject to a maximum ECR subsidy of £5,000 in any one year. With assistance from the ECR and by removing a line of rails from the Great Chesterford-Six Mile Bottom section, the Cambridge branch from Newmarket was finally completed on 9th October 1851. The same day the former Newmarket main line some 11½ miles in length from Great Chesterford to Six Mile Bottom was closed to all traffic, although powers to finally dismantle this section were not obtained until 1858.

In 1852 further powers were obtained for the extension from Newmarket to Bury St. Edmunds and this railway was subsequently opened to traffic on 1st April 1854. This line involved the construction of Warren Hill Tunnel, 1100 yards in length and the longest on the GER, which carried the line under Newmarket Heath.

In the ensuing years the ECR leased or took over the working of all the major railways in East Anglia and a scheme was subsequently prepared for the amalgamation of the Eastern Counties, Eastern Union, East Anglian, Newmarket and Norfolk Railways into a new undertaking to be known as the Great Eastern Railway. The Act sanctioning this amalgamation — the Great Eastern Railway Act 1862 (25 and 26 Vic Cap CCXXIII) obtained the Royal Assent on 7th August 1862 but took effect retrospectively from July of that year.

The tract of country left vacant by the failure of the Newmarket Railway to build their line to Ely and authorised by Parliament in 1847 was finally penetrated by the Ely and Newmarket Railway, which was incorporated on 11th August 1875 with a capital of £100,000 in £10 shares and borrowing powers of £33,333. The chairman of the new company was John Pugh Bridgewater with

Thomas Ellis and J. Elliot, fellow directors. The railway was opened to traffic on 1st September 1879 with stations at Soham and Fordham, together with a junction at Snailwell allowing direct access to both Newmarket and Bury St. Edmunds. The line joined the erstwhile Cambridge-Bury line at both Chippenham Junction and Warren Hill Junction. The new railway was operated by the GER from the outset, then leased on a £5,000 annual rental before being absorbed by the parent company in 1898.

In April 1885 a special station was opened near the latter on the 'down' or west side of the line, between the north portal of the tunnel and the junction, to handle race traffic and horse-box specials.

The opening of the Ely and Newmarket was a source of concern to various landowners and farmers within the triangle formed by this line and the GER main line between Cambridge and Ely and the Cambridge-Bury-Ipswich route. Trade was being lost because of the delay caused in forwarding commodities to and from markets. Steps had, however, been taken to rectify the position.

Twelve years earlier, in September 1867, Charles Peter Allix, JP, DL, MA, of Swaffham Prior, was of the opinion that a railway connecting the rural area with the main railway network at Cambridge would alleviate the hardship encountered from the earlier agricultural depression and restore trade and prosperity. Methodically gathering statistics relating to population, trade trends and other items, he compiled a memorandum which was duly signed by all the large landowners of the district to be served by the proposed line. The document was sent to the directors of the Great Eastern Railway for their comments and possible support. The GER was, however, at that time in considerable financial difficulty and the Board of the main line company were of the opinion that receipts from such a rural area were hardly likely to pay for the interest on borrowed capital. After some deliberation the request was politely but firmly refused.

Undeterred, Allix then approached the rival London and North Western Railway which had extended its line from Bletchley to Cambridge. To make the scheme attractive to the directors at Euston and in an endeavour to get the LNWR to build the railway, Allix even suggested the company might wish to use the line as a through route into East Anglia at Thetford. The LNWR, however, were mindful of the fact that they had gained access to, and the use of, Cambridge station over GER rails and had no wish to fall out with their hosts so that they were forced to build their own station in the university city. The directors at Euston, needless to say, turned the project down.

Allix continued to show an interest in the development of the rural area and over the next few years he backed various railway schemes. In 1875 the Ely and Bury St. Edmunds Light Railway was authorised by Parliament with Charles Allix as deputy chairman of the company. Unfortunately this scheme failed, overtaken by the Ely-Newmarket Railway, before being absolved by the Ely and Bury St. Edmunds Railway (Abandonment) Act of 1880. While in his capacity of deputy chairman, Allix obtained the backing of his cousin, Mr. Wilkinson of Hare Hall, and drew up plans for a railway connecting the Ely-Bury St. Edmunds line with Cambridge, at or near

Chesterton Junction on the northern edge of the city. Unfortunately, as with the Ely Light Railway plan, there was insufficient local capital to back the proposal and the scheme was abandoned.

Undaunted, Allix persisted in his attempts to provide a railway in the area. Worsening economic conditions on the farmlands made him intensify the campaign and he again approached the GER to renegotiate for a line. The stalling GER was in no hurry. However, in 1878 severe flooding and blockage of the railway near Lakenheath brought a change of heart at Bishopsgate when the authorities realised the proposal presented by Allix might provide the ready solution to their problem. Here was a line which could bypass the troubled area and shorten the mileage between Cambridge and Norwich. Six months after his contact with Bishopsgate, the GER directors requested Allix to provide an update of relevant information showing the need for the proposed railway.

The figures were duly sent to the GER Board who were still somewhat sceptical of the returns which would accrue from such a venture. Further flooding near Lakenheath finally forced an affirmative decision and an initial survey of the area from Barnwell through Bottisham, Burwell and Fordham to Mildenhall was made in the late summer and autumn of 1879.

Little progress was achieved during the early months of 1880 but by June the proposed line was included in a draft of proposed new railways for future presentation to the directors.

At the board meeting held on 18th August 1880 the policy regarding the construction of new lines was read to the GER directors when future applications to Parliament were considered. Amongst those under consideration was the railway to Mildenhall, and the GER general manager in his submission thought the proposed line would, as well as serving new agricultural districts with the possibility of expanded trade, offer the railway company an alternative route to Thetford and Norwich bypassing the particular trouble spot subjected to flooding near Lakenheath on the Ely-Norwich line.

'This is a rich and highly populated district separated from Ely and Newmarket by a hill and from Waterbeach by a river. Beyond there is Mildenhall and beyond there Thetford.' The general manager continued 'We have suffered and shall suffer again from floods stopping traffic on the main line at Lakenheath. The local parties have repaired the former damage with silt only and it will give way again. Two years ago it cost the GER a large sum of money in loss and diversion of traffic and this year it has cost £7,000 already. Altogether the flooding has cost the company £40,000.' The directors were then informed that the proposed route could become the main line between Cambridge and Norwich. 'The entire scheme is too large to be completed at one time but looking at the advantages to be gained, I think we ought to initially build part, expending £80,000-£100,000'. In subsequent discussion the Board were informed the line would ultimately extend for a distance of 30 miles through a district where the population was largely in favour of the scheme. After deliberating the merits of the proposal, a visit to the area was considered early in September.

The visit was subsequently made during the first week of September and at the Board meeting on the 14th Mr. George Wilson, the engineer of the GER, was requested to consider what course the line should take through the district, bearing in mind the railway was to form a relief route to avoid areas susceptible to flooding between Cambridge and Thetford. Wilson was asked especially to avoid the areas on the proposed route which were likely to flood.

The detailed surveys of the route of the proposed railway were carried out in October and November and the draft proposals for the line deposited in the Private Bill Office by the Parliamentary agents. The prospectus and plans were also sent to the Clerks of the Peace for the counties of Cambridge and Suffolk and to the parish councils through which the line was to pass, on the last day of November 1880.

Authority for the railway was included in the Great Eastern Railway Act 1881 (44-45 Vic Cap CXXXIV) which received the Royal Assent on 18th July 1881. Included in the Act was a clause authorising the making of certain railways from the Cambridge and Ely main line near Cambridge to the Ely and Newmarket Railway and thence to Mildenhall. Clause 8 of the Act confirmed the authority to build:

1. A railway (in this Act called Railway No. 2) 6 miles 4 furlongs 5 chains in length commencing by a junction with the Cambridge and Ely main line in the parish of St. Andrew-the-Less otherwise Barnwell in the County of Cambridge and terminating in the parish of Swaffham Prior in the same county near the White Droveway.

2. A railway (in this Act called Railway No. 3) 5 miles 2 furlongs 3.80 chains in length commencing by a junction with railway No. 2 at or near its termination and terminating in the parish of Fordham in the County of Cambridge by a junction with the Ely and Newmarket Railway.

3. A railway (in this Act called Railway No. 4) 7 miles 1 furlong 8 chains in length commencing by a junction with the Ely and Newmarket Railway at a point 80 yards or thereabouts north west of the end of the up platform at Fordham station in the said parish of Fordham and terminating in the parish of Barton Mills in the County of Suffolk in a field called Twelve Acre Piece owned by Abraham Peachey and occupied by Edward Savory.

The company were authorised to cross public roads on the level by gated level crossings at the following places:

Railway No. 2

Parish of Fen Ditton	1 road
Parish of Quy cum Stow	1 road
Parish of Bottisham	1 road

Railway No. 3

Parish of Burwell	1 road
Parish of Exning	1 road

In addition, the GER was to provide bridges to carry public roads over the railway at:

Railway No. 2

Parish of Fen Ditton   1 road — 20 feet wide

Railway No. 3

Parish of Swaffham Prior   1 road — 20 feet wide
Parish of Burwell   1 road — 20 feet wide

Railway No. 4

Parish of Fordham   3 roads — 2 at 15 feet
                                        1 at 20 feet wide
Parish of Isleham   2 roads — 15 feet and
                                        20 feet wide
Parish of Freckenham   2 roads — both 20 feet wide

Under an agreement dated 28th June 1881 between 'the Queen's most Excellent Majesty' on the first part, Charles Alexander Gore, a Commissioner of Her Majesty's Woods and Forests, on the second part, and the GER on the third part, the company was required to pay £868 15s 0d before taking over certain Crown farmlands in the Parish of Burwell. Under this agreement, the company was compelled not to damage or obstruct drains or watercourses on the west side of the railway when crossing the Crown farmlands. If watercourses were required, the GER was to construct sufficient culverts and drains as necessary for the proper drainage as required by the Commissioners. The company was also bound to construct suitable fencing alongside the railway and provide new gates.

The Act allowed the GER three years to complete the compulsory purchase of all land required for the line and five years for the completion of works. The cost of the new works including the Mildenhall line was to be financed by the creation of a new issue of £700,000 preference shares.

By 18th October 1881 proposals for the new route were so advanced to enable the GER solicitor to prepare legal documents for the acquisition of land. On 6th February 1882 the Board subsequently requested the solicitor to serve notice to all tenants and owners where drainage work was to be carried out on their land, between Chesterton and Swaffham Prior and Fordham to Mildenhall. At the same time the land agent was authorised to proceed with purchase of land required for the railway, stations, other buildings and signalboxes.

The claims of the GER for compulsory purchase of the land required for the railway had severe repercussions on some local landowners. At a public auction of land belonging to H. Knight, held in April 1882 at the premises of Henry Stanley at Tokenhouse Yard, London, it was established that one farm (Lot 3) would realise more if it were divided into more than one lot. Knight was of the opinion that he was forced to sell this land as the GER had given notice for 5 acres required for the proposed Cambridge-Mildenhall railway and this had effectively cut the farm in half. It was established, however, that the farm in question had remained uncultivated since the last Michaelmas and, far from losing on the transaction, the new buyer could negotiate over terms of purchase with the railway company with plenty of scope for heavy claims. Despite the pessimistic approach of the vendor, the farm was quickly sold to Mr. Grobbs of Chancery Lane for the handsome sum of £11,600.

Negotiations proceeded apace with little hindrance, so that by 6th June 1882 Charles F. Adams, the land agent, was able to present to the directors a list of purchases agreed on Railway No. 2 and also possession of some sections on Railway No. 3, together totalling 8 miles from the junction at Barnwell. At a board meeting on the same day Wilson reported that all working plans for the railway were completed, and the contract for construction could be let. The GER arranged for various meetings in parishes along the route of the railway for the purpose of appointing committees to agree compensation to be paid for the extraction of comparable and other rights over or on certain roadways and droveways.

The tenders for the construction of Railways Nos. 2 and 3 were to be delivered to the GER Liverpool Street Headquarters not later than 9.00 a.m. on 3rd July 1882, whilst the tender for No. 4 was to be delivered to the GER Liverpool Street Headquarters not later than 9.00 a.m. on Monday, 17th July 1882. At their meeting on the subsequent days, 4th July and 18th July, the directors examined the submissions. After due consideration, the offer of Henry Lovatt of Darlington Street, Wolverhampton was accepted.

Lovatt tendered at £45,494 2s 2d for Railways 2 and 3 and £30,833 9s 6d for the Fordham-Mildenhall section. The contract for Railways 2 and 3, subsequently awarded to Lovatt, stipulated that he was required to give notice to the GER of his intention to commence works at any time between 1st January and 1st October 1883 with completion by 1st April 1884. A breakdown of the schedule of prices forwarded by Lovatt to the GER engineer is given on page 5.

On 5th September 1882 the general manager reported to the Board that he had met with Mr. Lovatt who had agreed to undertake the three contracts for £76,327 11s 8d. By mutual agreement between the contractor and the GER, the first section contract was to date from 1st January 1883 with completion within 15 months. On the second section Lovatt was to give the railway company six calendar months' notice of intention to commence, such notice being given any time after the start on the first section but not later than November 1883. Completion of construction was required within twelve months from the date of completion of the first section. Lovatt was also required to adhere to the prices quoted on his tender except for fencing where an increase to 2/- per linear yard was agreed.

The GER surveyor exchanged the majority of contracts with landowners on railways 2 and 3 in August and the contractors' men obtained access for marking out the course of the line after completion of the harvest in early October 1882. Satisfied with such progress, the GER authorities and Allix then made plans for a small ceremony to commemorate the commencement of work on the new railway.

The ceremony of the cutting of the first sod arranged for 3rd January 1883 was given wide coverage in the area and between 500 and 600 spectators congregated to watch. During the morning a large company of landowners and gentry gathered at Swaffham Prior House and shortly after midday the company drove the short distance to the selected site about a quarter of a mile north of Swaffham

	Units of measure	Railway Nos. 2 & 3 Barnwell—Fordham				Railway No. 4 Fordham—Mildenhall			
		Amount	£	s.	d.	Amount	£	s.	d.
FENCING									
4 Rail Oak or Larch	linear yds	46,200	4,720	0	0	32,000	3,200	0	0
Wrought and painted 3 rail for station approaches	linear yds	2,300	517	10	0	3,650	821	5	0
Wrought and painted paled fencing 5 ft	linear yds	2,100	813	15	0	1,040	403	0	0
Wrought and tarred close board 5 ft	linear yds	100	50	0	0	100	50	0	0
Wrought fencing fixed and painted	linear yds	100	23	15	0	100	23	15	0
Wrought and painted 20ft gates	each	9	180	0	0	4	80	0	0
Wrought and painted 15ft gates	each	2	24	0	0	2	24	0	0
Wrought field gates 10ft	each	40	170	0	0	30	127	10	0
Wrought and painted wicket gates	each	25	75	0	0	15	45	0	0
Occupational crossing gates 12ft	each	32	640	0	0	17	340	0	0
Wrought and painted swing foot gates	each	1	4	0	0	10	40	0	0
EARTHWORKS									
Excavation earthworks	cubic yds	96,000	4,800	0	0	86,700	4,335	0	0
Excavation in diversion of streams	cubic yds	5,300	265	0	0	—	—	—	—
Embankments and approach roads	cubic yds	51,000	637	10	0	50,500	631	5	0
Excavation foundations of bridges, buildings, etc.	cubic yds	6,800	283	6	8	5,300	220	16	8
Dry rubble filling	cubic yds	250	12	10	0	350	17	10	0
Ballast	cubic yds	63,500	5,556	5	0	35,300	2,647	10	0
Metalled roads for yards and approaches 12in thick	sup yds	33,000	1,925	0	0	22,100	1,289	3	4
Screened and spread gravel on platforms	sup yds	300	15	0	0	300	15	0	0
Footpath gravel 4in thick	sup yds	200	10	0	0	200	10	0	0
Watching Lighting and forming Temporary roads	each	10	100	0	0	10	100	0	0
BRICKWORK									
Brickwork set — Greaves Blue lias lime mortar for bridges and culverts etc.	cubic yds	5,750	6,900	0	0	6,200	7,440	0	0
Bridgework in Portland Cement	cubic yds	100	145	0	0	50	72	10	0
Staffordshire Blue Brick coping for walls	linear yds	1,075	215	0	0	690	138	0	0
DRAINPIPES									
Best glazed stone or earthenware town made socket									
4 inch	linear yds	100	5	0	0	100	5	0	0
6 inch	linear yds	450	33	15	0	200	15	0	0
9 inch	linear yds	1,350	151	17	6	500	56	5	0
12 inch	linear yds	270	40	10	0	200	30	0	0
18 inch	linear yds	120	51	0	0	35	14	17	6
MASONRY									
Ashlar Stonework	cubic ft	470	82	5	0	670	117	5	0
Yorkshire self faced flags	sup ft	10		15	0	10		15	0
CONCRETE									
Concrete	cubic yds	2,090	940	10	0	1,333	599	17	0
ASHPHALT									
Ashphalt for coating arches, etc.	sq. yds	500	56	5	0	820	92	5	0
TIMBER									
Baltic	cubic	150	26	5	0	150	26	5	0
Best Memel	cubic	350	73	15	0	50	13	5	0
Best English Oak	cubic	50	17	10	0	50	17	10	0
Best Red Deal	sup ft	600	26	5	0	500	21	5	0
Parish Boundary Posts	each	30	30	0	0	15	15	0	0
Mile, quarter mile and gradient posts	each	100	100	0	0	50	50	0	0
Company Landmarks	each	20	10	0	0	20	10	0	0
IRONWORK									
Cast Iron	tons	2	24	0	0	2	24	0	0
Wrought Iron	tons	12	216	0	0	6	108	0	0
PERMANENT WAY									
Laying Single Line of Permanent Way	linear yds	26,100	1,196	5	0	15,000	687	10	0
Laying and fixing points and crossing	each	52	312	0	0	25	150	0	0
STATION BUILDINGS									
Stations	each £2,160	5	10,800	0	0	2 at £2,170	4,340	0	0
Granary at Mildenhall with 1 30cwt capacity crane							1,690	0	0
OTHER EQUIPMENT, ETC.									
Buffer Stops	each	6	150	0	0	5	125	0	0
Buffer Stops fixed to carriage dock	each	4	60	0	0	2	30	0	0
Wilkinson patent granite cement concrete paving for platforms etc.	sup yds	1,452	290	8	0	500	100	0	0
Level crossing cottages with 25ft gates at £350 each	each	6	2,100	0	0				
Cattle Pens	sets	3	310	0	0	2	260	0	0
Loading Gauges	each	5	37	10	0	2	15	0	0
Fixing of Pooley weighing machines	each	5	35	0	0	2	14	0	0
Catchpits for station yards	each	25	37	10	0	20	30	0	0
Chalk and cinders for coal allotments	sup yds	1,260	47	5	0	500	18	5	0
Lamp posts with oil lamp	each	100	250	0	0	30	75	0	0
Fixing one 45 feet diameter engine Turntable at Mildenhall							10	0	0
			£45,494	2	2		£30,833	9	6

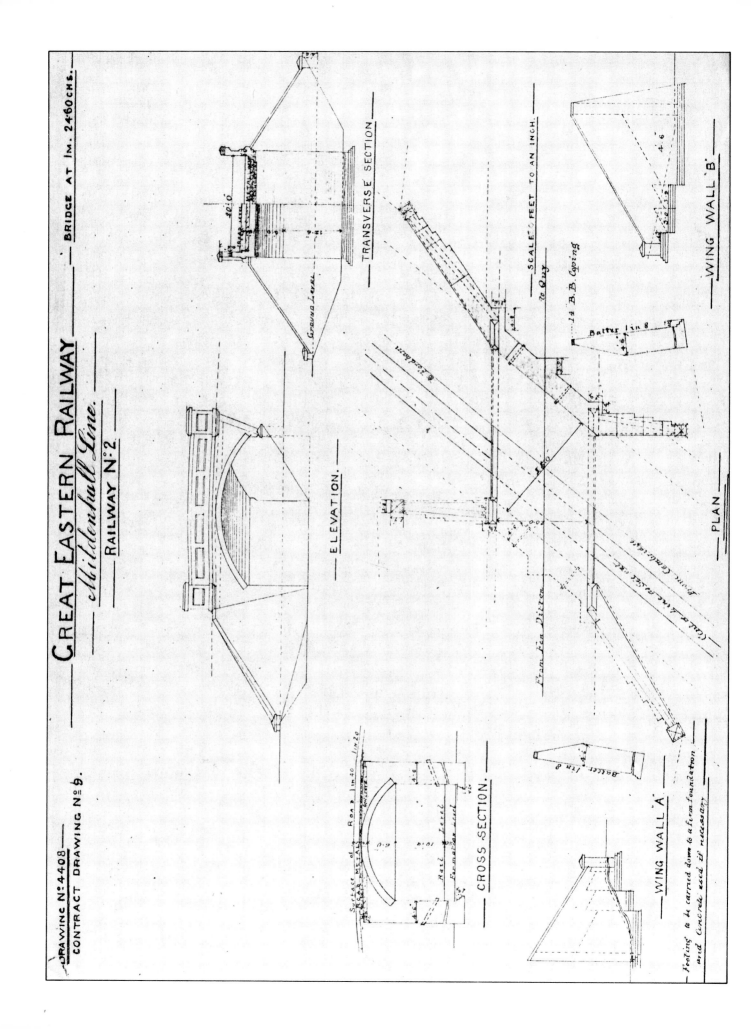

GREAT EASTERN RAILWAY

Mildenhall Line.

RAILWAY No 2

BRIDGE AT 1m. 24.60 chs.

DRAWING No 4408

CONTRACT DRAWING No 8.

TRANSVERSE SECTION

ELEVATION.

SCALE 8 FEET TO AN INCH.

PLAN

CROSS SECTION.

WING WALL "A"

WING WALL "B"

Batter 1 in 8

14 B.B. Coping

Footing to be carried down to a firm foundation and Concrete used if necessary

Prior village. On arrival the company were given a rousing cheer by the spectators. Mr. C. P. Allix then prayed that the sod would be turned in the faith of Jesus Christ and 'we pray that God for His sake will bless the undertaking and send prosperity to this countryside by these means.' The Reverend Canon Cockshott, vicar of Burwell, then gave the blessing before ten year old Master Charles Allix stepped forward to perform the actual ceremony. Using a handsome ceremonial spade and wheelbarrow supplied by Lovatt, the contractor, Charles Allix dug a spit of earth from the roadside on the route of the intended railway and then placed it in the wheelbarrow to the sound of much cheering and clapping. After he had completed his task, others present also dug small spits of earth into the wheelbarrow. The spade used at the ceremony is still preserved in private ownership and carries the following inscription:

'With this spade the first sod of the Cambridge and Mildenhall Railway was turned in the Parish of Swaffham Prior by Charles Israel Loraine Allix, aged 10 years of Swaffham Prior House on the 3rd day of January 1883'

Mr. Allix then reiterated to the gathering the problems he had encountered from the time of his first approach to the GER for a railway in the district in 1867, his later communications with the LNWR and again with the GER in his capacity of deputy chairman of the Ely and Bury St. Edmunds Light Railway Company, and finally to this first positive step in the construction of the new line. J. Wilson, the GER engineer, advised that work had already commenced on the railway. The main line company were of the opinion that it was better to push forward and open the Cambridge to Fordham section for traffic before completion of the Mildenhall section. Lovatt confidently forecast completion to Fordham within fifteen months.

Further cheers from the crowd feted the 50 or so ladies and gentlemen who returned by the carriages to Swaffham Prior House for luncheon. Among those who attended the ceremony were Mr. and Mrs. C. P. Allix, Master Charles Allix, Master John Peter Allix, Rev. Canon Cockshott, Mr. Hope, local agent for the new line, Messrs. Lovatt and Moseley, contractors for the new railway, and the following GER officers: J. Wilson, engineer, C. F. Adams, surveyor and land agent, and Mr. Dymant, solicitor. While luncheon was being served in the hall, about 50 of the estate workers were entertained in another part of the house, enjoying a meal of roast beef and plum pudding. To celebrate the event, the village church bells were rung at intervals for the remainder of the day.

After the event, work on the new line gathered momentum as Lovatt employed further local navvies to increase his workforce. Unfortunately continuous wet weather and subsequent flooding in February 1883 prevented progress. Drier weather by mid-March enabled construction to resume to the required schedule.

Problems over compensation for land purchased recurred when the Reverend J. Harlock disputed payment with the railway company. At the enquiry held at the Surveyors Institute, London, on Thursday, 22nd March 1883, it was revealed that compensation was required for damage done by the proposed railway practically bisecting a farm at Isleham and Freckenham. The claimant's witnesses requested compensation of between £888 and £989, whilst the GER representative thought the much lower figure of between £100 and £390 would suffice. After deliberating the legal arguments, the arbiter awarded the sum of £585.

In another dispute Cambridge Town Council complained to the GER authorities that the contractor had taken possession of a small pocket of land on Stourbridge Common before the council had granted permission. The matter was, however, amicably settled locally.

Construction during the spring proceeded apace, although some difficulty was initially experienced in subcontracting work as small contractors were reluctant to travel away from Cambridge, and by May 1883 local newspapers were advertising for bricklayers and carpenters to work on the new stations being built at Bottisham and Burwell. The general construction work progressed with only a few minor incidents but unfortunately this situation was marred by a fatal accident near Fen Ditton in July 1883. A carpenter, James Sydney, aged 36 or 37, had taken an unofficial ride in a wagon on a moving train. When it started to rain heavily Sydney jumped off to seek shelter but unfortunately landed on a slippery earth bank some two feet in height. Unable to gain a foothold, he slipped back under the wheels of the moving wagons. Other navvies working by the lineside and also on the wagons shouted to the engine driver to stop the train but on reaching the body, Sydney was found to be dead. At the inquest held at the Kings Head Public House, Fen Ditton, the jury recorded a verdict of accidental death, adding a rider 'that no blame of any kind could be attributed to the negligence of the contractor'.

Tenders for the signalling on the new line were sent out on 6th March 1883 and the contract was subsequently awarded to McKenzie and Holland Ltd. On 15th October C. L. Morgan at the company's Vulcan ironworks at Worcester, sent to John Wilson, the GER signal engineer, a schedule of prices. Included was the cost of each signalbox measuring 14ft by 11ft, with a working floor 6ft above rail level and estimated at £75 10s 0d each.

During construction of the railway, Mr. Allix made certain improvements and landscaping to the grounds of Swaffham Prior House including the planting of an avenue of elm trees from the house to the boundary of the GER Company's land close to Swaffham Prior station yard. Early in 1884 he wrote requesting the railway company to erect a small bridge across the stream which separated the station yard from his property, a gate made in the GER boundary fence and a path to the entrance of the booking office with the necessary steps.

The general manager reported to the Way and Works Committee on 5th February 1884 and received approval for the work to be carried out provided Allix bore the whole cost of the construction and the GER retained the right to remove the bridge and block off the gateway at any time they pleased. Allix subsequently offered no objection to the conditions, and work was completed later in the year. Much of the hedging and ditching along the line was subcontracted to John Gray who experienced difficulty in planting quickset hedges in some places.

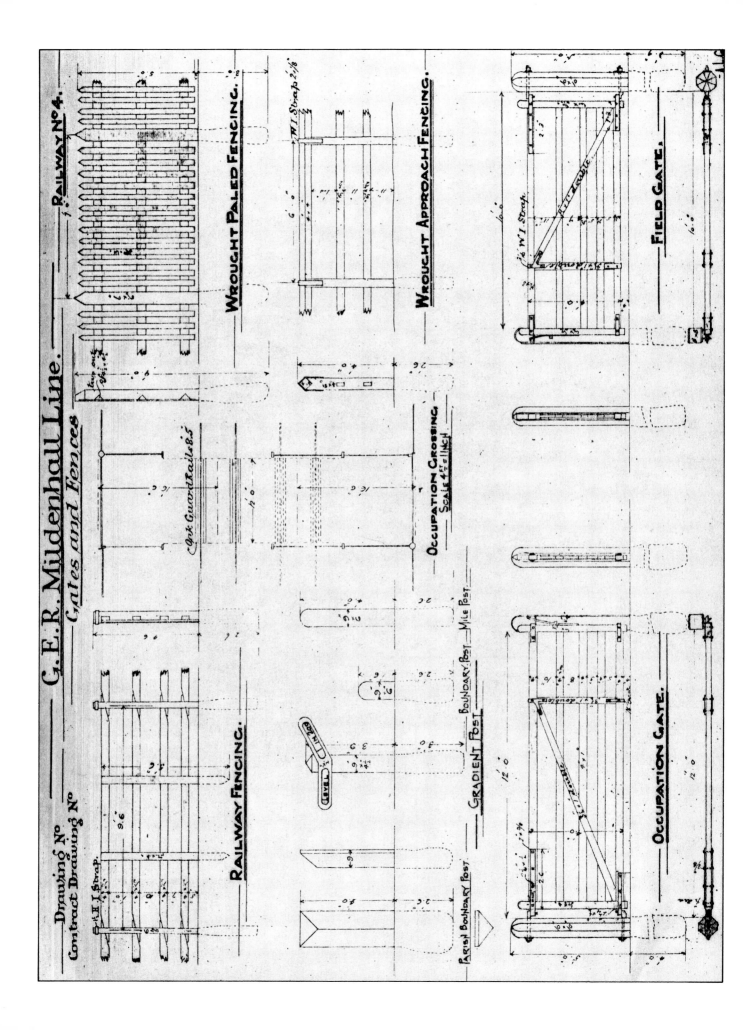

G.E.R. Mildenhall Line.
— Gates and Fences —

Drawing Nº
Contract Drawing Nº

— RAILWAY Nº 4. —

WROUGHT PALED FENCING.

WROUGHT APPROACH FENCING.

FIELD GATE.

RAILWAY FENCING.

OCCUPATION CROSSING.
Scale 4ft = 1inch

Cast Guard Rails 8.5

PARISH BOUNDARY POST.   BOUNDARY POST   MILE POST.

GRADIENT POST.

OCCUPATION GATE.

Further price alterations were made in 1884 when the porter's cottage accommodation and station master's house with bay windows at Swaffham Prior were increased to £296 and £308 respectively. These were accepted by the GER on 15th January, together with the cost of Quy station at £630 and the waiting shed at £182. In accepting these figures the GER authorities stipulated completion by 1st April 1884. On completion of the waiting shed at Quy, the railway officials decided like structures should be provided at Barnwell Junction, Burwell, Isleham and Mildenhall, and subsequently instructed Lovatt to add the charges to additional works outside the contract.

A further fatal accident occurred on the line in April 1884 when Samuel Benstead, a 19 year old labourer working for the contractor, jumped from a moving train near the site of Bottisham station and fell under the vehicles. He died three days later in Addenbrooke's hospital from his injuries. At the subsequent inquiry it was established that Benstead was in a hurry to get home as he wished to attend the circus at Cambridge and hitched a ride on the brake van of a ballast train. He asked the fireman on the engine to stop the train at Lode so that he could alight but through a misunderstanding the driver actually stopped the train at Swaffham Prior. It was when the train failed to stop at Lode that the labourer made his fatal leap.

In the same year, during Lent, the vicar of Quy, the Rev. Colbourne, obtained permission from the contractor and the GER officials to hold evening services each Sunday in the station waiting room.

Because of the close proximity of Swaffham Prior House and the association of C. P. Allix with the development of the railway in the area, the GER thought it appropriate to provide a more ornate station at Swaffham Prior. The engineer authorised the contractor to strengthen and re-pitch the angle of the roof of the station building and substitute tile roofing instead of slates.

In the later stages of construction of the line, the GER engineer was undecided as to whether tiles or slates should be used as roofing material on other buildings on the branch. After several verbal encounters, Lovatt wrote on 1st May 1884 that if tiles were to be supplied instead of slates on workmen's cottages, the extra pitch on the roofs and stronger timbers would cost an additional £24 each. A similar substitution on Mildenhall station was estimated at £15.

After some deliberation, the engineer advised Lovatt to only strengthen the roof timbers and tile the cottage at Swaffham Prior. All other cottages and Mildenhall station were to be equipped with slate roofing.

At the end of the first week of May, Lovatt advised the near completion of construction work and application was duly made to the Board of Trade for official inspection. Advice was subsequently received that this would take place on the last Wednesday of the month.

During a tour of the GER system by the directors on 26th and 27th May 1884, their special train passed over the new railway between Fordham and Barnwell Junction. A stop was made at all stations and one of the gatekeepers' houses was inspected. The layout of the structure so impressed the officers that they stipulated the building was to be considered as the model for future gatekeepers' cottages on the GER.

The official Board of Trade inspection was carried out by Major General C. S. Hutchinson on Wednesday, 28th May 1884. Accompanied by J. Wilson, Chief Engineer of the GE, Robertson, Superintendent of the line, and local officials of the GER, the inspector travelled by special train departing Cambridge at 9.40 a.m. to travel over the branch, calling at all stations and stopping to view the bridges. Hutchinson noted the 18 feet width of formation suitable for laying double track, if the increase of traffic so required. He noted the five overbridges, the largest with a span of 36½ feet, and inspected the brick abutments. The inspector also tested the deflection as the train passed over two stream bridges of 14½ and 20 feet spans and also six brick culverts with a span of 6 feet and remarked 'the works appear of substantial construction and are standing well, the girders have sufficient theoretical strength and give moderate deflections under test'.

The inspector also noted the four authorised level crossings over public roads were provided with the necessary gates and remarked that in three cases private roads of an important nature were also provided with similar protection. Hutchinson noted the fencing provided along the whole length of the line was formed of post and 4 rail timber type, the highest rail being 4 feet 2 inches above ground level. The stations provided on the new line at Barnwell Junction, Quy, Bottisham, Swaffham Prior and Burwell were found to contain all the necessary accommodation and the proper signal and telegraph arrangements. At Fordham Junction the new signal box was inspected and found to provide the requisite interlocking to ensure safety of trains entering and leaving the station on the new line and on the Ely-Newmarket line.

Luncheon for the inspection party was arranged in the waiting room at Fordham. Probably somewhat overcome by the occasion, Lovatt prophesied the railway would continue beyond Mildenhall to Thetford and 'he hoped they might meet each other at a future time to congratulate themselves upon that result'. After the meal, the special train conveyed the inspection party back to Cambridge.

Hutchinson, in his report, thought the construction of the line was well finished, although the following remedial work required attention. At Barnwell Junction station signal box Nos. 7 and 29 levers required interlocking whilst No. 30 lever when pulled should lock No. 12 points for the main line. At Fordham Junction station signal box, Nos. 36 and 38 levers required interlocking with No. 17, and No. 38 lever interlocking with No. 22. At Swaffham Prior station signal box, Nos. 13 and 18 levers required interlocking whilst additional fencing was essential for protection where the railway crossed culverts at 2 miles 46 chains, 3 miles 56 chains, 6 miles 58 chains, and 11 miles 2 chains. The inspector also stipulated the raising of the handrails on the underbridge close to Bottisham station whilst additional fencing was required at the back of the platform at Quy, Bottisham, Swaffham Prior and Burwell stations to prevent passengers falling into the carriage dock. To safeguard level crossings Hutchinson requested the provision of block telegraph repeater gongs on the level crossing houses at 5 miles 61 chains and 9 miles 76 chains.

The inspector concluded that subject to the prompt completion of the remedial work and the notification of the mode of working, he had no objection to the railway opening for traffic subject to the proviso that all trains were required to stop at all stations.

Lovatt and the GER engineer quickly arranged to carry out the remedial work and arrangements were made to open the line for passenger and goods traffic on Monday, 2nd June 1884, using the train staff and ticket method of working.

So important was the advent of the railway to the district that on Sunday, 1st June, the Vicar of Swaffham-prior, the Rev. T. Preston, made the opening of the line the subject of his afternoon sermon, quoting the text of Isaiah Chapter XI Verse 16 'And there shall be an highway for the remnant of his people'.

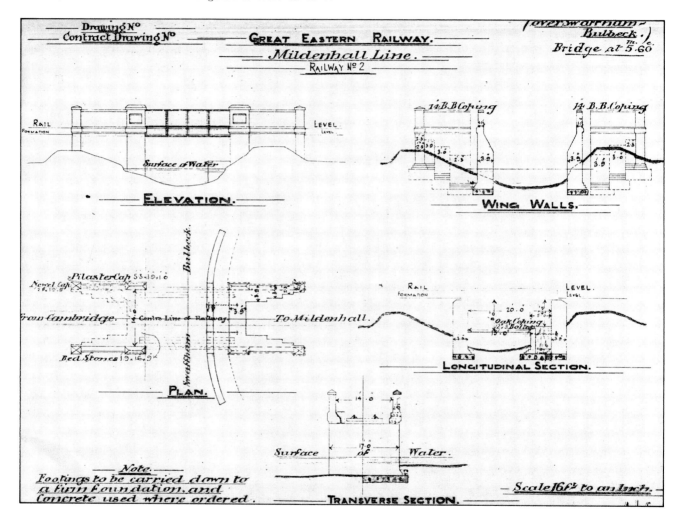

CHAPTER TWO

GREAT EASTERN OPERATION

THE new branch railway duly opened to traffic on Monday, 2nd June 1884. Four trains conveying first, second and third class accommodation were provided. Only one passenger was recorded travelling the full distance between Cambridge and Fordham whilst twenty-five used the first 'up' train to travel from the various stations to Cambridge. Burwell was particularly busy and each of the trains was greeted with hearty cheering and waving as they pulled into the platform at the branch stations. The *Cambridge Chronicle* reported: 'The approach of the first train into Swaffham Prior was welcomed with a burst of hearty cheering and much regret was felt at the absence of the squire (Charles Allix) in consequence of the illness of his son at Hunstanton.' The paper reiterated the wishes of many by concluding: 'It is to be hoped that the new venture will prove in all respects a prosperous one.'

The railway quickly settled down to provide the required service for farmers and growers of the area and proved a boon to the local populace who could travel to Cambridge in a quarter of the time taken by road. As well as providing connections for London and other East Anglian towns at Cambridge and Fordham, the GER also offered excursion facilities to Yarmouth, Lowestoft, Felixstowe, Hunstanton and Harwich. Response to these was mixed for many of the local people were employed on the land at a weekly wage of 10s 0d to 15s 0d and the fares charged amounted to almost a third of their wages. It was, therefore, the relatively few middle and upper class clientele who initially used the branch passenger services with any regularity. The exceptions were Cambridge and Newmarket or Bury St. Edmunds market days when the three or four coach branch trains were strengthened with an additional third class vehicle.

H. H. Holt, the officer in charge of construction, wrote from the contractor's office based at Worlington, to Lovatt on 21st October 1884, regarding No. 3 crossing keeper's cottage located at 5 miles 50 chains. Originally, the cottage, together with the 25 ft wide gates, was estimated at £340 but, as the cottage cost £310 and the gates £40, the work was costing £10 above the estimated price. Holt requested guidance. He also advised that now the line was opened for traffic, the GER was refusing to allow trains to stop to offload material. Delivery was made direct to Bottisham station goods yard where the material was offloaded into waggons before horses hauled the material 2½ miles by road to the cottage site, the last three-quarters of a mile along a droveway which was impassable in winter and bad weather. Holt was adamant that all material should be passed free of charge by rail.

There was also evidence of dissent over the works. 'The Cambridge foreman over the Cambridge men is not to be trusted' and Holt requested Lovatt to send down Bentley,

one of his foremen bricklayers, to take charge of the relatively small job to support the carpenter. Because of distance and other commitments, he was unable to oversee the work. Concluding, Holt suggested that as he was experiencing both transport and staff difficulties to the isolated site, the price of the cottage be raised to £350.

The difficulties over the construction of the cottage were later explained in a letter which Lovatt wrote to Wilson, the GER engineer, on 22nd October. The contractor also questioned the price of weighbridge offices being £30 for timber structures and not brick as originally quoted. On 25th October 1884, Wilson duly advised that he accepted the price of £30 for the weighbridges but was adamant the price of £340 for the crossing cottage and gates remain. Lovatt again raised the cost of transport of materials but Wilson, in a letter dated 29th October 1884, only conceded a price of £2 for carriage of items from Bottisham station to site.

Major General Hutchinson returned to the line on 22nd November 1884 and found that all the remedial work required was completed. As the line was being extended to Mildenhall, the inspector recommended the provision of a footbridge or tunnel to connect the platforms at Fordham before the further portion of the line was submitted for inspection. During the visit to Fordham, Hutchinson remarked that the water column at the 'down' end of the 'down' platform was too close to the edge of the rails and suggested 'this should be remedied by moving the water column or shortening the down platform'.

During outstanding construction work on the first section, the GER requested several modifications, one of which was the substitution of tiles for slates on the roof of the weighbridge at Swaffham Prior. Lovatt replied on 6th December 1884 that such work would cost an additional £3. This amount proved acceptable to the railway company.

As a result of Major General Hutchinson's visit to Fordham, the local superintendent supported the request to provide a footbridge to connect the platforms. The Way and Works Committee duly awarded a contract to Arrol Brothers who tendered at £215 on 16th December 1884.

On 4th February 1885 a further fatality occurred on the construction work when a navvy, David Heffer, suffered a haemorrhage and died shortly afterwards. Fifteen years earlier Heffer achieved considerable notoriety when he turned Queen's Evidence in the case of the murder of a gamekeeper at Eriswell. His companion was, however, found guilty and sentenced to death.

Lovatt forwarded the final account for construction of the railway from Barnwell Junction to Fordham to the GER directors on 9th March 1885. The breakdown of the expenditure of £52,574 9s 5d being as follows:

	£	s	d
Fencing	6777	2	6
Earthworks	16696	10	2
Brickwork	4356	18	0
Drainpipes	637	6	6
Masonry	669	8	3
Timberwork	227	8	6
Ironwork	175	14	0
Permanent Way	1561	1	3

Station Buildings

Barnwell Junction	2479	18	4
Quy	915	4	6
Bottisham	2554	14	0
Swaffham Prior	2412	12	0
Burwell	2339	2	0

	£	s	d
	10701	10	10
Buffer Stops	210	0	0
Granite cement or concrete on platforms	411	4	0

Level Crossing Cottages

at 2 miles 25 chains	353	6	0
at 3 miles 34 chains	353	6	0
at 5 miles 62 chains	378	16	6
at 5 miles 74 chains	353	6	0
Fencing	22	15	0

	£	s	d
	1461	9	6
3 Cattle Pens	270	0	0
5 Loading Gauges	37	10	0
6 Catch Points	9	0	0
400 sq yds Coal Allotments	15	0	0
57 Lamps and posts	142	10	0
Extras	332	17	9
Extra work over contract	4591	11	10
Waiting shed and Workers Cottages	3037	10	4
Weighbridge House and Pits	252	16	0
	£52574	9	5

By early March construction work on the Fordham-Mildenhall section was completed and the necessary application for inspection was made to the Board of Trade.

The official Board of Trade inspection on the Fordham-Mildenhall section was subsequently carried out by Major General C. S. Hutchinson on 28th March 1885. The formation of the 7 mile 20.8 chain extension was wide enough and bridges built for possible future doubling of the line. The permanent way was of similar formation as the Barnwell Junction-Fordham section and the inspector found the stations at Isleham and Mildenhall completed to his satisfaction. At Isleham, Hutchinson approved of the arrangement for the passing loop. The steepest gradient of 1 in 150 and sharpest curve (other than entry to stations) of 40 chains radius was not considered to present any problems in train working. During his journey the inspector noted the 11 overbridges constructed of brickwork, the largest span being 34¾ ft and the 3 underbridges, 2 built of brick with largest span of 14½ ft, and the third with brick abutments carrying wrought iron girders again with a span of 14½ ft. The wrought iron girders were found to have sufficient theoretical strength and gave moderate deflection under test. According to Hutchinson, the line 'was exceedingly well finished' and subject to the removal of a set of trap points at Fordham he recommended the opening of the railway to traffic.

Four days later, on 1st April 1885, the Mildenhall section was opened to passenger and goods traffic. The first train departed from the terminus at 8.08 a.m. conveying about 30 passengers. As the station was within five minutes walking distance from the centre of the town, a large number of people gathered to watch the departure and cheer the train on its way. The church bells were rung at intervals throughout the day to celebrate the event. The *Cambridge Observer and County Guardian* commented the railway 'will prove a great convenience to the inhabitants who have hitherto had to drive five and a half miles to the nearest railway station'. This station, Mildenhall Road on the Ely-Norwich line, was subsequently renamed Burnt Fen by the GER (renamed again in 1905 Shippea Hill). Kennett station on the Cambridge-Bury St. Edmunds line was also 5½ miles distant. The GER offered the new line five departures from Mildenhall to Cambridge and return weekdays only. On Thursdays only four trains were, however, offered in the 'down' direction as the 2.35 p.m. ex-Cambridge did not run.

Although the railway was favourably received, a correspondent to the *Cambridge Observer and County Guardian* was concerned with minor faults on the original section and in April 1885 wrote of inadequate signs to Swaffham Prior station and suggested the erection of a direction post at the corner of Fen Lane.

The day after the opening of the section to Mildenhall, Lovatt rendered his figures for the construction of Railway No. 4 between Fordham and Mildenhall to the GER Board.

	£	s.	d.
Fencing	4295	16	3
Earthworks	12278	7	4
Brickwork	7290	13	6
Drainpipes	92	10	6
Masonry	679	9	6
Timberwork	96	16	6
Ironwork	86	1	7
Permanent way	881	5	5

Station Buildings

Isleham	£2268 12s 0d
Mildenhall	£2322 16s 11d

	£	s.	d.
	4591	8	11
Granary and Goods Shed	1690	0	0
3 Buffer Stops	75	0	0
3 Wooden Buffer Stops	45	0	0
1041 cu. yds Granite cement	208	4	0
2 Cattle Pens	260	0	0
2 Loading gauges	15	0	0
433 sq yds Coal Allotments	16	4	9
17 Lamps and Posts	42	10	0
Fixing Locomotive Turntable	10	0	0
Extra Engineering Expenses plus 10 per cent	218	5	6
Extra work over contract	2183	13	1
Waiting sheds and Workmen's Cottages	1351	16	0
Weighbridges houses and pits	99	10	6
	£36507	13	4

The engineer submitted a report regarding the settlement of the contractor's account as at 30th June 1885, showing that of the £6870 outstanding, £3500 was certified as complete, leaving a balance of £3370 which was to remain with the Railway Company as indemnity until Lovatt had completed the maintenance of the line for one year after opening for traffic and to the engineer's satisfaction. The general manager concurred on 7th July 1885 and duly advised Lovatt of the decision.

During construction of the railway Lovatt had used a Manning Wardle 0—6—0 tank locomotive *Godfrey* (Works No. 533) on haulage of ballast and material trains, together with locomotives *Falcon* and *Berkeley*. It is uncertain how the latter were disposed of after completion of the main works but *Godfrey* was sent to the GER locomotive depot at Cambridge at the beginning of May 1885 for a thorough overhaul. On completion of the remedial work at the end of June, the engine with other items of equipment, was sent to work on the Poole and Bournemouth Railway. Remaining items of useful plant and machinery were forwarded for further use to the Woolsthorpe Branch Extension of the Great Northern Railway or the Skipton and Ilkley Railway, where Lovatt also had contracts. All plant and material not required by the contractor was gathered together at either Isleham or Mildenhall goods yards. These items were subsequently auctioned at 10.30 a.m. on Thursday, 30th July 1885, by Arthur T. Crow. Intending buyers were advised that a train left Cambridge for Isleham at 10.14 a.m. After the completion of the sale of the first 137 lots, the sale moved to Mildenhall and intending bidders caught the 1.16 p.m. ex-Isleham, returning after the auction by the 5.50 p.m. train.

The largest item for disposal at the auction, and entered as an afterthought as lot 137A, was the fourth locomotive to be utilised by Lovatt on the construction work. Six coupled tank locomotive *Scot* built by the Hunslet Engine Company (works No. 152) had also received shops attention over a period of six weeks which included a new set of tyres on all wheels, prior to the sale.

In August 1885 the general manager received complaints regarding the approach road to Quy station. Local officials confirmed that it was not a public road and that the narrowness caused problems for horse-drawn waggons approaching, turning and leaving the station. Land in the vicinity belonged to Mr. Musgrave Francis and others. After negotiating with the landowners, the GER authorities confirmed on 18th August that repairs would be executed, with costs shared between the railway company and Francis, at an estimated cost of £525 subject to the local authority adopting the roadway.

After several months it was evident to both the local authorities and the railway company that improvements were also required on the road approach to Mildenhall station. As a result of a site meeting, authority was given on 6th October 1885 for resurfacing and widening of the approach road at an estimated cost of £25. Despite the urgency of improvements before the heavy winter weather, the remedial work was not completed until the following spring.

The new railway quickly became one of the focal points of the rural community, especially for the arrival or departure of local people. On one such occasion, on 14th June 1887, Miss Preston departed from Swaffham Prior village on the 4 p.m. train to Cambridge on her way to the West Country and future marriage. Half the inhabitants, including the Sunday School children, wished Miss Preston a fond farewell from the flag bedecked station.

The Jubilee of Queen Victoria in June 1887 was celebrated throughout the length and breadth of the British Isles. Almost every town and village held a social gathering and at Mildenhall so great was the number of poorer folk to be entertained that no establishment was large enough to hold such a gathering except the church and the use of that building for a meal was definitely frowned upon. Evidently the next suitable building was the goods shed at Mildenhall station. After due representation by local organizations, the GER authorities agreed to the use of the building for other than goods transit and, after due cleaning, the shed was decorated. Three hundred and forty of the poorer inhabitants subsequently sat down to a free meal provided by the local gentry. Ironically, the gathering attended the church for a full choral service immediately before the meal.

From the opening of the line, freight traffic handled at Swaffham Prior had been increasing and it soon came to the notice of the local goods manager that wagons for the station were being detained short of their destination until adequate room could be found in the goods yard to handle the traffic. Empty wagons awaiting loading were equally delayed. To obviate the complaints voiced by local farmers and growers, authority was given on 6th March 1888 for the provision of an additional siding at a cost of £131. Further down the line at Isleham, similar difficulties were being experienced with the siting of coal and coke stacks for local fuel merchants. In order to improve the general tidiness of the yard and appease the local coal merchants, the provision of coal and coke bays at a cost of £81 was authorised on 1st May 1888.

Two months later a further source of complaint at Swaffham Prior was settled. As at Mildenhall three years earlier, the approach road was considered insufficiently wide or adequately surfaced to handle the horse and waggon traffic using the station. After due investigation, the GER Way and Works Committee authorised the widening of the approach road and other remedial work, on 3rd July 1888, at a cost of £51. All three projects were completed by November of the same year.

An accident which might have had more serious repercussions occurred at Fordham Junction in dense fog on 13th December 1889 when a passenger train standing in the 'down' platform 225 yards inside the 'down' home signal was run into by another 'down' train which had passed signals at danger. At the subsequent inquiry the driver of the second train, who had been on duty for 11½ hours, admitted he had lost sight of his usual bearings in the fog and thought the protecting home signal was the distant signal. The inspecting officer thought the accident could have been prevented had the 'down' home signal been attended by a fog signalman.

The increase of staff required to handle traffic at Fordham station brought its own disadvantages. Housing in this rural area of Cambridgeshire was scarce and personnel

CAMBRIDGE AND MILDENHALL RAILWAY.

There is only a Single Line of Rails between Barnwell Junction and Mildenhall.

The Trains on this Single Line are worked by Train Staff and Train Staff Ticket, according to the "Train Staff Regulations" contained in the "Appendix" to this Working Time Book. No Engine or Train is to be run on this Branch without a Train Staff or Train Staff Ticket. The Train Staff Stations are Barnwell Junction, Bottisham, Burwell, Fordham, Isleham & Mildenhall.

Miles	DOWN TRAINS. Week Days.		1	2	3	4	5	6	7	8	9	10	11	12	13	14	15	16	17	18	19	20	21	22	23	24	25	26	27	28	29	30	31
			Mxd.	Pass.	Pass.	Pass.	A Gds.	B Pass.	Pass.	C Pass.																							
			a.m.	a.m.	p.m.	p.m.	p.m.	p.m.	p.m.	p.m.																							
—	**Cambridge**	dep.	7 15	9 15	12 25	....	12 30	3 0	....	5 53																							
1¼	Barnwell Junction	arr.	7 20	9 19	12 29	...	12 45	3 4	...	5 57																							
		dep.	7 22	9 20	12 30		12 38	3 5	....	5 58																							
4½	Quy	,,	7 33	9 27	12 37	Tuesdays only.	1 17	3 12	Thursdays only.	6 5																							
6	Bottisham	arr.	7 38	9 30	12 40		1 22	3 15		6 8																							
		dep.	7 43	9 31	12 41		1 40	3 16		6 9																							
8	Swaffhamprior	,,	7 55	9 36	12 47		2 0	3 22		6 15																							
10	Burwell	arr.	8 1	9 40	12 51		2 10	3 26		6 19																							
		dep.	8 10	9 41	12 52		2 25	3 27		6 20																							
13¼	**Fordham**	arr.	8 20	9 48	12 58	...	2 55	3 36	...	6 26																							
		dep.	8 35	10 6	1 1	2 5	3 15	4 10	5 10	6 31																							
16¾	Isleham	arr.	8 44	10 13	1 8	2 12	3 25	4 22	5 17	6 38																							
		dep.	8 52	10 14	1 9	2 13	3 38	4 23	5 18	6 39																							
20¾	**Mildenhall**	arr.	9 5	10 23	1 18	2 22	3 50	4 35	5 27	6 48																							

A No. 5. To call at Coldham Lane Siding (near Cambridge) when required.
B No. 6 does not run on Thursdays between Cambridge and Fordham.

C No. 8. On Mondays may work not exceeding 2 Trucks of Cattle from Cambridge. On Tuesdays to work forward from Fordham to Mildenhall the Cattle arriving by 6.15 p.m. Train from Newmarket.

Miles	UP TRAINS. Week Days.		1	2	3	4	5	6	7	8	9	10	11	12	13	14	15	16	17	18	19	20	21	22	23	24	25	26	27	28	29	30	31
			Pass.	D Pass.	E Pass.	Pass.	Pass.	Pass.	F Gds.	G Pass.																							
			a.m.	a.m	a.m.	p.m.	p.m.	p.m.	p.m	p.m.																							
—	**Mildenhall**	dep.	7 45	9 43	11 55	1 38	3 28	4 40	4 50	6 8																							
4	Isleham	arr.	7 51	9 51	12 3	1 43	3 36	4 45	5 2	6 16																							
		dep.	7 52	9 52	12 4	1 44	3 37	4 49	5 20	6 17																							
7½	**Fordham**	arr.	8 0	10 0	12 12	1 52	3 45	4 57	5 40	6 25																							
		dep	8 3	10 15	12 22	Tuesdays only.	3 47	Thursdays only.	6 0	6 40																							
10¾	Barwell	arr.	8 8	10 20	12 27		3 52		6 10	6 45																							
		dep.	8 9	10 21	12 28		3 53		7 0	6 46																							
12¾	Swaffhamprior	,,	8 15	10 27	12 34		3 59		7 15	6 52																							
14¾	Bottisham	arr.	8 20	10 32	12 39		4 4		7 22	6 57																							
		dep.	8 21	10 33	12 42		4 5		7 40	6 58																							
16¼	Quy	,,	8 25	10 37	12 46		4 9		8 5	7 2																							
19½	Barnwell Junction	arr.	8 33	10 45	12 54	...	4 17	...	8 15	7 10																							
		dep	8 34	10 46	12 56	....	4 18	....	8 20	7 11																							
20¾	**Cambridge**	arr.	8 38	10 50	1 0	...	4 22	...	8 25	7 15																							

D No. 2. On Mondays, Tuesdays, Wednesdays, and Thursdays not exceeding 4 Trucks of Cattle may be worked from Mildenhall by this Train for the Cambridge, Newmarket, Bury, and Ely Markets respectively.

E No. 3 Up does not run on Thursdays between Fordham and Cambridge.
F No. 7. To shunt at Burwell for No. 8 Passenger Train.
G No. 8. Not exceeding 2 Trucks of Goods may be worked from Mildenhall by this Train.

185

GER Working Timetable for 1890

transferred to the junction found difficulty in acquiring accommodation. After representation by staff, the GER authorities agreed on 4th February 1890 to the provision of two staff cottages. Estimated to cost £490, work was completed the following year when the premises were occupied by permanent way gangers.

Early in 1890 Mr. Musgrave Francis and other interested parties working Coprolite fields near Quy, approached the GER authorities and requested the provision of a siding to serve the Quy Coprolite works. After investigation it was found that a suitable facility could be installed leaving the main single branch line half a mile east of Quy station. The general manager agreed to the proposal and the Traffic Committee authorised the expenditure on 15th April 1890 subject to the following conditions:

1. The GER Company will undertake to provide the siding at the expense of Mr. Francis and others at a cost of £340.
2. The land necessary for the siding to be conveyed to the GER Company free of charge.
3. The Ordinary Quy rates to be charged to all traffic to and from the siding and at the end of each year, a rebate to be made of 2d per ton upon every ton of traffic forwarded or received from the siding.
4. This allowance to be continued until such time as the Railway Company recoup £340.
5. Mr. Francis and others to have the right to send 6 months notice to require the siding to close at any time and have conveyed back to them the land and also have a portion of the amount realised on old materials as well as recouping them to the balance of £340, unless the half yearly payment of 2d per ton has covered the £340, in which case the old material becomes the property of the railway company.

Coprolite formed of phosphatic nodules was once believed to be fosillized dinosaur dung but was later found to be the remains of aquatic creatures.

After the company had agreed to provide the siding half a mile from Quy station, Mr. Musgrave Francis requested alterations to the original plans. The changes increased the cost from £340 to £410 with Francis and his associates willing to bear the additional cost. The Way and Works Committee agreed the alteration on 5th August 1890 and work on the siding began early the following year.

Traffic through Fordham, on both the Ely-Chippenham Junction line and Mildenhall branch, was steadily growing and it became increasingly clear that facilities on both the passenger station and in the goods yard were inadequate. To ease the situation authority was given on 3rd February 1891 for general improvements estimated at £350 to be carried out. The work took some years to complete and included resurfacing of the platforms on the station and general tidying up of the goods yard to facilitate smooth loading and unloading of freight consignments.

On 13th September 1891 train services on the branch were suspended for some four hours after a suicide near Barnwell Junction.

Traffic on the branch was showing an increase, with just over 10,000 passengers departing from Mildenhall station in 1890. Two years later the figure had advanced to 10,175. However, despite the improvement, receipts from certain lines of the GER were causing considerable concern at Bishopsgate. Compared with earnings on the main line of £107 per mile per week, the average branch and cross country line was earning £14 per mile per week. The best of the branch lines from Southend to Shenfield showed receipts of £46 per mile whilst at the other end of the scale the line from Downham to Stoke Ferry earned a meagre £4. At the review of receipts held during a Traffic Committee meeting, the Mildenhall branch fared little better with takings of £6 per mile per week and like the other smaller earners was subject to closer scrutiny. After investigations, the general manager reported to the Traffic Committee on 15th February 1895 that he proposed to implement a scheme for savings of £370 on the original operating costs of the Cambridge-Mildenhall services, by reducing the number of trains.

By 1895 freight trains passing through the junction at Fordham were increasing to such a length that it was impossible to shunt a slower goods service for a passenger or express freight train to pass if the crossing loop was occupied. Delays to services were becoming such an embarrassment that the Way and Works Committee readily agreed on 15th October the extension of the Trap siding at a cost of £345 to accommodate the longer trains.

The large number of occupational crossings on the branch were always a source of problem to railwaymen, and accidents or near accidents were commonplace, as it appeared the local populace always attempted to cross the railway when one of the infrequent trains was passing. One of the unfortunate ones was a labourer, William Hart, who was crossing the line near Fen Ditton on 28th September 1896. Driver William Precious, noting Hart on the crossing, sounded the engine whistle and shut off steam but failed to prevent the accident. Hart obviously thought he was clear of the train and moved only slowly with the result that the left hand buffer of the locomotive struck him and threw him to one side, leaving him badly injured. He was quickly carried to the halted train for conveyance to Cambridge and hospital but he died later of his injuries.

Operation of the branch was rarely inconvenienced by inclement weather but on 15th and 16th January 1897 services were affected when drifting snow blocked various shallow cuttings along the line. Traffic was delayed for some hours on both days before platelayers and gangers managed to shovel the snow clear of the track.

On 22nd April 1897 the GER finally acknowledged that the branch served the locality of Lode and renamed Bottisham station 'Bottisham and Lode', despite the fact that the station was actually in the village of Lode, Bottisham being 2 miles distant.

The station master at Fordham regularly complained of inadequate accommodation of the station house. His plea for additional room was upheld on 5th April 1898 when the GE authorities agreed to the provision of a wash house and other accommodation at a cost of £45, the work being completed later in the same year.

By 1898 some of the branch stations were decidedly shabby and remedial action was finally taken on 20th September 1898. The contracts for the painting and repair work at Burwell was awarded to Vigor and Company of Poplar who tendered at £149 10s 0d while A. Coe of Ipswich attended to Isleham and Mildenhall stations tendering at £105 and £130 respectively.

Following earlier application for a rail connection, the installation of the Commercial Brewery siding near Barnwell Junction was completed in September 1898 at a cost of £365, the work being inspected and passed for the Board of Trade by Colonel Addison in April 1899. As traffic increased so the local freight trip working, both to the Barnwell Junction yard siding and the Commercial Brewery siding across the branch, was considerably delayed by lack of crossover facilities from the 'down' main line yard at Barnwell Junction. To obviate light locomotive movements and subsequent blockage of the main line and the Mildenhall branch, a new crossover was authorised on 19th September 1899 at an estimated cost of £220.

The infrequent service operated by the GE was little affected by a derailment which occurred at noon on Thursday, 30th January 1900 near Quy station. The locomotive and 12 wagons of the 11.50 a.m. Cambridge-Mildenhall goods left the rails at a speed of under 20 mph when the points failed to lock correctly and moved under the weight of the engine. The Cambridge breakdown train was quickly summoned and managed to clear a path for the later passenger services. Some of the derailed wagons were, however, pushed to one side of the running line and rerailed the following day.

Adverse weather again caused problems when a severe blizzard blocked the line between Barnwell Junction and Swaffham Prior, and Fordham and Isleham on 14th February 1900. The branch remained closed for over 24 hours before permanent way staff managed to clear the line. Roads were impassable and, once cleared, the branch provided the only means of communication with the surrounding area for some days.

The programme of repairs and painting of stations, which commenced in 1898, continued with the renovation of Fordham station by A. Coe of Ipswich who was awarded the contract on 13th June 1900 tendering at £198 10s 0d.

Early in 1901 Mr. R. Stephenson of Burwell wrote to the GER requesting the provision of a siding to his recently established cement works near Fordham. After due investigation and consultation with Stephenson, the general manager reported to the Way and Works Committee that the provision of the siding costing £480 on GER land would be advantageous to future traffic growth. Stephenson was prepared to pay the cost of the siding on his own land as well as £48 per annum for the provision of the facility, subject to the usual 5 per cent rebate on traffic tonnage handled. The Way and Works Committee saw no objection to the proposal and, after the private siding agreement was signed on 13th April, authority for work to proceed was given on 16th April 1901. The work was completed somewhat quickly by railway standards and was inspected and passed for working by the Board of Trade inspector on 17th September 1901.

Early in February 1903 the GER were advised by the local Gas Company that after some years of increased pricing, the cost of gas supplies to Mildenhall station were to be reduced by 5d per 1000 cubic feet.

Fordham station, which opened in 1879, 69 miles 8 chains ex Liverpool Street and 13 miles 36 chains ex Cambridge, was the junction for the Ely-Newmarket and Bury St. Edmunds routes, and the Mildenhall branch. The station and goods yard covered an area of five acres. In this view facing Ely, the Mildenhall branch curved away to the east beyond the level crossing.   *Lens of Sutton*

As the train service on the Mildenhall branch tended to be infrequent, many local people still persisted in using the railway as a right of way, unfortunately all too often at their peril. On one such occasion William Parmenter, the platelayer stationed at Swaffham Prior, proceeding along the line at 6.30 a.m. on 31st March 1903, stumbled across a body near Clarks Crossing. The deceased, George Gray aged 50, a gamekeeper of Swaffham Prior, was evidently taking a short cut along the line from the nearby crossing when he was struck by the early morning train. At the county coroner's inquest held the following day at the Allix Arms, Swaffham Prior, Parmenter advised that he had found Gray lying in the 'four foot' with one leg across the rails and severed from the rest of the body. The jury duly recorded a verdict of accidental death.

A further fatal accident occurred at Barnwell Junction on the evening of Tuesday, 30th June 1903, when booking clerk Ernest Watson, after attending to business in the goods yard, stood on the 'down' main line waiting for an 'up' goods train to pass. The noise of the passing wagons distracted Watson from noticing an approaching 'down' main line train which hit him and killed him instantly. At the inquest held on Friday, 3rd July, it was established that Watson had crossed the line for unknown reasons and should not have endangered himself by standing on the 'down' main line. The line was straight in the direction of the approaching train and Watson should have noted its approach. A verdict of accidental death was recorded.

From the opening of the railway, two sets of footplate crews were established at Mildenhall and sought lodging locally. As the years progressed and men were transferred, it became evident that there was a shortage of housing in the district for any newcomers. Matters came to a head in 1903 when James Holden, locomotive superintendent of the GER, complained to his general manager of the scarcity of suitable houses at Mildenhall and requested the urgent provision of two cottages for the driver and acting driver stationed there. The request was passed to James Wilson, the engineer, who estimated the cost of cottages on GER land at £452. Holden reported that the men were willing to pay a weekly rent of 4s 0d producing a 2¼ per cent return on outlay. Authorization for the provision of the cottages was given on 21st July 1903, but it was 17th November before E. Willmott and Sons of Cambridge received the contract after tendering at £425. Change of specification caused a delay in the commencement of the work and the cottages were not completed until October 1905 at a cost of £508, £56 in excess of estimates.

Delays to trains passing through Fordham station continued to cause concern at GER Headquarters. Not only branch trains were involved but lengthy coal trains from Stanground yard, near Peterborough, and Whitemoor, and the resultant empty wagons returning from the Essex and Suffolk stations meant holding trains back at Ely and Bury St. Edmunds until a clear path was available between Chippenham Junction and Ely Dock Junction. To facilitate smoother working and after consultation with the

Mildenhall station, 76 miles 31 chains from Liverpool Street and 20 miles 59 chains ex Cambridge, with its 365ft long platform on the down or north side of the main single line in 1905. Built as a through station in case the railway was extended to Thetford, it ultimately never served such a purpose as the single branch terminated at buffer stops just beyond the end of the platform 76 miles 41 chains ex Liverpool Street.

Isleham station, 72 miles 30 chains ex Liverpool Street and 16 miles 58 chains from Cambridge, was almost identical in design to Burwell. Situated almost a mile south of the village, the station had up and down side platforms served by a crossing loop 850ft in length. Station master Henry Kitchen and his staff pose on the down platform in 1905. *Lens of Sutton*

Operating Department, the engineer announced on 18th December 1906 the plan to alter the layout at Fordham. The scheme included the lengthening of the loop through the station to allow the longest of the freight trains to pass each other if necessary and a reception siding alongside the Newmarket line to accommodate a locomotive and 55 trucks. Approval for the scheme costing £1300 against the Way and Works Committee budget and £650

earlier scheme enabled the work to be completed at a cost of £518, giving a saving of £212 on the siding, and work was completed in April 1910.

Thefts from branch station booking offices were rare as most station masters lived on the premises. However, between 11 p.m. on 1st April 1909, when relief station master Harry Fields locked up Barnwell Junction booking office for the night, and 7 a.m. on 2nd April 1909 when

Holden's 'Y65' class 2—4—2Ts were utilized on Mildenhall services for a number of years after their introduction in 1909/10. Their large cab towering above a small boiler soon earned them the nickname 'Crystal Palaces'. No. 1307, with Mildenhall driver B. Coe on the footplate, stands gleaming in its GER livery, near the goods shed at Mildenhall on 19th May 1911.

against the Traffic Committee budget was given the same day.

The remedial work and provision of a longer loop at Fordham only partially resolved the traffic congestion. In 1908 the goods manager and his operating counterpart advised the general manager that traffic and exchange traffic at or near Fordham had grown and other branch traffic was also increasing. This latter was aggravated by consignments from Stephenson's new intermediate siding between Fordham and Burwell and the proposed siding for Colchester and Ball's chemical, manure and brick siding being installed between Soham and Fordham. Traffic from these sidings required sorting at Fordham and only the shunting spur for the 'up' sidings was available for storage and refuge of wagons. If this was occupied shunting had to be performed on the main single line which required clearing for the passage of trains. These movements also halted the shunting into and out of the goods yard. Despite the plea no action was taken and the following year application for a new siding was mooted. The engineer, after investigation, approved the proposal at an estimated cost of £730 for the siding and electrical costs for lighting the yard at £54, giving a total cost for the Fordham scheme of £2734.

The provision of the new siding followed on from the other work at Fordham and excess equipment from the

he reopened, the office was ransacked and 5s 1d in coppers and 43 halfpenny stamps were stolen. Within hours of reporting the incident, James Rowlands, an unemployed labourer from London, found wandering the streets of Cambridge, was arrested and charged with the offence.

After some thirteen years the branch stations were again repaired and painted. Clark and Sons of Cambridge received the contract for Barnwell Junction on 15th June 1911 after tendering at £115 2s 0d. The same firm also received the contracts for Swaffham Prior and Bottisham and Lode on 5th October 1911 at costs of £83 15s 0d and £114 19s 6d respectively, whilst Burwell and Isleham were contracted on 18th April 1912 for £121 and £102. The stations at Fordham and Mildenhall were painted and repaired by A. Coe of Ipswich who tendered at £167 and £119 10s 0d and received the contract on 5th October 1911. All the work was carried out in 1912.

The poor passenger traffic receipts earned by the Mildenhall line were always a source of concern to the GER authorities and, in an attempt to reduce the operating deficit, the branch was chosen for experiments with a push-pull auto-train. For some years many of the British main line railways had been experimenting with steam railcars and auto-trains on lightly used lines. The GER lagged behind in the development programme until 1914 when James Holden adapted one of the 'Y65' 2–4–2T locomotives, No. 1311, for compressed air operated auto-train working, and coupled it to two converted coaches to form a push-pull train with the locomotive pulling the two coaches in one direction and pushing them in the other. The train was formed of a 48 ft 3 ins clerestory corridor composite coach seating nine 1st class and thirty 3rd class passengers next to the engine, and a clerestory 3rd driving trailer with end compartment for driver and guard with accommodation for forty-six 3rd class passengers. The two coaches weighing 25 tons 8 cwt and 26 tons 10 cwt respectively, were well within the capabilities of the 'Y65' locomotive. The auto-train commenced trial running on the Mildenhall line on 5th October 1914 but after several weeks the trial was transferred to the Ramsey High Street branch. Unfortunately, the auto-train was unsuitable for either branch where mixed train working was established as it operated only as a self-contained unit and it was impossible to strengthen the train on market days and other busy periods, especially if the engine was propelling. The train was subsequently transferred to the temporarily restored service between White Hart Lane and Cheshunt, on the reopened Churchbury loop line.

The outbreak of the First World War on 4th August 1914 found the GER with other British Railways companies under government control. Train services continued to run to the pre-war timetables as passengers travelled to business or on pleasure. Goods traffic quietly flourished as increased produce was despatched from the farmlands to towns and cities to make up for the loss of imported food. Several local railwaymen quickly answered the call to arms and joined the colours in the first few months.

Soon after the beginning of hostilities, the GER set up a War Relief Fund with collections made at the company's stations. The first call resulted in 13s 6d being collected at Mildenhall. Other station collections included Fordham 7s 3d, Burwell 3s 9d, Bottisham and Lode 1s 10d, and Barnwell Junction 7s 0d.

On the outbreak of the First World War British farmers were urged to increase production of vegetables and fruit to offset the deficit of imported foodstuffs caused by enemy action against shipping. Growers and cattle breeders of Cambridgeshire and West Suffolk, like their counterparts all over the country, rallied to the call and as a result a considerable number of additional freight trains ran across the branch. As the war years progressed, hay traffic also increased as fodder and bedding was required by the many military establishments in London and East Anglia. The Mildenhall line was not so strategically placed as many other East Anglian branches and few military personnel were carried on the branch trains. For the few military exercises conducted in the area most men were conveyed by lorry whilst horses were conveyed by special trains.

Serving an agricultural and farming community, the GER was keen to assist with the efforts to increase production. To this end the railway company organised an egg and poultry demonstration train, and during 1916 the train visited the Mildenhall branch when a total of 653

CAMBRIDGE, FORDHAM AND MILDENHALL.

Single Line between Barnwell Junction and Mildenhall.

people attended the exhibition, 381 adults and 272 children, many of the latter no doubt more through curiosity than real interest.

The strain of the war years was taxing the resources of the railways and in December 1916 the Railway Executive Committee issued an ultimatum to the effect that they would only continue if drastic reductions were made to ordinary services. Locomotive power was short through lack of coal supplies. The Lloyd George Coalition thus agreed to the reduction of passenger services from 1st January 1917. Despite this edict, the Mildenhall branch services remained virtually intact.

After the cessation of hostilities on Armistice Day flags were displayed at the branch stations. The festivities, as far as the branch was concerned, were short-lived for from 26th September to 8th October 1919 a railway strike halted services on the line. Two years later the miners' strike affected coal supplies, although services were not curtailed. This industrial action and the later general strike of 1926 began the decline in railway services. Farmers and growers realised that with improved roads, goods could be conveyed by lorry, using, in some cases, vehicles purchased second-hand from the army, thus permitting short haul journeys at cheaper rates than charged by the GER. The door to door services were more convenient than double handling caused by loading and unloading into and out of railway wagons. The primitive commercial vehicles of the day were not, however, capable of continuous long hauls and the middle and long distance freight traffic remained safely in the hands of the railway company.

In the early war years it became increasingly evident that economies would have to be made in the operation of the Mildenhall line. Staff reduction was subsequently arranged and, to assist the remaining staff to deal with their work more efficiently, it was agreed on 13th December 1921 that long-burning signal oil lamps would be provided in place of gas or one-day oil lamps at Barnwell Junction, Bottisham, Swaffham Prior, Isleham and Mildenhall stations. Authority was given for the work costing an estimated £190 and replacement was completed the following spring.

On 26th June 1922 Musgrave Francis renewed his private siding agreement whilst two years earlier on 28th October 1920 H. & D. Taylor had taken over the siding agreement formerly signed by the Commercial Brewery Company.

The seeds of competition against the railway, sown by Mr. George Mansfield of Burwell before the First World War, came to fruition in July 1922 when he introduced a bus service linking Burwell with Cambridge via Reach, Commercial End, Bottisham and Lode Church. Prior to hostilities, Mansfield expanded his cobbler's business to take over the supply and repair of bicycles. He later acquired a motor cycle and sidecar and was contracted to convey the bank clerk from Newmarket to Burwell and back for the bank's weekly visit to the village. Flushed with such success, a model T Ford taxi was acquired but soon trade had flourished beyond the vehicle's capabilities and a Ford T with a larger body was bought to enable the

carriage of both goods and passengers, the latter sitting on tip-up seats. The first passenger runs were made in 1921 but Burwell and District bus services were truly established the following year when Mansfield purchased a similar dual purpose vehicle built by Garner's of Moseley Bank from the maker's stand at the Royal Show at Cambridge. The vehicles were immediately placed on Route 1, Burwell to Cambridge, in direct competition with the Mildenhall train service. Within weeks a service was also introduced between Burwell and Newmarket, running on Tuesdays only for the local market.

With a view to counteracting the bus competition and working its branch line with utmost economy, the GER operating and commercial superintendent proposed, along with other lines on their system, the introduction of conductor-guard method of working on the Mildenhall branch. The Traffic Committee was advised that the Ministry of Transport had given their approval to the modification required for working existing branch lines. In view of the fact that the Downham-Stoke Ferry branch had been operated under such conditions since 1895 and the Somersham-Ramsey High Street line had changed over to conductor-guard working in the spring, the Traffic Committee duly approved of the expenditure of £2,500 for modification and alterations to signal boxes and booking offices on the line on 18th June 1922. Against the expenditure, the annual estimated saving for all lines involved in the scheme was £7,000.

At the same meeting the operating and commercial superintendent reported that at several places served by road transport there was no rail facility to offer. It was well known and all too obvious that a further reduction in passenger receipts had been caused by the introduction of motor buses serving such localities. The cost of providing a large station was hitherto expensive but with the Ministry of Transport's relaxation it was possible to provide cheap halts. On the Mildenhall line petitions had been received requesting stations to serve the villages of Fen Ditton and Horningsea, Exning, and Worlington village and golf links. After investigation it was found possible to site cheaply built halts, adjacent to overbridges, to serve these villages, the estimated cost for low clinker, timber-fronted platforms, with oil lamp and nameboard, being at £80-£150. The CME estimated that the cost to provide steps on the side of coaching stock to enable passengers to join and detrain at the platforms would be £14 per coach per set. The total expenditure to provide enough stock for the introduction of conductor-guard working on the various lines was estimated at no more than £400. This sum was considered by the Traffic Committee and due authority was given.

Thus the GER, prior to amalgamation with other companies to form the London & North Eastern Railway, opened three new halts at Fen Ditton, Exning Road and Mildenhall Golf Links on and from 20th November 1922. At the same time the conductor-guard method of working, forerunner of today's pay trains, was introduced with the guard issuing tickets for the halts. All the halts were extremely simple 'structures' merely consisting of a platform of clinker raised to rail level only with timber

Fen Ditton Halt in 1922 showing the clinker platform with oil lamp and nameboard. Note the sleeper front has yet to be installed.

Conductor-guard operated train at Fen Ditton Halt in 1922 with a passenger alighting from the brake third by using the steps on the side of the coach. Note the guard's rack of tickets, also the side notice on the vehicle denoting Mildenhall Golf Halt as well as Fen Ditton and Exning.

CAMBRIDGE, FORDHAM AND MILDENHALL.
Single Line between Barnwell Junction and Mildenhall.

DOWN WEEK DAYS

Miles from Cambridge	Station	1 Pass. a.m.	2 Gds. a.m.	3 Pass. a.m.	4	5	6 Pass. p.m. M S O	7	8 Pass. p.m.	9	10 Pass. p.m.
—	Cambridge .... dep.	—	9 0	10 30	—		1 45	....	4 20	—	7 36
1 46	Barnwell Junction... Ⓢ { arr.	—	9 6	10 33	—		1 48	....	4 23	—	7 39
	{ dep.	—	9 12	10 34	—		1 49	....	4 24	—	7 40
2 33	Fen Ditton Halt........... „	—	—	10 37	—		1 52	....	4 27	—	7 43
4 49	Quy .... ⓃⒷ „	—	9 30	10 44	—		1 59	....	4 34	—	7 50
6 7	Bottisham and Lode Ⓢ { arr.	—	10 0	10 47	—		2 2	....	4 37	—	7 53
8 3	Swaffhamprior ...... ⓃⒷ „	—	10 20	10 53	—		2 8	....	4 43	—	7 59
9 75	Burwell .... Ⓢ „	—	10 25	10 57	—		2 12	....	4 47	—	8 3
10 50	Exning Road Halt ...... „	—	—	11 1	—		2 16	....	4 51	—	8 7
13 39	Fordham .... Ⓢ { arr.	7 24	11 20	11 7	—		2 22	....	4 58	—	8 14
	{ dep.	7 26	12 0	11 10	—		2 24	....	5 0	—	8 16
16 61	Isleham .... Ⓢ „	7 33	12 10	11 17	—		2 31	....	5 7	—	8 23
19 69	WorlingtonGolfLinksHalt „	7 34	—	11 25	—		2 39	....	5 15	—	8 31
20 62	Mildenhall .... Ⓢ arr.	7 42	12 40	11 29	—		2 43	....	5 19	—	8 35

UP WEEK DAYS

Miles from Mildenh'll	Station	1 Pass. a.m.	2 Pass. a.m.	3	4	5 Gds. p.m. SO	6 Pass. p.m.	7 Gds. p.m. MSO	8 Pass. p.m. NS	9	10	11 Pass. p.m.
—	Mildenhall .... Ⓢ dep.	7 51	11 36	—		1 45	3 7	3 0	5 27			8 45
— 73	WorlingtonGolfLinksHalt „	7 54	11 40	—			3 11		5 31			
4 1	Isleham .... Ⓢ { arr.	8 0	11 46	—		1 55	3 17	3 10	5 37			8 52
	{ dep.	8 1	11 47	—		2 10	3 18	3 20	5 38			8 53
7 23	Fordham .... Ⓢ { arr.	8 11	11 54	—		2 20	3 25	3 30	5 45			9 0
	{ dep.	8 14	11 56	—		3 0	3 27	4 15	5 50			9 2
10 12	Exning Road Halt .... „	8 21	12 3	—			3 34		5 57			
10 67	Burwell .... Ⓢ { arr.	8 23	12 5	—		3 20	3 36	4 35	5 59			
	{ dep.	8 24	12 6	—		3 48	3 37	5 5	6 0			
12 59	Swaffhamprior ...... ⓃⒷ „	8 29	12 11	—		4 3	3 42	5 26	6 5			
14 55	Bottisham and Lode Ⓢ { arr.	8 33	12 15	—		4 8	3 46	5 31	6 9			
	{ dep.	8 34	12 16	—		4 12	3 47	5 45	6 10			
16 13	Quy .... ⓃⒷ „	8 38	12 20	—		4 55	3 51	6 0	6 14			
18 29	Fen Ditton Halt .... „	8 45	12 27	—			3 58		6 21			
19 16	Barnwell Junction Ⓢ { arr.	8 49	12 33	—		5 3	4 4	6 10	6 26			
	{ dep.	8 50	12 34	—		5 8	4 5	6 15	6 27			
20 62	Cambridge .... arr.	8 55	12 39	—		5 15	4 10	6 23	6 32			

=1 From Cambridge, via Newmarket, at 6.45 a.m. See page 22. May work not exceeding 2 trucks of important goods from Cambridge to Mildenhall if the trucks are fitted with Westinghouse brake pipes. 3 To shunt at Burwell for 4. To work traffic for Ipswich and district to go forward from Fordham on 11.35 a.m. ex Whitemoor. =10 May work horses London to Burwell, or cattle from Cambridge or Fordham to Mildenhall only, if the trucks are fitted with Westinghouse brake pipes.

=2 To work cattle from Mildenhall to Fordham and Cambridge only, if the trucks are fitted with Westinghouse brake pipes. 5 To shunt at Burwell for 6. 7 To work traffic to or from Francis siding (between Bottisham and Quy), and Stephenson's siding (between Burwell and Fordham). To attach traffic at Barnwell Junction. On Mondays to follow 6 from Mildenhall. =10 To Cambridge, via Newmarket. See page 25.

Passenger trains are worked on the "Conductor Guard" principle.

LNER Working Timetable for 1924

facing and all situated on the 'up' side of the line. To facilitate passengers alighting and joining the train, the branch was allocated six wheel brake third vehicles equipped with retractable steps operated by the guard. Other six wheel vehicles, third class and first/third composite formed the rest of the train and each vehicle had a central gangway and end drop plates, which enabled the guard to walk through the vehicles to collect fares and check tickets. To assist passengers joining and alighting at the halts, notices were provided inside the vehicles stating that 'Passengers for Fen Ditton, Exning Road and Mildenhall Golf Halts must not attempt to alight until the steps have been fixed and the guard has opened the door'. The brake third was also labelled externally with the notice 'This car for Mildenhall Golf, Exning and Fen Ditton Halts'.

6-wheel brake third No. 221, showing the side steps in the running position flush with the side of the vehicle.

CHAPTER THREE

GROUPING AND DECLINE

FROM 1st January 1923 the GER was amalgamated with the Great Northern, Great Central and several smaller railways to form the London & North Eastern Railway. The new ownership brought few changes to the branch although Mildenhall Golf Links halt was more appropriately renamed Worlington Golf Links halt from the first day of the new régime, and from 1st May 1923 the LNER relinquished the maintenance of three bridges on the branch when West Suffolk County Council took over the responsibility for the structures. The three concerned were Freckenham Road No. 2255 at 74 miles 75 chains, Manor Farm No. 2256 at 75 miles 33 chains, and Worlington Halt No. 2257 at 75 miles 42 chains.

Industrial action soon affected affairs when a seven day railway strike from 20th January 1924 brought a further decline in traffic. Passengers who had regularly patronised the railway service for short journeys turned to the competitive bus services operated by Burwell and District and Ortona Omnibus Companies. Some never returned to use the branch line. Two years later services were once again affected by the General Strike in early May 1926. Union members withdrew their labour in support of the miners and subsequently train services could not be guaranteed. On several days the Mildenhall branch services were suspended. As with other main line companies, at times it was possible for the LNER to offer a skeletal train service by using volunteer labour. The Mildenhall line was one which was fortunate to be operated in such a way and extracts from a diary kept by a volunteer engine driver, Colonel Frank H. Keats, later published in the *Cambridge Chronicle* make interesting reading.

'At 8.55 a.m. on the Tuesday, I received instructions to report for duty as early as possible. Commandeering a lift in the first car passing I arrived at Cambridge station at 9.10 a.m. After a general welcome from the various gentlemen in the 'train office' I was told to book on at the shed. After more friendly greetings I was handed over an engine and told to take the 11.30 a.m. to Mildenhall. I had two firemen, Messrs. Rason and Bing, good lads, who entered into the spirit of the thing. It proved a somewhat tedious journey owing to having to open several crossing gates ourselves en route. However we arrived at Mildenhall eventually, and then returned to Cambridge.'

Fortunately, within a week or so regular railwaymen returned to work and the volunteer labour ceased. The impact of the continuing miners' strike, however, meant coal stocks available to the railway companies were low. The LNER authorities decided on the only course of action available and reduced train services to conserve their supplies of coal. From 31st May 1926, when the revised timetable was introduced, only two passenger trains made the return trip from Cambridge to Mildenhall instead of the previous five.

Despite the introduction of conductor-guard working, the loss of traffic, caused by the various strikes and the attractions of an almost door to door service operated by the competitive bus companies, was always a source of concern to the railway company. The decline suffered on the Mildenhall branch is evident by the receipts earned at the branch stations in the years 1923-28 inclusive:

	Passengers	Passenger Receipts £	Parcel Receipts £	Season Ticket Receipts £	Total £
1923					
Barnwell Junction	4145	235	51	2	288
Quy	1002	8	185	1	194
Bottisham & Lode	5974	316	498	27	841
Swaffhamprior	3905	274	56	14	344
Burwell	8957	786	292	137	1215
Fordham	13110	1166	466	33	1665
Isleham	6096	658	612	123	1393
Mildenhall	9183	1832	1229	60	3121
1924					
Barnwell Junction	3512	177	53	6	236
Quy	692	7	159	–	166
Bottisham & Lode	5105	288	481	23	792
Swaffhamprior	3185	256	56	12	324
Burwell	6937	756	213	61	1030
Fordham	11945	990	528	42	1560
Isleham	6170	656	671	105	1432
Mildenhall	8702	1785	1179	52	3016
1925					
Barnwell Junction	3873	249	440	5	694
Quy	484	6	153	–	159
Bottisham & Lode	6779	350	353	33	736
Swaffhamprior	2666	237	66	31	334
Burwell	6594	752	246	82	1080
Fordham	11754	1013	655	57	1725
Isleham	6405	650	665	50	1365
Mildenhall	8278	1697	1272	66	3035
1926					
Barnwell Junction	1700	104	911	11	1026
Quy	499	30	48	–	78
Bottisham & Lode	5330	288	105	59	452
Swaffhamprior	1732	160	66	45	271
Burwell	4694	584	352	82	1018
Fordham	8862	856	877	77	1810
Isleham	5486	551	726	66	1343
Mildenhall	6701	1304	1194	53	2551
1927					
Barnwell Junction	1936	133	694	1	828
Quy	410	7	41	4	52
Bottisham & Lode	5370	293	124	66	483
Swaffhamprior	1838	151	49	25	225
Burwell	5075	643	290	118	1051
Fordham	7558	777	570	111	1458
Isleham	5724	548	618	100	1266
Mildenhall	6898	1313	892	39	2244
1928					
Barnwell Junction	1425	104	590	–	694
Quy	578	28	17	6	51
Bottisham & Lode	4872	264	105	60	429
Swaffhamprior	1541	154	47	25	226
Burwell	4627	567	295	57	919
Fordham	6880	677	568	109	1354
Isleham	5622	508	465	116	1089
Mildenhall	6796	1219	741	25	1985

A severe snow storm during the afternoon of Christmas Day 1927 caused a blockage of the Mildenhall branch. The timing was most inconvenient for all the railwaymen at branch stations had retired from duty for the day to enjoy their festive fare. The swirling snow quickly filled the shallow cuttings and in the absence of train movements, packed hard across the track. Any attempt to clear the line by the following morning was futile and it was mid morning of Boxing Day before permanent way gangs

'E4' class 2—4—0 No. 7441 waiting at Mildenhall in 1935 with train formed of four 6-wheel vehicles modified for conductor-guard working and a centre brake 6-wheel coach behind the tender.
J. E. Kite

LNER Working Timetable for 1935

and other staff began clearing operations. The railway authorities attempted to run a train but it stuck in a drift near Lode and had to be dug out. It then returned to Cambridge. As soon as most of the top snow was cleared from the track a light engine was utilized to run across the branch to keep the rails clear of snow, and services resumed later in the evening of the same day.

The LNER at this period was suffering traffic losses which deemed it necessary for the management at Marylebone and Liverpool Street to seek economies. Various branch lines in East Anglia were investigated as to their viability in the future passenger railway network. Fortunately, despite the withdrawal of passenger services from Somersham to Ramsey East and Downham to Stoke Ferry on 22nd September 1930, and Ely to St. Ives and Mellis to Eye on 2nd February 1931, the Mildenhall line was considered viable enough to continue its useful service to the local community.

The railway company continued to negotiate on the maintenance of bridges in an effort to save money, and, after due negotiations, Suffolk County Council agreed to take over the responsibility of another bridge from the LNER on 21st May 1931 when Four Cross Ways bridge, No. 2254 at 73 miles 78 chains, was transferred to the Council for maintenance.

By agreement with Cambridgeshire County Council, the LNER relinquished maintenance of a number of bridges to the Council from 17th April 1934 including Fen Ditton Road No. 2236 at 58 miles 6 chains, High Ditch Road No. 2237 at 58 miles 43 chains, Reach Road No. 2240 at 64 miles 39 chains, Burwell Road No. 2241 at 65 miles 48 chains, Exning Road No. 2242 at 66 miles 23 chains, Cambridge Road No. 2244 at 69 miles 41 chains, Lark Hall No. 2245 at 69 miles 71 chains, Soham Road No. 2246 at 70 miles 13 chains, Fordham Moor Road No. 2248 at 71 miles 2 chains, Fordham Road No.

An 'E4' class 2—4—0 approaching a flag-bedecked Burwell station with a Cambridge-Mildenhall train formed of four 6-wheel coaches and a van.
Courtesy Mrs. D. Grainger

2249 at 71 miles 72 chains, Isleham Station Road No. 2250 at 72 miles 35 chains and Beck Row No. 2251 at 73 miles 2 chains.

The value of the Mildenhall branch to the community was referred to in a report on Cambridgeshire Regional Planning by W. R. Davidge published in 1934. The paper reported the branch 'an asset of considerable importance in the region'. The report also recommended the replacement of Fordham level crossing by a road bridge but the suggestion was never acted on.

By the mid 1930s the competitive bus services operated by Burwell and District Motor Services was going from strength to strength with two services running on parallel routes and in opposition to the railway. The original route 1 from Burwell to Cambridge via Reach, Commercial End, Bottisham, and Lode Church ran each weekday whilst service 11 linking Mildenhall and Cambridge via Isleham and Burwell, ran on Mondays, Wednesdays, Saturdays and Sundays only.

The strikes of 1919, 1924 and 1926 had left their toll on the branch and traffic continued to decline. Services remained unaltered after the reduction in the late 1920s and, with no imminent sign of increase by the mid 1930s, the LNER authorities were again seeking ways of reducing operating costs. After investigation, the divisional general manager of the southern area announced in November 1934 the introduction of the 'train staff and metal tickets' method of single line working. This enabled keys to be attached to tickets as well as the staff to open and close the intermediate sidings on the branch and thus obviate delays which were occurring. At the same time the closure of Quy and Swaffham Prior signal boxes was mooted as for some years they had only been switched in and operated by porter/signalmen as and when trains were required to shunt the sidings. The cost of the scheme, £305 with a saving of £75 per annum on operating and renewal charges, included the provision of ground frames at Quy and Swaffham Prior. The new method of working was subsequently introduced on 1st July 1935.

Just prior to the outbreak of the Second World War, the LNER came under the control of the Railway Executive Committee with all other major railway companies. Within weeks of the commencement of hostilities local bus services were reduced and some removed from the road by petrol rationing. The Mildenhall branch services again carried an increased number of passengers, but by 1941 first class facilities were withdrawn and remained so for ten years. Cheap day tickets were also withdrawn.

In order to safeguard against air raids, especially at night when station lamps remained dimmed, staff utilized

Four views of an immaculate Burwell station in various states of decoration for either the Silver Jubilee of 1935 or the 1937 Coronation.

Mrs. D. Grainger

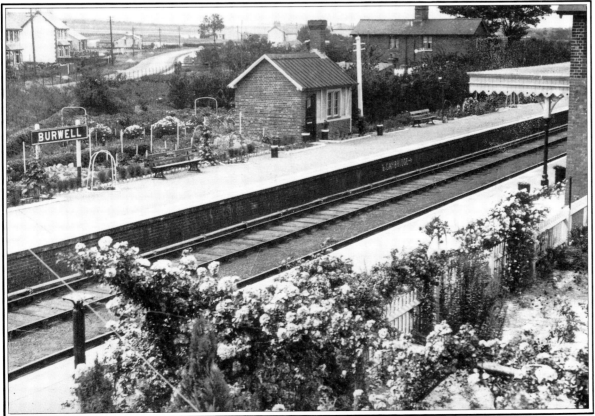

K 28

CAMBRIDGE, FORDHAM AND MILDENHALL
Single Line between Barnwell Junction and Mildenhall

DOWN — WEEKDAYS

No.		3	7	9	12
Description		OP	OP		OP
Class					
Miles from Cambridge / M.C.	Station	am	am	am	PM
	Cambridge	6 33	10 28	10 35	4 27
1 56	Barnwell Junction (S)	6 36	10 31		4 30
	Barnwell Junction	6 37	10 32	10 45	4 31
2 31	Fen Ditton Halt		10 35		4 34
4 49	Quy	6 45	10 41	✶	4 40
6 5	Bottisham & Lode (S)	6 50	10 44	11 10	4 43
	Bottisham & Lode	6 51	10 45	11 20	4 44
8 2	Swaffhamprior	6 56	10 50	11 35	4 49
	Burwell (S)	7 1	10 54	11 40	4 53
9 75	Burwell	7 3	10 55	11 50	4 54
10 50	Exning Road Halt		10 58		4 57
13 36	Fordham (S)	7 11	11 5	12 0	5 4
	Fordham	7 14	11 10	12 20	5 10
16 58	Isleham (S)	7 21	11 16	12 30	5 16
	Isleham	7 22	11 17	12 50	5 17
19 68	Worlington Golf Links H.		11 24	12 50	5 24
20 59	Mildenhall (S)	7 31	11 27	1 0	5 27

Passenger trains between Cambridge and Mildenhall are worked on the "Conductor-Guard" principle.

MILDENHALL, FORDHAM AND CAMBRIDGE
Single Line between Mildenhall and Barnwell Junction

UP — WEEKDAYS

No.		2	4	8	11
Description		OP	OP		OP
Class					
Miles from Mildenhall / M.C.	Station	am	am	PM	PM
	Mildenhall (S)	7 42	11 50	3 0	5 48
71	Worlington Golf Links H.	7 46	11 54		5 52
4 1	Isleham (S)	7 52	12 0	3 10	5 58
	Isleham	7 53	12 1	3 20	5 59
7 23	Fordham (S)	7 59	12 7	3 30	6 6
	Fordham	8 6	12 9	4 15	6 7
10 9	Exning Road Halt	8 13	12 16		6 15
10 66	Burwell (S)	8 15	12 18	4 35	6 17
	Burwell	8 16	12 19	4 55	6 18
12 57	Swaffhamprior	8 20	12 23	✶	6 22
14 54	Bottisham & Lode (S)	8 25	12 27	5 15	6 26
	Bottisham & Lode	8 26	12 28	5 30	6 27
16 10	Quy	8 30	12 32	✶	6 31
18 28	Fen Ditton Halt	8 35	12 37		6 36
19 13	Barnwell Junction (S)	8 37	12 39	5 55	6 38
	Barnwell Junction	8 38	12 40	6 0	6 39
20 59	Cambridge	8B47	12 45	6 5	6 43

Passenger trains between Mildenhall and Cambridge are worked on the "Conductor-Guard" principle.

shielded hand lamps to attend to the train and shunting duties. As a precaution against enemy attacks, the station nameboards were removed and stored in lamp rooms and signal boxes constantly under lock and key.

The agricultural nature of freight handled at all branch stations was of utmost importance as the vital provisions of home grown food, grain, vegetables, fruit and sugar beet traffics were despatched and conveyed to home markets. In addition to the outward flow of traffic, the war years brought an influx of tinned foods and dried milk for distribution to the Ministry of Food storage depots in the area.

The close proximity of RAF Mildenhall, opened in 1934 as the first of the new style bomber bases, brought a steady flow of armaments and stores for the personnel stationed at the airfield. Ammunition dumps were located at well camouflaged sites away from the airfield, and bombs and other armaments were conveyed by night to Mildenhall to be offloaded under the cover of darkness for transit by road to site. Because of the heavy weight of these trains, the freights were routed via Newmarket or Ely to Fordham and thence to Mildenhall, thus avoiding the main centres of population. The Luftwaffe must have had knowledge of the movement of some of these trains for on one occasion the Mildenhall ammunition train took refuge in Warren Hill tunnel until the investigating German aircraft had departed.

The closeness of the branch to Mildenhall, Lakenheath, Duxford and other airfields, did not render the line immune from air attacks. On Friday, 4th December 1940, the 4.25 p.m. Cambridge to Mildenhall train was attacked by a Luftwaffe aircraft soon after passing Exning road bridge. Swooping out of the low cloud, the aircraft jettisoned three bombs which blew up the track 50 yards behind the train. The coaching stock roofs and door locks were damaged or blown off and sidelights broken. The train continued on its journey across the open fenland but with no available cutting or tunnel for cover, the aircraft turned again for a second attack using its machine guns. Two Royal Air Force personnel who were leaning out of the windows, suffered bullet wounds in the neck and hands respectively. However, despite this second attack, the train managed to reach Fordham station, where an ARP ambulance was obtained to convey the casualties to White Lodge Hospital, Newmarket. At least two other attacks were made on the branch trains but fortunately with no serious consequences, whilst some bombs fell near the line at Quy.

The branch enjoyed the honour of a royal visit on Saturday, 13th June 1942, when, during a tour of the Eastern Counties, King George VI and Queen Elizabeth visited fen land reclaimed by the Cambridgeshire War Agricultural Executive Committee at Swaffham Prior Fen and Adventurers Fen, Burwell. Their Majesties arrived in the royal train during the mid morning and alighted at Swaffham Prior station to commence their tour of inspection. Needless to say, as with all royal visits in the war, the tour by 'Mr. and Mrs. Grove' (Grove being the coded telegraphic message for the royal train conveying the king) was not publicised until after the event.

Later in the year, on 5th November, Mr. L. B. Turner, station master at Mildenhall, suffered fatal injuries in a shunting accident. At the inquest held on Friday, 6th November, the Bury St. Edmunds coroner, Mr. T. Wilson, heard that during the visit of the freight trip from Cambridge, wagons were being shunted in the goods yard. In the course of manoeuvres, the open door of a wagon became wedged and the station master attempted to release it. Unfortunately, the engine driver had not been advised to stop in time, with the result that as the wagons continued moving, the door moved forward and pinned Turner against a wall, killing him almost instantly. A verdict of death by misadventure was recorded.

By 1944 Barnwell Junction station was established as the unloading point for several ambulance trains conveying the war wounded from the Italian war front. The casualties were then forwarded by ambulances and buses to various hospitals in Cambridgeshire and the surrounding counties.

As a result of petrol rationing, the competitive Burwell and District bus route 11 from Mildenhall to Cambridge was withdrawn and the buses diverted to contract work linking the airfields at Stradishall, Kimbolton, Molesworth and Bottisham as well as Mildenhall. When peace was restored, service 11 was subsequently reinstated to link Isleham and Cambridge via Burwell on Saturdays and Sundays only.

After the war the railways resumed peacetime activities with run-down and life-expired rolling stock and equipment, and stations in need of maintenance. Questions were raised in Parliament regarding the deteriorating service given by the LNER and the poor condition of rolling stock, and the Mildenhall branch was no exception.

The severe weather early in 1947 with heavy snowfalls brought delays to services. In February the line was partially blocked between Swaffham Prior and Burwell. The Cambridge snowplough succeeded in clearing the line which then required the use of a locomotive to run up and down the branch all night to keep the line clear for the following day's services.

The Mildenhall branch was spasmodically used as a diversionary route during engineering work on Sundays and on various other occasions, when a derailment occurred, for instance. Never was the importance as a relief line demonstrated more than during the 1947 fen floods. On Monday, March 17th 1947, the main line between Cambridge and Ely became impassable when the banks of the Ouse at Little Thetford broke and flooded the surrounding area. For several days until the floods subsided and the track and ballast was replaced, many trains were routed from Cambridge via Burwell and Fordham to Ely. During this period Cambridge and Ely drivers were provided as pilotmen for Stratford, Norwich, March and Kings Lynn crews, who did not have the necessary route knowledge for the branch.

As petrol rationing eased, so Burwell and District Bus Company and the Eastern Counties Omnibus Company improved the frequency of their services in the area. Most of the branch stations were well away from the centres of population they were supposed to serve and the combination of poor infrequent rail services and the cheaper fares charged on the buses succeeded in transferring a large proportion of the remaining passenger traffic from the railway to road.

BARNWELL JUNCTION 1922

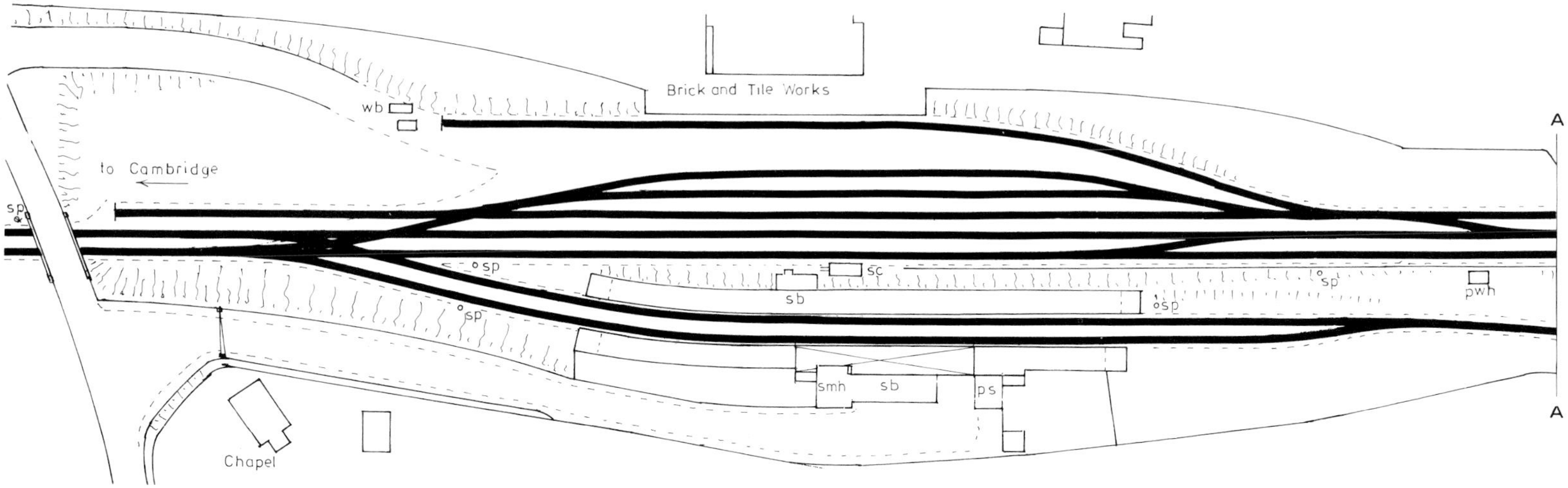

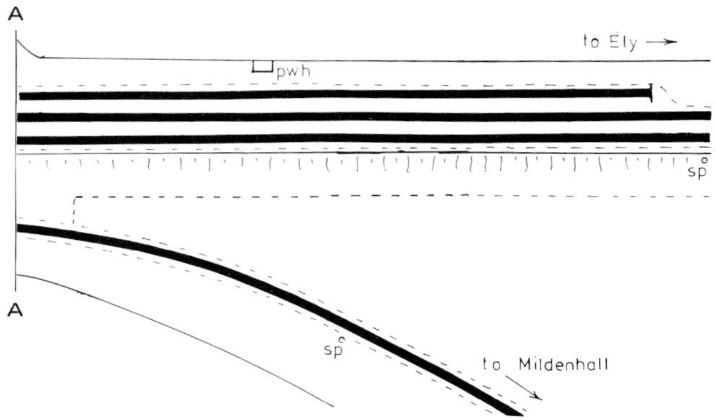

Brick and Tile Works

Chapel

to Cambridge

sp

sp

sp

sp

sp

sp

sb

sc

ps

sb

smh

wb

pwh

A

A

to Ely →

to Mildenhall

pwh

sp

sp

A

A

CHAPTER FOUR

THE ROUTE DESCRIBED

Barnwell Junction station and goods yard, to the right and left respectively of the Cambridge to Ely main line. View facing Ely on 16th August 1911.   *Collection M. Brooks*

MOST travellers began their acquaintance with the Mildenhall branch at Cambridge station where the bay platforms Nos. 5 and 6 at the north end were used for the majority of departures. If for any reason those platforms were occupied, the unsuspecting passenger was directed to Platform 4, the north end of the main single platform, where the two- or three-coach branch train was waiting. All three platforms were also used for departures to destinations as diverse as Kettering, March, Wisbech, Kings Lynn, Peterborough, Ipswich, Norwich, Lincoln, Doncaster and York. At no time did Mildenhall services have exclusive use of them.

As the mileposts erected alongside the branch gave the distance from Liverpool Street via Hackney Downs and Clapton Junction, the following description of the route quotes these distances; station distances from Cambridge are also shown.

From Cambridge station, 55 miles 52 chains, branch trains negotiated the pointwork at the north end of the station to join the down main line as far as Barnwell Junction. In the opposite direction, Mildenhall—Cambridge trains used the up main line between these points. Climbing initially at 1 in 3111 past Cambridge North signal box, which controlled all points and signals at the country end of the station, the main lines passed under Mill Road overbridge No. 1546 at 56 miles 0 chains before descending at 1 in 176 on a straight course parallel with the goods avoiding lines on the up side. At the 56¼ mile post, the descending gradient sharpened to 1 in 148 falling, and at 56 miles 29 chains the junction points for the Newmarket and Ipswich lines (controlled from Coldham Lane Junction signal box, which was located on the up side) swung away to the right to join the goods lines. The four tracks continued on a parallel course to pass under Coldham Lane overbridge No. 1547 at 56

miles 50 chains. The down goods loop, which also ran parallel, joined the down main line just before the bridge, whilst immediately north of the structure, the up and down Newmarket branch swung sharply away to the east. In 1958 Coldham Lane diesel maintenance depot was built on land previously used as sidings in an area east of the Newmarket lines and south of the road. It was responsible for the maintenance of the diesel railbuses and multiple units used on the Mildenhall line in later years.

Beyond Coldham Lane bridge, the up and down main lines continued on a 1 in 148 falling gradient, easing to 1 in 273 at the 56¾ mile post. The Mildenhall branch finally left the main line at 57 miles 12 chains immediately after passing under the Newmarket Road overbridge No. 1548. The line was on the level through Barnwell Junction station (57 miles 28 chains ex-Liverpool Street, 1 mile 56 chains ex-Cambridge), where platforms were only provided for branch services. Although the 380 ft down platform backed onto the up main line, no platform edging was ever provided for the latter. A small waiting shelter was provided whilst trees and shrubs gave a landscaping effect.

The up side platform, 370 ft in length, served the main station buildings, which included booking office, waiting room, ladies waiting room, parcels office, staff room and toilets, whilst alongside was the station master's house. The station buildings were fronted by an ornate pierced wooden canopy supported by half fluted iron pillars and ironwork brackets. Separate vehicular access roads were provided from the Newmarket Road to the station and goods yard, the latter being located on the down or west side of the main line to Ely directly opposite the branch station. The yard was connected with the customary trailing connections from up and down running lines and comprised two loop sidings, each 440 ft in length, giving

Barnwell Junction station, 57 miles 28 chains ex Liverpool Street and 1 mile 56 chains from Cambridge. View facing Mildenhall from the down platform, showing signal box to the left and main station buildings and station master's house on the up side.
Collection Geoff Pember

The 380ft down side platform backed on to the up main line but only possessed a platform face to the down branch line. Barnwell Junction signal box is partly obscured by the small ornate waiting shed. In the left background is Barnwell Junction goods yard which was only accessible from up and down main lines.
Lens of Sutton

Barnwell Junction station up platform, 370ft in length, showing the ornate canopy supported by half-fluted cast iron pillars which fronted on to the main station buildings. The branch curves away to the right in the background.   *Lens of Sutton*

The up platform at Barnwell Junction showing main station buildings and station master's house. The lock-up store with pitched roof to the left was common to the larger stations on the Mildenhall branch.

Lens of Sutton

The north end of Barnwell Junction station viewed from an approaching train.   *R. Powell*

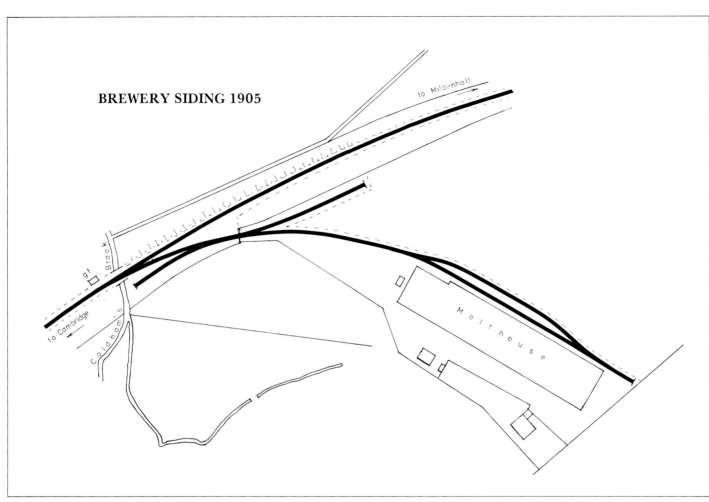

BREWERY SIDING 1905

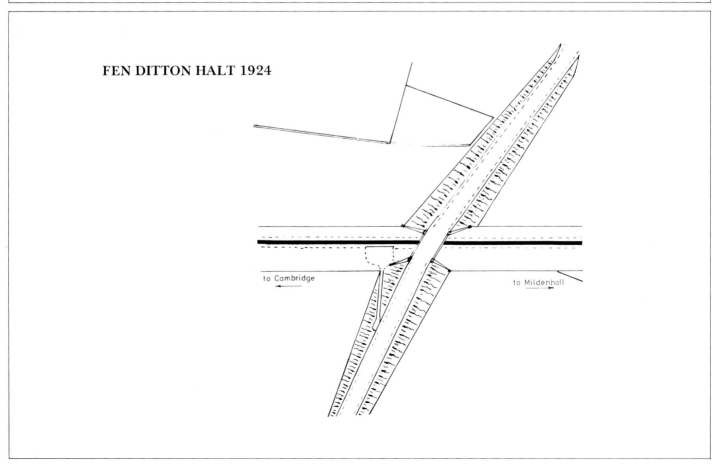

FEN DITTON HALT 1924

accommodation for 22 and 24 wagons, and a 510 ft 'back road' which served coal and coke stacking grounds used by local fuel merchants.

Points and signals on both the main line and the branch were worked from the 34-lever Barnwell Junction signal box located on the up side of the up main line backing on to the down side Mildenhall branch platform.

Leaving Barnwell Junction station, the Mildenhall branch became single, negotiating a 40 chain radius right-hand curve, passing the single connection on the up side of the line leading to the sidings of the Commercial Brewery Company (later H & D Taylor and now Flitwick Oils Terminal). After climbing a short section of 1 in 200, then straightening out for a quarter mile, the line reached Fen Ditton Halt, 58 miles 3 chains ex Liverpool Street and 2 miles 31 chains ex Cambridge. Located on the south or up side of the line, the halt was opened by the GER on 20th November 1922. The 30ft platform at rail height was formed of clinker with sleeper edging facing the track and a large nameboard. As at the other halts opened when conductor-guard working was introduced, the guard was responsible for lighting and extinguishing the solitary oil lamp. Access to and from the main road to the halt was by a clinker footpath which climbed the embankment beside the adjacent Fen Ditton Road overbridge, which

provided the only protection from the elements for intending rail passengers.

Beyond the overbridge No. 2236, at 58 miles 6 chains, the line climbed at 1 in 100 round a 35 chains left-hand curve through a cutting, to pass under High Ditch Road overbridge No. 2237 at 58 miles 43 chains. Descending a short stretch at 1 in 1000, and then on level track, the line followed a straight course across a shallow embank-

Fen Ditton Halt, 58 miles 3 chains ex Liverpool Street and 2 miles 31 chains from Cambridge, opened by the GER on 20th November 1922. View facing Mildenhall.

Lens of Sutton

The Commercial Brewery Company Sidings, a few chains east of Barnwell station, in August 1911. The hut containing the ground frame controlling the points is on the left, whilst the Maltings are on the right.   *Collection M. Brooks*

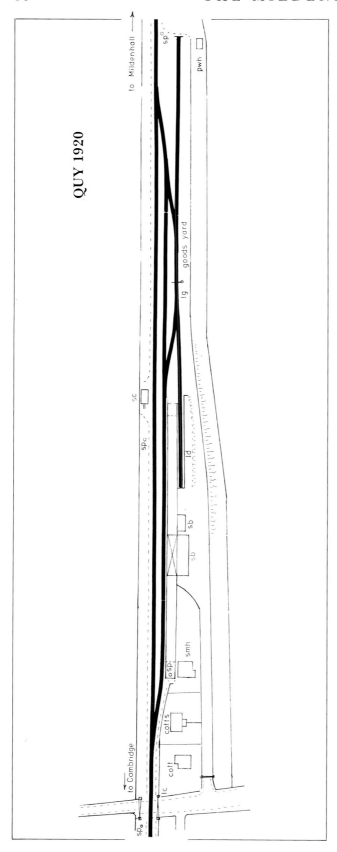

QUY 1920

to Mildenhall →

sp

pwh

lg goods yard

sc

sp

ld

sb

sb

smh

sp

cotts

cott

lc

to Cambridge

sp

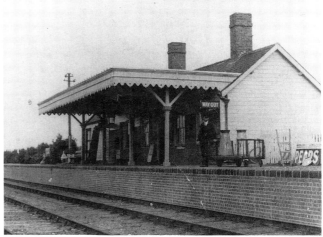

Quy station, 60 miles 21 chains from Liverpool Street and
4 miles 49 chains from Cambridge, soon after the opening of the
railway. Station master Richard Gray is on the platform. The
ornate canopy fronting on to the wood-cladded station building
was later removed, as was the 920ft goods loop shown in the
foreground.   *Cambridgeshire Collection*

ment before falling at 1 in 200 and bisecting Honey Hill
by a cutting. No. 1 gatehouse crossing (crossing No. 8) at
59 miles 66 chains was passed before the branch continued
across fields and open fen country to cross a public road
(crossing No. 10) at 60 miles 16 chains and enter Quy
station (60 miles 21 chains ex Liverpool Street, 4 miles
49 chains from Cambridge).

Located a mile north of the centre of the village of
Stow-cum-Quy, the station enjoyed the least passenger
patronage on the branch, with the exception of the halts,
with corresponding low receipts. The single platform,
380ft in length, on the up or south side of the main
single line, had a single storey timber-framed and cladded
station building with slate roof, containing the booking
office, waiting rooms, staff accommodation and toilets.
In the early years a station master's office was also
included. A small ornate wooden canopy also fronted the

GER cast fireplace at Quy station.   *J. Watling*

The approach road to Quy station and the adjacent goods yard. The latter for many years dealt with considerable tonnages of sugar beet despatched to Ely, Felstead and Bury St. Edmunds sugar factories. October 1957.   *H. C. Casserley*

Quy station building in May 1962. The short wooden nameplate with cast letters shared with Eye and Ely the distinction of bearing one of the shortest names for a station on the GER system.   *J. Watling*

Situated a mile north of the village of Stow-cum-Quy, the station saw little passenger traffic in later years. Soon after opening, the waiting room was used by the local vicar to hold the service of Evensong.   *J. Watling*

Quy signal box, containing a 22-lever frame, was closed in 1935 as part of the rationalisation programme to improve the operation of the line. After that date it was used as a P.W. store.

J. Watling

buildings over the platform but this was later removed. The track layout at the station originally featured a 920 ft goods loop on the down side, but this was removed in June 1935. Facing and trailing crossovers led from the platform line (later main single line) to serve a 240 ft refuge road at the east end of the yard, which was generally used for coal traffic, and a 220 ft dock road at the west end of the yard, backing on to the passenger station platform. This served the cattle dock and pens and was used in later years for loading sugar beet and vegetable traffic.

The signal box, originally containing 22 levers and controlling all points and signals at Quy, was located on the down side of the goods loop line opposite the Mildenhall end of the platform. It was closed on 1st July 1935

Ornate GER post-mounted platform oil lamp case at Quy station.
J. Watling

Quy station, looking towards Mildenhall. Unlike other stations on the branch, Quy station building was of wood-cladded construction with slate roof, which contained booking office, waiting room, staff accommodation and toilets. Only two station masters served at Quy before the post was downrated to porter-in-charge by the GER.

The east end of Quy station, again facing Mildenhall. To the left is the signal box which fronted on to the 920ft goods loop removed in June 1935. Beyond the platform is Quy goods yard and in the far distance Francis Siding on the down side of the line and adjacent No. 2 gatehouse on the up side.

Collection G. Pember

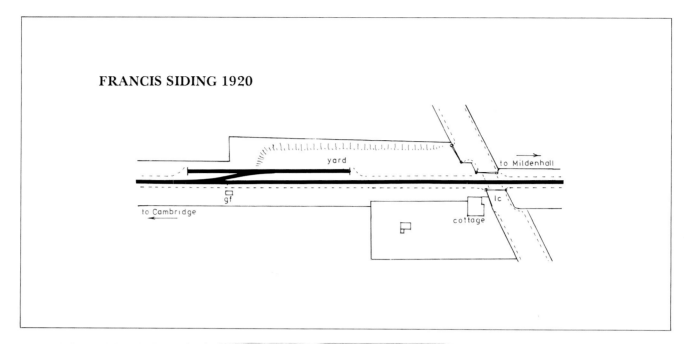

FRANCIS SIDING 1920

'J15' class 0—6—0 No. 5350 passing Bottisham down home signal and over Bottisham Lode underbridge with the 10.35 a.m. Cambridge-Mildenhall goods on 15th October 1949.

LCGB/Ken Nunn Collection

View from a down train approaching Bottisham and Lode. The down home signal stands in advance of Bottisham Lode
underbridge No. 2238, protecting Bottisham station level crossing and the station crossing loop.   *R. Powell*

when all signals were dismantled and points reconnected
to a ground frame released by a key attached to the train
staff and to each of the metal tickets. The structure
remained *in situ* until the late 1950s, by which time it had
taken over the dual role of greenhouse and permanent
way tool shed.

From Quy the line followed an almost straight course,
initially on the level, before passing Francis siding 550
yards east of Quy station. With a trailing connection from
the up direction, the single siding on the down side of the
line was worked by a 4-lever ground frame, released by
a key attached to the train staff or metal tickets. Beyond
the siding, level crossing No. 11 (No. 2 gatehouse) at
60 miles 54 chains, took the line over the road from
Stow-cum-Quy to the local fen. From here there was a
quarter of a mile descent at 1 in 400 across the south edge
of Stow-cum-Quy Fen, followed by a straight and level
course passing over Bottisham Lode underbridge No. 2238
at 61 miles 52 chains, followed immediately by Bottisham
station level crossing No. 17, to enter Bottisham and Lode
station (61 miles 57 chains from Liverpool Street and
6 miles 5 chains from Cambridge).

Situated on a 50 chain radius right-hand curve, this
was the first train staff station beyond Barnwell Junction,
and boasted a 600 ft long crossing loop which could
accommodate a train of 24 wagons with engine and brake.
The down platform, 360 ft in length, was provided with
only a small brick-built waiting shelter for intending

passengers, whilst the main station buildings were on the
350 ft up side platform. The brick-built structure was late
Victorian in style with heavy half-lipped roofs and heavy
bargeboards on the gable ends. The station master's house
was complemented by the usual station building which
included booking office, station master's office, waiting
rooms, staff room and toilets. The station was originally
incorrectly titled 'Bottisham' but the GER aptly amended
the title to 'Bottisham and Lode' from 22nd April 1897
as the premises were situated adjacent to Lode village, yet
two miles away from Bottisham. The goods yard was
located on the up side of the line on the east of the
station and was connected by trailing connections from
the up and down platform roads. A 250 ft dock road
served the loading and cattle dock, and pens located
behind the up platform, whilst at the east end of the yard
a 250 ft refuge road served the coal wharves of the local
fuel merchants. The points at the Mildenhall end of the
goods yard also gave direct access by a crossover to the
down loop line. Signals and points at Bottisham and Lode
were controlled from the station signal box, which was
equipped with a 22 lever frame and located at the Mildenhall end of the down platform.

Away from Bottisham and Lode, the single track
branch followed a right-hand curve for a short distance
before descending at 1 in 300 to a level and straight
course across the southern edge of Bottisham Fen.
Swaffham Bulbeck Lode underbridge No. 2239, adjacent

Bottisham and Lode station, facing Mildenhall and showing the 600ft long crossing loop serving down and up side platforms. The tall GER up starting signal protects the up loop.

R. Powell

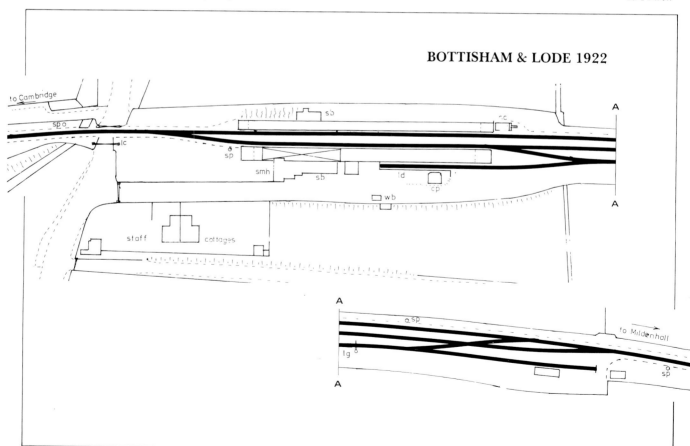

BOTTISHAM & LODE 1922

The entrance road to Bottisham and Lode station and goods yard. The station master's house fronting on to the garden is typical of the structures erected by Lovatt. Beyond the station master's house is the booking office and other station buildings. The original wooden fencing erected by the contractor has been replaced by rail post and tubular fencing so favoured by the Great Eastern.

H. C. Casserley

A closer view of Bottisham and Lode station master's house, station buildings and store. As with most other stations on the Mildenhall branch, the platforms were illuminated by oil lamps at night, although more often than not in the final few years Tilley lamps were used.

M. Brooks

Bottisham and Lode station, facing Cambridge, on 28th May 1957, showing the up starting signal in the usual GER drooping off position. Note also the shorter down home signal repositioned on the up side of the line beyond Bottisham station level crossing.   *H. C. Casserley*

Waiting room and station nameboard on down side platform at Bottisham and Lode.   *J. Watling*

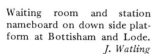

A study of the station buildings and station master's house on the up side platform at Bottisham and Lode. The ornate canopy which fronted the buildings was removed in the late 1920s. The station was actually located on the north edge of Lode village and Bottisham was two miles away to the south-east.

Lens of Sutton

View from up platform at Bottisham and Lode, facing Mildenhall, in July 1961, showing the signal box which controlled all points and signals as well as the east end of the 600ft crossing loop. To the right is the goods yard devoid of traffic.   *J. Watling*

A closer view of Bottisham and Lode signal box of brick and timber construction.   *Collection J. Watling*

'E4' class 2—4—0 No. 62796 trundling along the branch near Swaffhamprior with a Cambridge-Mildenhall train composed of two GER bogie coaches and 6-wheel parcels van. The tender cab proved welcome for the diagram involved an evening round trip from Mildenhall to Newmarket which had to be run in one direction tender first.

Dr. I. C. Allen

Swaffhamprior station, 63 miles 54 chains from Liverpool Street and 8 miles 2 chains from Cambridge, facing Mildenhall soon after the railway opened to traffic. The station master Robert Arnold is on the platform with his leading porter. The station was built with additional refinements because C. P. Allix, who first mooted the Mildenhall line, lived at nearby Swaffham Prior House. To the left of the picture is the 850ft goods loop which was removed in June 1935. Beyond the station is Swaffhamprior station level crossing.

Cambridgeshire Collection

to the 63 mile post, was crossed as the gradient altered to 1 in 130 rising/level/1 in 160 falling, to carry the branch over the waterway. Immediately beyond the bridge the branch continued on an embankment to cross a public track leading to the fen at No. 3 gatehouse (level crossing No. 23 at 63 miles 2 chains). The branch then skirted the north-western edge of the grounds of Swaffham Prior House before entering Swaffhamprior station (63 miles

54 chains from Liverpool Street and 8 miles 2 chains from Cambridge).

The rather remote station served the villages of Swaffham Prior and Swaffham Bulbeck ½ mile and 1½ miles to the south and south-west respectively. The single platform, 360 ft in length, on the south or up side of the main single line, served ornate station buildings designed in a T plan with the two-storey station master's house

The road approach to Swaffhamprior station, again soon after the opening of the railway. Station master Robert Arnold stands with his wife by the gate of the station house.

Cambridgeshire Collection

Swaffhamprior station, facing Mildenhall in 1956. The canopy fronting on to the main station building has been removed, as has the goods loop and signals. The station nameboard pronounced 'Swaffham Prior' correctly as two words but the GER and later the LNER and BR usually referred to the station title as one word 'Swaffhamprior'.
Collection G. Pember

Swaffhamprior station, facing Cambridge in May 1962. The kink in the main single line shows where the connection to the goods loop had been.
J. Watling

Exterior view of Swaffhamprior station from the entrance road.
M. Brooks

complemented by the single-storey station buildings containing the usual offices and waiting rooms. As at Quy, a wooden canopy, supported by cast iron columns, originally provided protection over the platform for waiting passengers but this was later removed.

The track layout at Swaffhamprior again included a goods loop line, 850 ft in length, on the down or north side of the main single line, later removed as part of the 1935 rationalisation programme. The goods yard was located on the up side of the main single line west of the station and accessed from facing and trailing crossovers. The yard was served by three sidings, a refuge road at the west end, 100 ft in length, a 200 ft Dock Road at the east end of the layout serving the loading dock and cattle pens, and a 180 ft long Coal Road which ran parallel to the Dock siding.

Again until 1935 signals and points at Swaffhamprior were originally controlled by a 22-lever signal box located on the down side of the goods loop at the Cambridge end of the station, opposite the end of the platform. After removal of the signals, points were operated by ground frame released by a key attached to the train staff and to the metal tickets.

Beyond the station, the line crossed the public road leading from the village to Swaffham Prior Fen by Swaffhamprior station level crossing No. 27 at 63 miles 59 chains, with the adjacent Allix Arms public house a few yards away on the up side of the line, east of the crossing. It then followed a straight course for three-quarters of a mile, initially on a shallow embankment and then through a cutting, climbing at 1 in 300, before passing under Reach Road overbridge No. 2240 at 64 miles 39 chains. The gradient stiffened to 1 in 100

Swaffhamprior station from the west, showing the 360ft single platform and behind that the dock road siding and cattle dock. The former signalbox, which before 1935 contained a 22-lever frame controlling points and signals at the station, differed from others on the branch by having a steeper pitch to the roof. This was to bring it in line with the ornate station building constructed for the benefit of the Allix family.   *R. Powell*

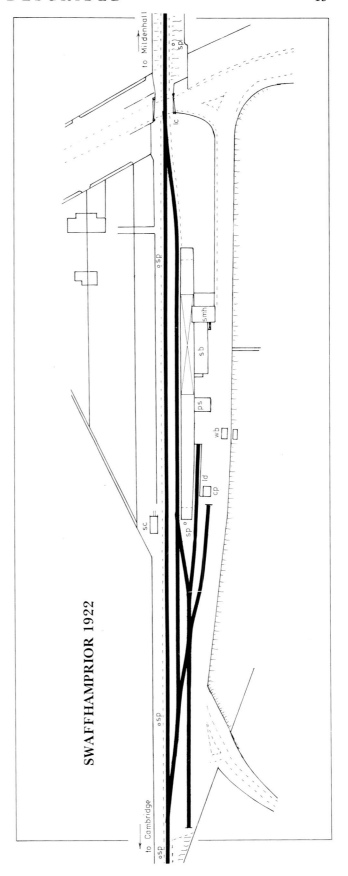

SWAFFHAMPRIOR 1922

Cambridge-Mildenhall goods approaching Burwell in the 1930s with the leading porter in the near foreground waiting to assist in shunting wagons into the goods yard.

Cambridgeshire Collection

through the cutting to where the branch bisected Devils Dyke, a defensive earthwork built to protect the pre-historic Icknield Way. Where the railway cut through the ramparts in a south-westerly to north-easterly direction, the cutting was 120 ft wide. On the down side of the railway, west of the Dyke, the remains of a Roman villa were unearthed together with a well preserved hypocaust for warming the villa by hot air. Archaeological

observations concerning the origin of the Dyke were carried out during construction of the railway and later in 1923-4 by Sir Cyril Fox.

Leaving the cutting, the line levelled out for a short distance whilst negotiating a 44 chain radius right-hand curve, before falling at 1 in 500. A straight level section followed before the railway ascended a short rise of 1 in 400 to Burwell (65 miles 45 chains ex Liverpool Street

'J17' class 0—6—0 No. 65528 standing on the down loop line at Burwell opposite the signal box before shunting vans into the goods yard on 23rd March 1961.

J. Watling

A view across the station gardens to the up platform at Burwell with 'J15' class 0—6—0 No. 65438 waiting with her 2-coach Mildenhall-Cambridge train on 5th October 1957. Empty wagons in the goods yard are waiting to be loaded with sugar beet. *H. C. Casserley*

and 9 miles 73 chains from Cambridge), the second train staff station from Barnwell Junction. Situated on the southern edge of the town, the station boasted a crossing loop 680 ft in length, serving up and down platforms and capable of holding a train of 29 wagons with engine and brake van. The up platform, 345 ft in length, was only provided with a small waiting shelter, whilst the 350 ft down side platform was host to the main station buildings and adjacent station master's house. Constructed of red brick on the T plan principle, the building housed the usual offices, waiting room and toilets, whilst an ornate

canopy spanned the platform in front of the station buildings. As at Bottisham, beneath Burwell station house was a cellar where station master Reginald Gates and his family sheltered during air raids in World War Two. The GER also provided two cottages adjacent to the station for traffic staff.

The goods yard, situated at the west end of the station on the down side of the line, was accessed by two crossovers, both trailing from the down direction from the down loop line. Again three sidings served the yard, a 150 ft Dock Road, which led behind the down platform

Burwell signal box was equipped with a 23-lever frame and was located at the Cambridge end of the up platform.
Collection J. Watling

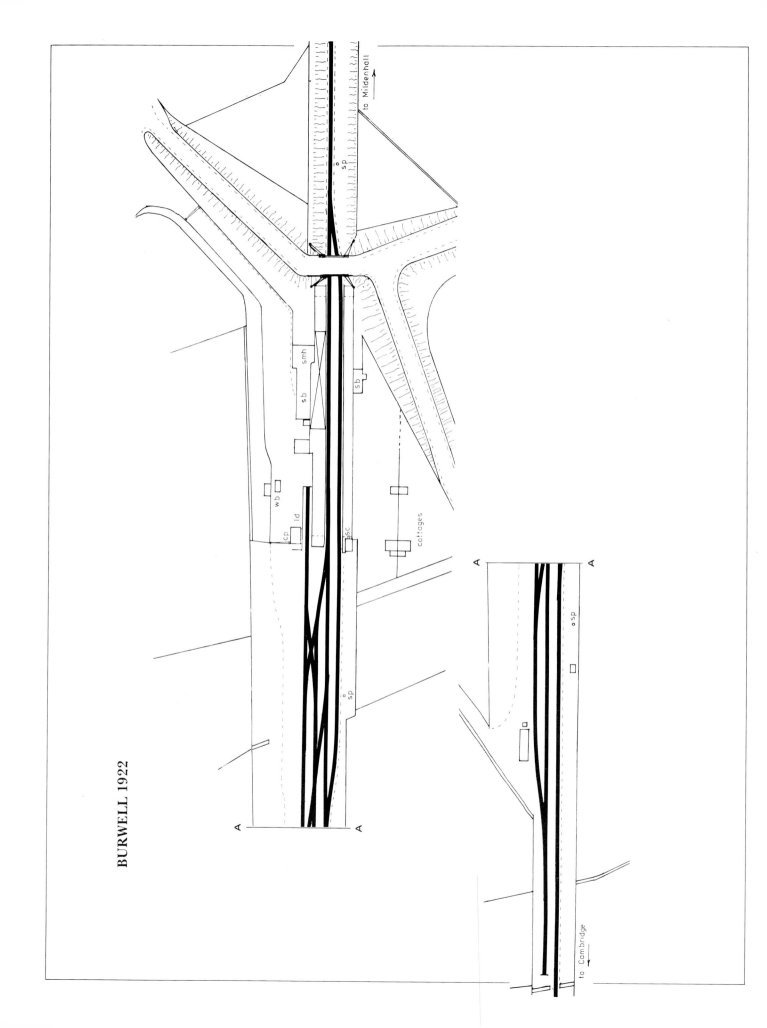

BURWELL 1922

to Mildenhall

to Cambridge

Burwell station (65 miles 45 chains from Liverpool Street and 9 miles 73 chains ex Cambridge) facing towards Mildenhall. This was the second train staff station after Barnwell Junction. The crossing loop was 680ft long. Note the original wooden fencing supplied by Lovatt in this 1905 study.

A view across the platforms at Burwell c.1905. Beyond the station master's garden is the approach road leading to the village, whilst the tall GER down starting signal protects the end of the crossing loop.

A general view of Burwell station facing Mildenhall in the 1950s.
Collection J. Watling

The original canopy on the down platform at Burwell was supported by nine columns. At some time around World War I it was shortened by a third, leaving just six columns. It survived in this state until the late 1950s as is evident by this photograph facing towards the east end of the station and Burwell road overbridge No. 2241.
Lens of Sutton

The waiting room on the up platform at Burwell in May 1962. At one time the building was longer and had two chimney stacks with a central door similar to Isleham.   *J. Watling*

A Mildenhall to Cambridge train departing from Burwell on 5th October 1957. The lengthy 680ft crossing loop could accommodate a freight train of 29 wagons with engine and brake van. In earlier years of the branch this was often necessary as the goods yard at Burwell handled considerable vegetable and fruit traffic in addition to horses and cattle.   *H. C. Casserley*

In the 1950s the Mildenhall branch was opened again on Sundays for the passage of excursion trains which proved very popular. Here Class 2 2—6—0 No. 46467 pulls into Burwell with the Cambridge-Fordham portion of a Skegness excursion. Even the signalman exchanging the Burwell-Fordham staff is wearing his Sunday best!
                                                                    Dr. I. C. Allen

The approach path to Exning Road Halt viewed from the top of the embankment.   *Collection P. Turner*

and served the loading dock and cattle pens, a down refuge siding, 330 ft in length, and leading from this line to the Dock Road a yard loop siding, 370 ft between entry points and points to the Dock Road. Unlike other goods yards on this section of the branch, it was not possible for an up freight train to reverse directly into the goods yard clear of the crossing loop.

Points and signals at Burwell were controlled from the station signal box equipped with 23-lever frame and located at the Cambridge end of the up platform.

On leaving the station, the branch immediately passed under Burwell Road overbridge No. 2241 at 65 miles 48 chains which carried the B1102 Fordham to Stow-cum-Quy road over the railway. Climbing at 1 in 100 for a quarter of a mile through a cutting, the line reached its summit before negotiating a slight left-hand curve and levelling out to Exning Road Halt (66 miles 22 chains ex Liverpool Street and 10 miles 50 chains ex Cambridge). Situated west of Exning Road overbridge, on the up and south side of the single line, the halt was the most isolated on the branch, 1¼ miles west of the village it was supposed to serve. Construction was similar to the halt at Fen Ditton with the 30 ft long ash and clinker platform with timber edging raised to rail height. Facilities at the halt were completed by a nameboard and post oil lamp. Access to the main road was via a footpath up the embankment beside the bridge.

Leaving Exning Road Halt, the branch passed under Exning Road overbridge No. 2242 at 66 miles 23 chains and continued on a left-hand curve, falling at 1 in 100 to follow a north-easterly course across open fen farmland. Straightening out, the line levelled and then fell at 1 in

Exning Road Halt, 66 miles 22 chains from Liverpool Street and 10 miles 50 chains from Cambridge, was opened by the GER on 20th November 1922 as part of a programme to increase traffic and counteract competitive bus services which were then in their infancy. The halt was the most isolated on the branch, being 1¼ miles west of the village it was supposed to serve and consequently saw little traffic.   *Lens of Sutton*

150/400 to cross the Exning–North Street road at No. 4 gatehouse (level crossing No. 41) at 67 miles 14 chains. The general open farmland continued as the line descended at 1 in 400 past the site of a Roman villa to a level section where Stephenson's siding was located on the down side of the line at 67 miles 39 chains, with access via a trailing connection from the up direction. The points were operated by a 6-lever ground frame released by a key attached to the train staff. No fewer than eight occupational crossings punctuated the line on the next section

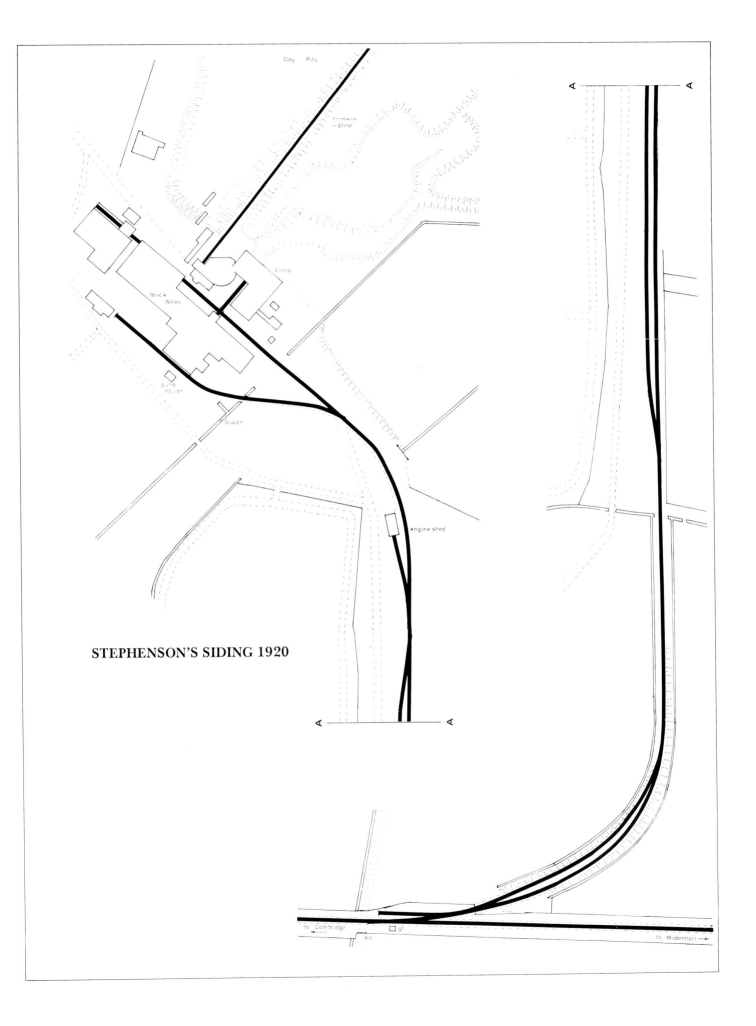

Clay Pits

tramway incline

A ——— A

Kilns

Brick Works

pump house

Sluice

engine shed

STEPHENSON'S SIDING 1920

A ——— A

to Cambridge   gf

to Mildenhall →

'J17' class 0—6—0 No. 65528 heading away from Fordham with the branch freight *en route* to Cambridge. The tall down branch distant signal was fixed and the signal lamp was halfway down the post and separate from the signal arm. This arrangement was considered to give the best sighting for enginemen looking for the arm during daylight and the lamp at night. The lamps were difficult to light during high winds and the lampman or porter also often found these tall signals swaying if a gale was blowing.

Dr. I. C. Allen

as the gradient fell at 1 in 400 over a stream bridge No. 2243, at 68 miles 20 chains, and then level/1 in 500 falling/level, before the branch swung to the left on a 20 chain radius curve to the junction with the Newmarket/Bury St. Edmunds—Ely line at Fordham South Junction 69 miles 5½ chains from Liverpool Street.

Occupying an area of some five acres, Fordham Junction station, 69 miles 8 chains ex Liverpool Street and 13 miles 36 chains from Cambridge, was built in 1878 and opened for traffic as 'Fordham and Burwell' on 1st September 1879. On the opening of the Mildenhall branch the station reverted to plain 'Fordham'.

The down side platform, 370 ft in length, was equipped with a small timber-built structure housing waiting rooms and staff room. The up platform, 375 ft long, in contrast boasted the main station buildings including booking and parcels office, waiting rooms and toilets, station master's office and staff room. Both up and down side platform buildings were fronted by ornate canopies supported by cast iron columns or brackets. Adjoining the up side station buildings was the station master's house, whilst at the south end of the station buildings on the same platform was the signal box with its 40-lever frame controlling all points and signals at the

Fordham station from the south, looking towards Ely, with the signal box on the up platform towering above other buildings. The footbridge was removed shortly after the withdrawal of Mildenhall branch passenger services whilst Fordham station was closed on 13th September 1965.   *Collection G. Pember*

Fordham signal box was equipped with a 40-lever frame to control the signals and points at the junction of the Mildenhall branch with the Ely-Newmarket/Bury St. Edmunds lines.   *R. Powell*

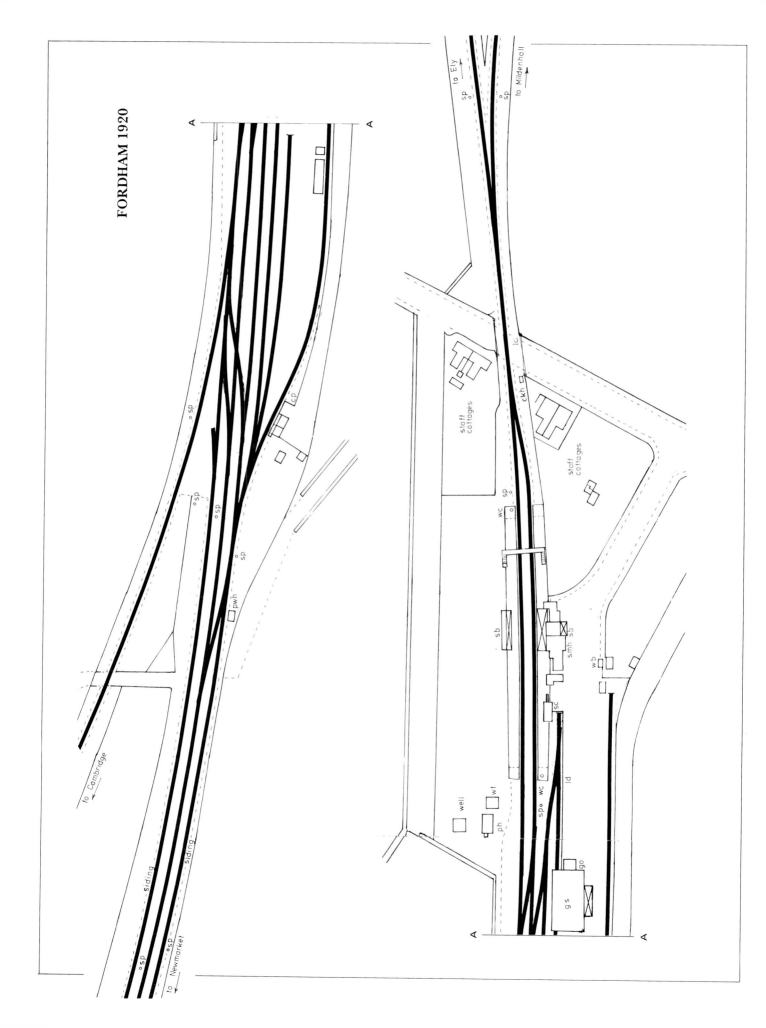

FORDHAM 1920

'E4' class 2–4–0 No. 62796 waiting to depart from Fordham with a Cambridge to Mildenhall train on 22nd September 1956. Fordham station initially illuminated by oil during the hours of darkness, later received a gas supply. *H. C. Casserley*

station. Originally the station was located on a crossing loop 700 ft in length but from June 1938 the line between Snailwell Junction and Soham was doubled.

In accordance with the instructions of the Inspecting Officer of Railways, a footbridge No. 2229, connecting up and down platforms, was provided at the Ely end of the station. Water columns for replenishing locomotives were provided at the Ely end of the down platform and Newmarket end of the up platform, the latter also serving the straight road siding in the goods yard.

Compared with other stations in the area, the goods yard at Fordham was quite large. Its siting south of the station on the east side of the Newmarket line precluded any direct access to and from the Mildenhall branch.

German-built diesel railbus E79962 on a Cambridge–Mildenhall working waiting to pass an up train at Fordham before continuing its journey on 23rd August 1960.
Collection J. Watling

After the withdrawal of the GER corridor bogie coaching stock, the Mildenhall branch train was formed of Gresley LNER corridor vehicles. A few of the brake thirds were equipped with side steps for use at the halts but the majority were devoid of the necessary item. It was for this reason that halts were supplied with a portable set of steps. Here 'J15' class 0—6—0 No. 65451 working tender first with a wagon sheet as a tarpaulin shelter, pulls away from Fordham with a Newmarket-Mildenhall train formed of Gresley corridor brake third and composite in 'plum and custard' livery.

Dr. I. C. Allen

'J15' class 0-6-0 No. 65425 accelerating away from Fordham with the branch freight in 1955. The train is approaching Lark Hall overbridge whilst Cambridge Road overbridge No. 2244 is in the background. The Fordham-Mildenhall section of the branch differed noticeably from the Barnwell Junction-Fordham section, for the GE engineer and Lovatt abandoned level crossings in favour of bridges to carry roads across the railway. In all there were eleven overbridges after the branch left Fordham. *Dr. I. C. Allen*

Entry to the sidings was by two trailing connections from the up direction and a trailing connection from the down loop. Sidings included a straight road 500 ft long, a 480 ft shed road serving the goods shed, 340 ft coal road, and the 710 ft long back road. Running parallel to the single line at the Newmarket end of the station was a 640 ft long shunt spur whilst on the down side of the single line south of the Mildenhall branch junction was an 1100 ft down reception road which became part of the down Newmarket—Ely line when this section was doubled in 1938.

Immediately north of Fordham station, on the other side of Station Road level crossing, the Mildenhall branch veered away from the Ely line at 69 miles 15 chains in a north-easterly direction. From the junction, the railway climbed for a short distance at 1 in 660, around a 20 chain right-hand curve, before levelling out and passing under Cambridge Road overbridge No. 2244 at 69 miles 41 chains. Thirty chains further on was a long cutting, and Lark Hall overbridge No. 2245 at 69 miles 71 chains carrying a small minor road over the railway. The line

then negotiated a slight right curve before straightening out, climbing at 1 in 1500 for almost a mile. At 70 miles 13 chains the railway passed under Soham Road overbridge No. 2246 carrying the A142 Newmarket—Ely main road over the line. The cutting gave way to open farmland and just beyond the 70¾ mile post the gradient levelled out as the branch crossed the infant River Snail on underbridge No. 2247 at 70 miles 66 chains. The railway continued on a straight course and at the 71 mile post the gradient fell for a short distance, passing under Fordham Moor Road overbridge No. 2248 at 71 miles 2 chains. A slightly rising gradient of 1 in 3000 for half a mile was abruptly followed by a climb of 1 in 150 as the branch negotiated a cutting passing under Fordham Road overbridge No. 2249 at 71 miles 72 chains. Leaving the cutting, the line then crossed a short level section before entering Isleham station 72 miles 30 chains ex Liverpool Street, 16 miles 58 chains from Cambridge.

Situated almost a mile south of the village, this station had up and down side platforms served by a crossing loop 850 ft in length and long enough to accommodate a train

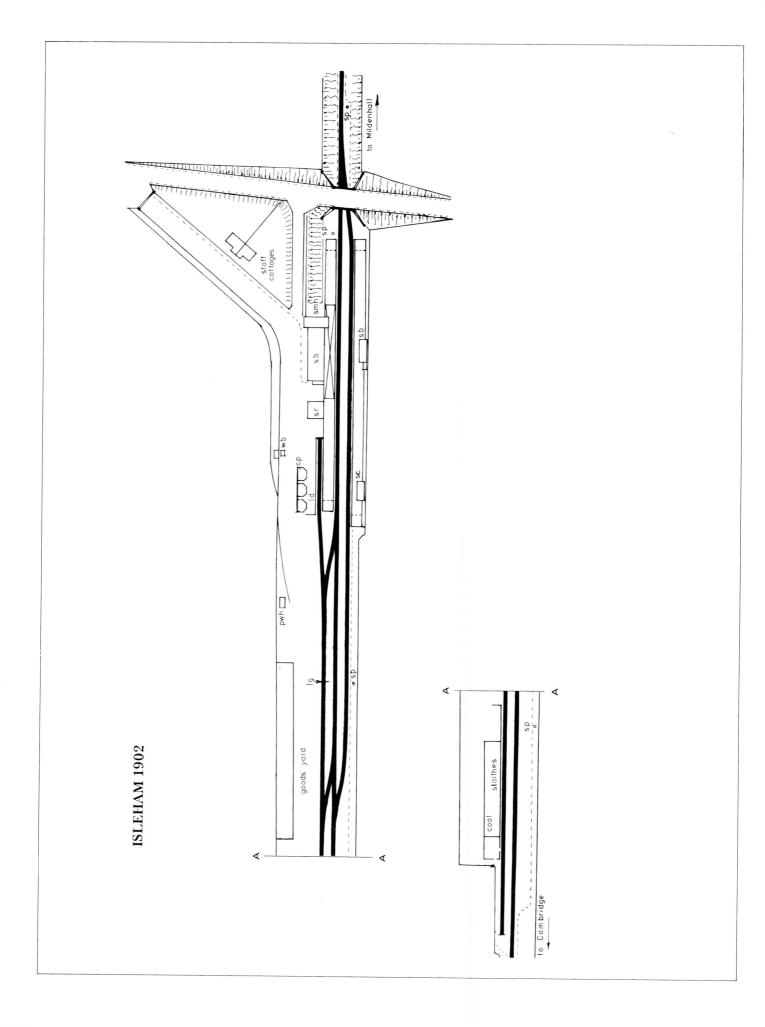

ISLEHAM 1902

to Mildenhall

staff
cottages

goods yard

pwh

lg

wb

cp

ld

sr

s b

smh

sp

sc

sb

sp

A

A

coal
staithes

sp

to Cambridge

A

A

Isleham station, facing towards Cambridge. The branch followed a straight course to the horizon, passing under Fordham Road and
Fordham Moor Road overbridges. The down starter is an upper quadrant signal on concrete post.   *R. Powell*

Coal merchants at Isleham were provided with a covered coal shed, and this wooden structure, located at the west end of the yard and
shown here in dilapidated condition in March 1961, was the only one at any of the branch goods yards.   *J. Watling*

The flat rural area served by the Mildenhall branch is evident in this photograph taken from the train of the up side platform and signal box at Isleham.

R. Powell

of 24 wagons with engine and brake van. The down side platform, 360 ft long, served the main station buildings including booking and parcels office, waiting rooms, staff accommodation and toilets. Again the buildings were fronted and covered by an ornate canopy. Adjoining the station buildings at the east end was the station master's house of similar construction to that at Burwell. The 380 ft up platform was only equipped with the usual small waiting shelter. In addition to the platform buildings, two staff cottages were located in the approach road to the station.

The goods yard at Isleham was at the west end of the station on the down side of the line. Two trailing crossovers from the down loop line gave access to a 580 ft refuge road, or if part of this was occupied with wagons and only the west end trailing points were used, the siding

The decorative timber and brick waiting shelter on the up side platform at Isleham.

Collection D. Taylor

Isleham, facing towards Cambridge, showing the 850ft crossing loop serving both platforms. The signal box is located at the west end of the up platform whilst the goods yard is on the down side beyond the station.
Lens of Sutton

A closer view of the brick and timber waiting shelter. The platforms were illuminated by oil lamps.   *Lens of Sutton*

Isleham down side platform with station master's house and main station buildings including booking office, waiting rooms and toilets. Note the modified chimneys from earlier years, also the rail post and tubular fencing which has replaced the original wooden fence. The width of formation beyond Station Road overbridge was wide enough for double track but the branch was always single. *Lens of Sutton*

The flat terrain of the Fen border country is evident in this view of 'J15' 0—6—0 No. 65438 approaching Isleham with a Mildenhall-Cambridge train on 5th October 1957. No. 65438 was one of five fitted with side window cabs and tender cab in 1934/5, for working the Colne Valley line but often saw use on the Mildenhall line. The tall GER signal with lower quadrant arm is the Isleham up home.

H. C. Casserley

was only 310 ft to the buffer stops. The west end of the siding otherwise served coal wharves. At the east end of the goods yard was the 180 ft long Dock Road which ran behind the down side platform and served the loading dock and cattle pens.

Signals and points at the station were controlled from Isleham station signal box equipped with a 20-lever frame and located at the Fordham end of the up platform.

Away from Isleham the branch passed under Station Road overbridge No. 2250 at 72 miles 35 chains, climbing at 1 in 150 through a short cutting to reach a minor summit of the line. Level gradients were then followed by a short fall at 1 in 160 across open farming country, then a 40 chain radius right-hand curve took the line into a short cutting before passing under Beck Row overbridge No. 2251 at 73 miles 2 chains. A straight course across the valley of a small stream took the line in quick succession over two underbridges No. 2252 at 73 miles 24 chains, an occupational path and Lee Brook by bridge No. 2253 at 73 miles 29 chains.

For the next two miles the branch continued its straight course across open country and here the difference between the two sections of the Cambridge—Mildenhall line was most noticeable. West of Fordham the GER Engineer and Lovatt, the contractor, decided on few bridges and many level crossings. The folly of providing expensive-to-man level crossings was abandoned east of Fordham where all public roads crossed the railway by overbridges. The last four of these structures spanned the single track branch railway in the last three miles to the terminus.

At 73 miles 78 chains the branch negotiated the first of these, Four Cross Ways overbridge No. 2254 where the railway had cut neatly through a four-way cross roads. The resultant banking necessitated by diverting the country roads to the bridge was a noted local landmark. From that bridge the line commenced a short 1 in 200 climb before a half-mile of level track. A descent at 1 in 100 to another short level section took the branch under Freckenham Road overbridge No. 2255 at 74 miles

'J15' class 0—6—0 No. 65442 approaching Worlington Golf Links Halt with a Cambridge-Mildenhall train in 1955.

Dr. I. C. Allen

'E4' class 2—4—0 No. 62781 on a Mildenhall-Cambridge train waiting for passengers to board by using the steps on the side of the brake third at Worlington Golf Links Halt.

Dr. I. C. Allen

75 chains, after which the line curved to the left and at the 75¼ mile post the gradient altered to 1 in 260 falling through a cutting under Manor Farm occupation overbridge No. 2256 at 75 miles 33 chains. Skirting the southern boundary of the village of Worlington, the branch ran along a short straight section to Worlington Golf Links Halt 75 miles 40 chains ex Liverpool Street and 19 miles 68 chains from Cambridge.

Similar in construction to the halts at Fen Ditton and Exning Road, with clinker platform, large nameboard and single post oil lamp, it was located nearer to the centre of population and consequently provided more traffic to the branch than the other two halts. Another beneficial factor was the Royal Worlington and Newmarket Golf Course located on the up side of the line west of the adjacent overbridge. Although the club was founded in 1893 and despite many petitions for a railside halt, members had to wait until 20th November 1922 before facilities were provided. As with the other halts, passengers awaiting trains had to seek shelter under the arch of the bridge in inclement weather.

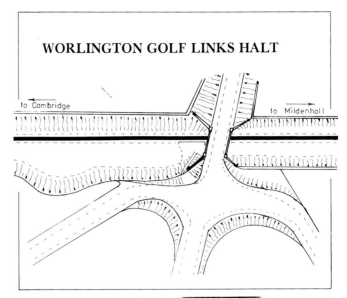

WORLINGTON GOLF LINKS HALT

to Cambridge

to Mildenhall

A passenger joining a train at Worlington Golf Links Halt using the extended steps on the side of the brake third. The steps were operated by the guard and the brakes could not be released until the steps were pulled back flush with the side of the vehicle.

Cambridgeshire Collection

Worlington Golf Links Halt, opened by the GER on 20th November 1922 to serve the Royal Worlington & Newmarket golf course and the local village. Known as Mildenhall Golf Links Halt until 1st January 1923, only basics were provided, with clinker platform and sleeper facing at rail height. An oil lamp and nameboard completed the facilities. It is viewed here facing Mildenhall with Worlington Road overbridge No. 2257 adjacent. In inclement weather this bridge was the only shelter available to passengers.   *Lens of Sutton*

This picture shows the access path from adjacent road. The oil lamp shown in earlier views was superseded by a Tilley lamp provided during hours of darkness.
                                                                                          Lens of Sutton

Mildenhall signal box was located on the up side of the loop road opposite the west end of the station platform.
Photomatic

Mildenhall turntable and engine inspection pit, looking towards the buffer stops. The signal box is to the left.

R. Powell

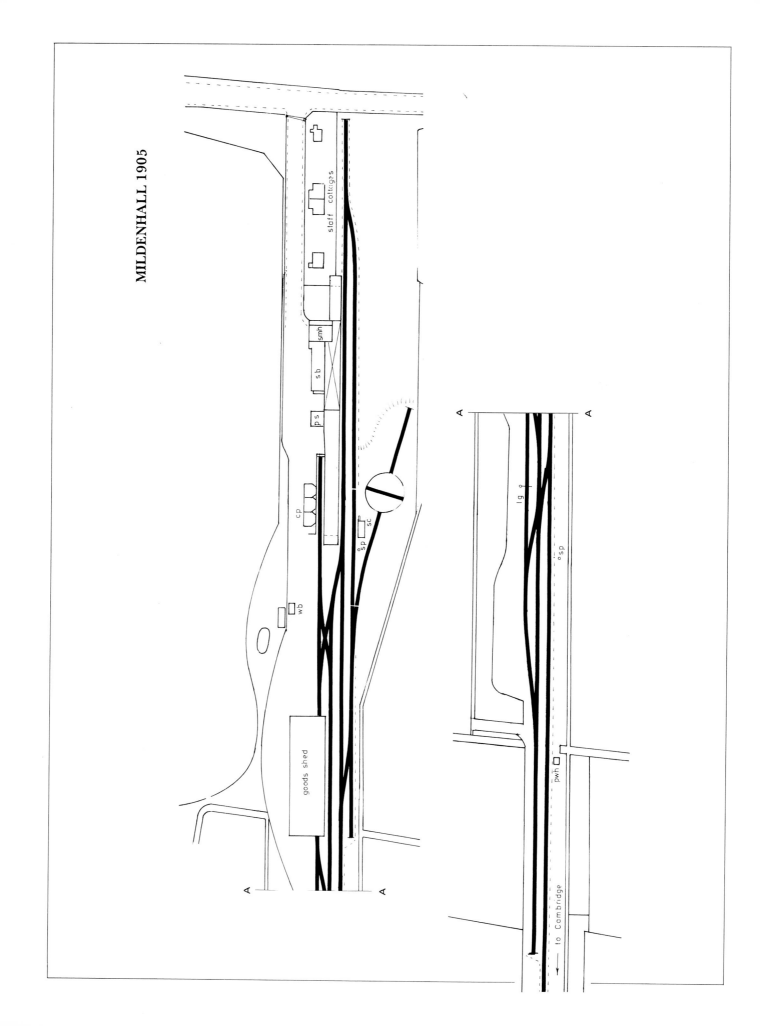

From 1885 to 1915 a locomotive was outbased at Mildenhall to work some of the branch services. After initially allocating small tank engines to work the line, the GER found from experience that tender locomotives provided greater reliability especially as no water supplies were made available at Mildenhall and engines had to top up at Fordham. A hand-operated turntable of 50ft diameter (later reduced to 49ft 6in) and an inspection pit were the only facilities provided by the motive power department and are shown here on the turntable road in May 1962.   *J. Watling*

The 49ft 6in turntable and pit at Mildenhall with station in the background. Footplate crews always tried to position their locomotive correctly on the table so that balancing made the turning an easy operation. It could otherwise prove very difficult to turn.   *J. Watling*

'E4' class 2–4–0 No. 62785 leaving Mildenhall with a train for Cambridge on 3rd May 1958. By this time she was the last of the class and consequently often used on Cambridge University Railway Club specials across the branch, when, under supervision, members tried their hand at driving. The train is formed of GER brake third and Gresley corridor composite.

Dr. I. C. Allen

No. 65473 with a Cambridge train at Mildenhall in 1951. *O. H. Prosser*

'E4' No. 62785 on an afternoon Cambridge train on 19th September 1953. *I. L. Wright*

Exterior view of Mildenhall station with the approach road to the left and Station Cottages beyond. Mildenhall station was actually located in the parish of Barton Mills although it was not far from the town of Mildenhall.   *R. Powell*

Unlike later years when few passengers travelled, Mildenhall station platform is quite busy on 18th April 1949 as 'E4' class 2—4—0 No. 62791 awaits departure with the 5.48 p.m. to Cambridge.
                                                                        W. A. Camwell

The station buildings and station master's house were of similar design to those at Burwell and Isleham. The lock-up store originally used for parcels and later oil and coal, was located at the west end. The gardens opposite the platform and adjacent to the loop road were let to the staff. *Lens of Sutton*

The ornate canopy fronting onto the station building at Mildenhall was originally supported by nine columns. The canopy was later shortened by removing the section in front of the station master's house and also a small portion at the west end. *Lens of Sutton*

Mildenhall station building including booking office, waiting rooms, toilets and station master's office with ornate canopy over the platform. This view is taken facing the buffer stops in July 1961.

J. Watling

The end of the line — the buffer stops located beyond the platform. On the left are the two cottages, Nos. 1 and 2 Station Yard, provided in 1905 for loco crews outbased at Mildenhall.   *R. Powell*

Looking back towards the station from the buffer stops in June 1962.   *R. Powell*

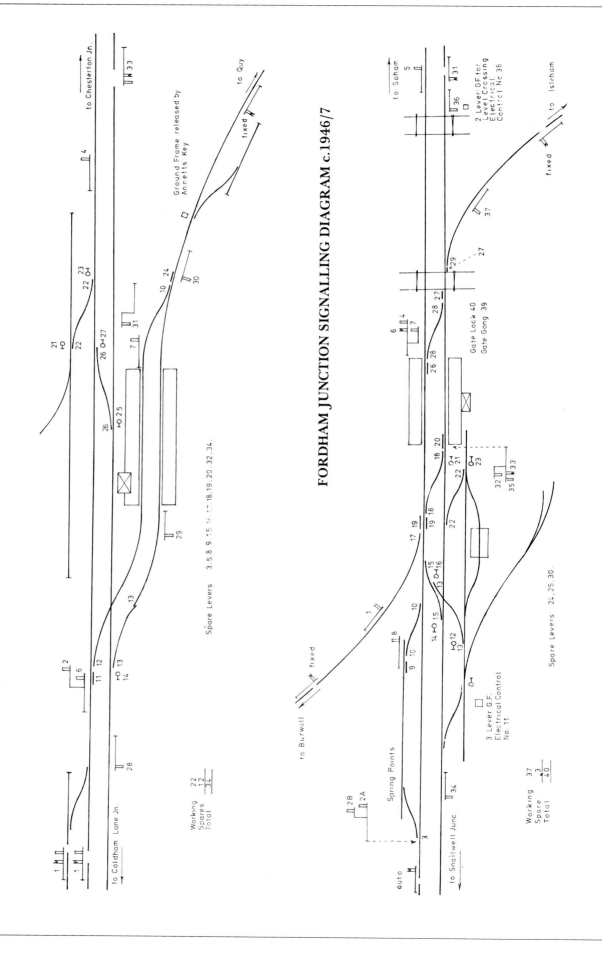

BARNWELL JUNCTION SIGNALLING DIAGRAM c.1946/7

FORDHAM JUNCTION SIGNALLING DIAGRAM c.1946/7

PERMANENT WAY AND SIGNALLING

THE overall speed limit on the branch was 30 mph with 10 mph restrictions when entering and leaving the crossing loops at Bottisham and Lode, Burwell, Isleham and Mildenhall. Mileposts were located on the down side of the branch whilst gradient posts were sited on the up side of the line.

PERMANENT WAY

According to Major General Hutchinson, the original permanent way on the branch was of the 'GE type for new lines', and consisted of 80 lbs per yard bullhead rails in 24 ft lengths, laid in chairs weighing 38 lbs fastened by iron spikes and wooden trenails to creosoted sleepers measuring 8 ft 6 in by 10 in by 5 in. The rails were connected by fishplates weighing 40 lbs per pair. The track was laid on gravel ballast to a depth of 1 ft below sleeper level.

Around the turn of the century, 85 lbs and 90 lbs per yard bullhead rails gradually replaced the original track and these sufficed with replacement of worn out rails until just before the grouping. From 1923 the LNER commenced replacing the 24 ft lengths with 30 ft and 45 ft rails, initially weighing 85-87 lbs per yard, but just before the Second World War 90 lbs per yard rails were introduced on certain sections. Much of the track on the branch was secondhand after use on the main line. Bullhead track remained in use until closure of the branch and latterly short sections of 95 lbs per yard rails were introduced.

Originally gravel ballast was used for the fairly light traffic carried, but, as tonnages increased, the GER introduced ashes and clinker to the formation, having found that ashes were adequate for the ballasting of many of their branch lines and supplies were readily available from the motive power depots on the system. When supplies of ashes or clinker were not available from locomotive sheds, wagon loads were obtained from Tate and Lyle's sugar refinery at Silvertown and, after 1925, from the British Sugar Corporation factories at Ely, Felstead, Bury St. Edmunds and Wissington.

From 1884 the maintenance of the permanent way was covered by two gangs with a third added the following year for the extension to Mildenhall. One gang covered the Barnwell Junction to Swaffhamprior section, the second Swaffhamprior exclusive to Fordham and the third from the junction inclusive to Mildenhall. Each gang comprised a ganger and four lengthmen. In the early 1920s the Barnwell-Swaffhamprior gang had David Day, who lived in No. 2 Gatehouse as ganger, with 'Tommy' Atkin, who lived in No. 1 Gatehouse, J. Howard, S. Symons and Charlie Bradley as lengthmen, whilst the Swaffhamprior-Fordham section was manned by William Parmenter, Thomas Camp, Samuel Thurlborne and George Turner under the charge of ganger Charles Betts. At the east end of the line were George Peachey, William Frost and three others. In the early years each gang possessed their own transport in the form of a hand pump trolley on which they and their tools travelled to site.

After rationalisation in the early 1930s, the Barnwell Junction-Swaffhamprior and Swaffhamprior-Fordham gangs were amalgamated under the control of ganger David Day. To cover the extended section, an additional lengthman was employed, bringing the team total to six men. Improved transport was introduced soon after, on 22nd January 1934, when a petrol-driven motor trolley replaced the hand trolley. Members of the Barnwell-Fordham gang in later years included Bert Moulding, Frank Coxall, Arthur Bradley, Charlie 'Wag' Chapman, Reg Hulyer and Den Baker. David Day retired after 27 years as ganger on reaching his 65th birthday in 1949 but continued as lengthman for a further five years.

The Mildenhall gang was also later disbanded and the area covered by a gang based at Fordham. Unlike their fellow P.W. colleagues, the Mildenhall gang never had use of a motor trolley for the section from Fordham to Mildenhall. In addition to day-to-day track maintenance and relaying, the permanent way gangs were also responsible for cleaning toilet systems where no mains sewerage existed as well as maintenance of gates and fences. On hot and dry summer days they also patrolled the line, acting as beaters to extinguish fires caused by stray sparks from passing locomotives.

The Mildenhall branch was always under the control of the District Engineer, later District Civil Engineer, at Cambridge.

SIGNALLING

Tenders for signalling work on the Mildenhall line were distributed on 6th March 1883 and the contract subsequently awarded to McKenzie and Holland Ltd. of Worcester on 15th October of the same year. John Wilson, Signal Engineer of the GER, was sent a schedule of prices by the company and noted that included were the costs of signalboxes each costing £75 10s 0d. From the outset, block signalling was provided and the line was worked on the train staff and ticket principle. The single line staffs provided were Barnwell Junction to Bottisham, round in shape and coloured green; Bottisham to Burwell, square and yellow; Burwell to Fordham, triangular and red; Fordham to Isleham, hexagonal and blue; Isleham to Mildenhall, square and yellow, the paper tickets corresponding in colour with the train staffs.

On the branch Barnwell Junction station was provided with distant, home and starter signals in the down direction and fixed distant, home and starter and advanced starter signals for up trains. Bottisham and Burwell stations were protected by distant, home and starter signals in each direction. Before closure Quy and Swaffhamprior station signal boxes controlled the same. At Fordham Junction, distant and home signals were provided for the Mildenhall branch trains from each direction, whilst starting signals were provided on the up and down platforms at the station.

The simple layout at Isleham included the provision of working distants and home and starter signals for each

BOTTISHAM & LODE SIGNALLING DIAGRAM c.1946/7

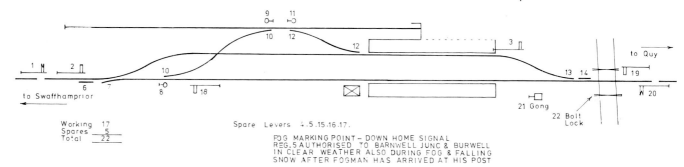

Working 17
Spares 5
Total 22

Spare Levers 4.5.15.16.17.

FOG MARKING POINT – DOWN HOME SIGNAL
REG.5 AUTHORISED TO BARNWELL JUNC & BURWELL
IN CLEAR WEATHER ALSO DURING FOG & FALLING
SNOW AFTER FOGMAN HAS ARRIVED AT HIS POST

BURWELL SIGNALLING DIAGRAM c.1946/7

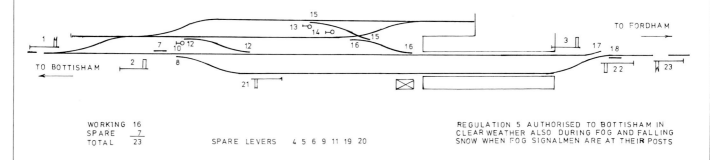

WORKING 16
SPARE 7
TOTAL 23

SPARE LEVERS 4 5 6 9 11 19 20

REGULATION 5 AUTHORISED TO BOTTISHAM IN
CLEAR WEATHER ALSO DURING FOG AND FALLING
SNOW WHEN FOG SIGNALMEN ARE AT THEIR POSTS

ISLEHAM SIGNALLING DIAGRAM c.1946/7

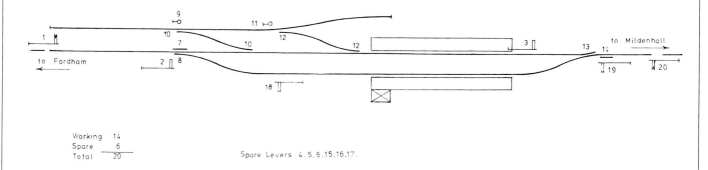

Working 14
Spare 6
Total 20

Spare Levers 4.5.6.15.16.17.

MILDENHALL SIGNALLING DIAGRAM c.1946/7

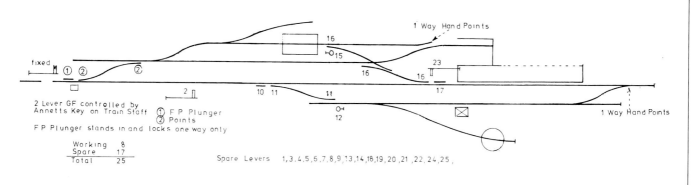

2 Lever GF controlled by
Annetts Key on Train Staff ① F P Plunger
② Points
F P Plunger stands in and locks one way only

Working 8
Spare 17
Total 25

Spare Levers 1,3,4,5,6,7,8,9,13,14,18,19,20,21,22,24,25,

direction. Mildenhall was protected by a fixed distant and a home signal on the approach to the station, whilst up services required only the clearance of the starting signal before setting off for Isleham.

Barnwell Junction signalbox, controlling the main line and branch, boasted a 34-lever frame with 31 operating levers and 3 spare (later 22 working and 12 spares). Quy signalbox had a 22-lever frame with 16 working levers and 6 spares. The crossing loop at Bottisham and Lode with associated signalling and sidings was controlled by the station signalbox with a 22-lever frame with 17 operating levers and 5 spares. Swaffhamprior signalbox also boasted a 22-lever frame with 20 working levers and 2 spares. The signalbox at Burwell, governing the crossing loop and all points and signals, had a 23-lever frame with 18 working levers and 5 spares (later 17 and 6 respectively). Fordham Junction signalbox had the largest frame of 40 levers with 37 operating and 3 spares. On the extension to Mildenhall, Isleham signalbox had the smallest frame on the branch with only 20 levers, 14 working and 6 spares. The signalbox at the terminus was provided with a 25-lever frame with 17 operating levers and 8 spares, later vastly reduced to 8 working and 17 spares. All frames were McKenzie and Holland.

All the signalboxes on the branch were of brick and timber construction with individual dimensions as under:

	Length	Width	Height of operating floor above rail level
Barnwell Junction	26ft	12ft	10ft
Quy	22ft	12ft	5ft 6in
Bottisham and Lode	22ft	12ft	6ft
Swaffhamprior	22ft	12ft	6ft
Burwell	20ft 4in	12ft	6ft
Fordham	28ft 6in	9ft 6in	13ft
Isleham	22ft 9in	13ft	8ft
Mildenhall	26ft	12ft 6in	8ft

During GER days Barnwell Junction signalbox was closed and switched out from 10 p.m. until 6 a.m. on weekdays and all day on Sundays, whilst the rest of the branch station signalboxes including Quy, which was not a block station, were closed at night and on Sundays. By 1910, because of its position on the Ely-Newmarket line, Fordham Junction signalbox was open continuously on weekdays but closed from 10 a.m. until 12.00 midnight on Sundays between the running of booked and special trains. By 1919 Barnwell Junction signalbox was open from 6 a.m. until 10 p.m. on weekdays, whilst all the other branch signalboxes were open for the running of trains shown in the Working Timetable and for trains specially advised. Fordham Junction was the exception, being open continuously from 10 p.m. on Sunday until 10 a.m. the following Sunday, and at other times on Sunday for the running of trains shown in the Working Timetable and for trains specially advised. The LNER initially made few alterations except that Fordham Junction was opened later at 6.00 a.m. on Mondays and then remained open continuously until 6.00 a.m. the following Sunday and then for the running of trains shown in the Working Timetable or those specially

advised. A decade later the only alterations in timing affected Barnwell Junction and Fordham signalboxes. Barnwell Junction was now open on weekdays from 6.15 a.m. until 10 p.m. Monday to Friday, and after the passage of the 11 p.m. ex Cambridge on the main line if the latter was running late, so at Fordham the signalbox was open continuously on weekdays and until the 'train out of section' was received for the 10.15 p.m. goods ex Parkeston on Sunday mornings. Between that time and 10.45 p.m., when it was due to re-open, it was also open on Sundays for the running of branch trains shown on the Working Timetable and specials. Minor adjustments were made during the war years to suit traffic conditions and it was not until after nationalisation that specific opening times were given for all the branch signalboxes. By 1961 the position was as follows:

Barnwell Junction	6.15 a.m. to 10.25 p.m. weekdays
Bottisham and Lode	7.45 a.m. to 5.00 p.m. weekdays
Burwell	7.35 a.m. to 5.00 p.m. weekdays
Fordham — Winter	9.30 p.m. Sunday to last freight Sunday morning, then 5.05 p.m. to 7.50 p.m. Sunday
Summer	5.05 p.m. Sunday to last freight Sunday morning, then 10.00 a.m. to 10.30 a.m. Sunday
Isleham	6.45 a.m. to 7.50 p.m. weekdays
Mildenhall	7.00 a.m. to 7.50 p.m. weekdays

The points to the various intermediate sidings on the Mildenhall branch were released and locked by Annett's key attached to the train staff for the relevant section of line. The method adopted to work these sidings was often quite complex, especially in the days before the adoption of metal tickets. The GER set out detailed instructions in its Appendix to the Working Timetables.

Francis Siding, about 550 yards to the west of Quy station on the down side of the line, was served by points trailing from the up direction. The points were controlled from a 4-lever ground frame released by Annett's key attached to the Barnwell Junction and Bottisham train staff; the same key also released the ground frame to the Commercial Brewery Company's siding at Barnwell Junction.

All trucks for Francis Siding were required to be worked from Bottisham station and special working arrangements were made for up freight trains to shunt the siding. When the driver of the train appointed to work the siding was only in possession of the train staff ticket, when leaving Bottisham for Cambridge the station master at Bottisham was required to hand the Bottisham-Barnwell Junction train staff to a competent member of his station staff who then accompanied the train to the siding. After shunting was completed, it was the responsibility of this man to see that all wagons were placed inside the catch points, clear of the main single line, and the points locked before allowing the train to proceed. This completed, the member of station staff then returned on foot to Bottisham station to deliver the staff to the station master.

When the engine driver was in possession of the Barnwell Junction-Bottisham staff, the member of station staff was still required to accompany the train to the siding to ensure the wagons were clear of the trap points and the points locked for the main single line before handing the staff to the driver and allowing the train to continue.

Similar arrangements were in operation at Stephenson's siding, located on the down side of the branch between Burwell and Fordham, where the points again trailed from the up direction. The points were controlled by a 6-lever ground frame released by Annett's key attached to the Burwell and Fordham train staff, and wagons for the siding were worked from Fordham station. It was then the responsibility of the Fordham station master to provide a competent member of staff to accompany the up goods train to the siding to ensure the wagons were safely clear of the running line. The competent member of staff then returned to Fordham with the train staff if the driver was in possession of a ticket only, or empty-handed if the driver was in possession of the Burwell-Fordham train staff.

Unlike other private sidings on the line, which were shunted by the branch freight, the Commercial Brewery Company's (later H. & D. Taylor's) siding near Barnwell Junction was worked by the pilot engine from Cambridge. Trucks for the siding were propelled from Barnwell Junction yard sidings with the brake leading. According to the 1919 WTT Appendix, between 1.00 p.m. and 1.50 p.m. or 3.50 p.m. and 4.20 p.m., the pilot engine shunted on the rear of the trucks in Barnwell Junction sidings and, after the departure of the up Mildenhall branch passenger train, and on authority of the signalman, drew the trucks out on to the up main line at Barnwell Junction. The driver was then authorised, on receiving the correct signals, to set the train of wagons into the up loop line at the station. On receipt of the Barnwell Junction-Bottisham single line staff, the driver carefully backed the trucks to the Commercial Brewery siding located on the up side of the line with points trailing from the up direction. On completion of shunting, the train of wagons, with the brake van in the rear, returned to either Barnwell Junction goods yard or Cambridge as appropriate.

It was mandatory for a competent shunter to accompany the pilot engine shunting the sidings and it was his responsibility to obtain the keys for the gate to the Commercial Brewery siding from the Barnwell Junction station master and the train staff from the driver. On arrival at the siding, the shunter duly unlocked and opened the siding gates and unlocked the 4-lever ground frame controlling the points with the Annett's key attached to the train staff. On completion of the shunting, he was responsible for ensuring all trucks were placed within the catch points and that the gates, ground frame and points were locked in position to enable normal branch line working to continue. The staff was duly returned to the driver and the gate key to the station master.

The original signalling equipment supplied by McKenzie and Holland included conventional lower quadrant home and distant signals with pitch pine posts, cedar arms and cast and wrought iron fittings. In common with GER practice, each signal arm was stamped on the reverse with the name of the controlling signalbox. Around the turn of the century modifications were made to the operating distant signals on the branch. At that time the GER distants were painted the same red as stop signals and showed the same red and green aspects to drivers at night.

To avoid confusion with the home and starter signals, the distant signals were fitted with Coligny-Welch lamps which displayed an additional white 'V' at night that was actually horizontal (thus >) beside the signal aspect.

With the advent of the LNER, the distant signals were gradually repainted the familiar yellow with black 'V' and the Coligny-Welch lamps removed or modified to serve as ordinary lamps. After World War Two some of the signal posts on the branch were found to be rotting and were replaced by those of tubular steel. Lower quadrant arms were replaced by LNER or BR upper quadrant arms on the same post, including Isleham down starter, Mildenhall down home and up starter, and Fordham down and up starter signals for both main line and branch.

By the mid-1930s the LNER authorities were seeking further economies in the working of the branch. The train staff and ticket method of working was also causing delays, especially when the intermediate sidings were shunted. The signalboxes at Quy and Swaffhamprior were only switched in and operated by the porter/signalman when trains required to call to shunt the station sidings.

Under the original system of using paper tickets to authorise all the trains (except the last) in a group to travel through a single line section in succession — the space interval between them being maintained by block working — only the last train, which carried the staff, could work an intermediate siding where the ground frame was released by an Annett's key on the staff. Some companies, notably the Great Northern, adopted re-usable metal tickets in the form of metal plates (rectangular or oval) but they made no contribution to overcoming the problem. In the LNER 'Train staff and metal ticket system' the tickets were more akin in form to a key token, with a key to the in-section ground frames on every ticket, so that any train could work at any ground frame. It then became so much simpler to abolish a little used (but expensive to man) signal box and replace it by ground frames.

The Traffic Committee found that considerable savings could be achieved and on 21st November 1934 the Divisional General Manager of the Southern Area sought approval for the introduction of the train staff and metal ticket method of working. At the same time it was proposed to close Quy and Swaffhamprior signalboxes. The estimated gross cost of the scheme was £305 but the net cost was reduced to £262 if the estimated value of recoverable material of £43 was offset against expenses. The saving of renewal and maintenance charges was estimated at £75 and the committee readily gave their approval to the scheme. The modifications and alterations were completed by late June and the signalboxes at Quy and Swaffhamprior duly closed on 1st July 1935. The staff sections were thus altered and became Barnwell Junction to Bottisham, and Bottisham to Burwell, new staffs being provided.

In later years the staff and metal ticket box at Barnwell Junction was in the station master's office, and the station master had an electric release on the down starting signal. As at some of the branch signalboxes, Barnwell Junction was equipped with a Tyer's two-position block instrument with a three-way commutator indicating 'Train on Line' and 'Train arrived'. Trains were accepted from Bottisham with the special bell signal 1—3—3 ('Train may enter section') but the indication on the instrument was not altered until the ordinary 'Train entering section' (2 bells) was received.

After the withdrawal of passenger services on 16th June 1962, Isleham and Mildenhall signalboxes were closed the following day and the section Fordham Junction to the terminus worked on the 'one engine in steam' principle, with some points modified for hand working. 'One engine in steam' was also introduced on the Barnwell Junction-Fordham section, although signalmen were retained at the junction signalboxes as well as Bottisham and Burwell to operate the points for the remaining weekday freight service. Later in the year further rationalisation took place and marker boards were provided 600 yards on the approach to each public level crossing and drivers were advised that they might find the gates across the railway. At Quy No. 2 Gatehouse and Exning Road No. 4 Gatehouse, the level crossing gates were removed and whistle boards erected on the approach side of these crossings in each direction. The speed of trains was restricted to 10 mph within these distances. At Quy station crossing a 'stop board' was positioned on the Mildenhall side of the crossing and up trains were required to stop at the board before proceeding over the crossing.

At the same time 'pilot guard' working was introduced for the weekday only goods service between Fordham and Barnwell Junction. The Mildenhall branch freight was re-routed on the down journey from Cambridge via Newmarket and Fordham. On the up run the train was booked via Burwell with the 'pilot guard', nominally the Fordham station master, joining the train at Fordham. As the points to the goods yards at Swaffhamprior and Quy and Francis Siding were operated by ground frame released by a key, it was still a requirement to carry a train staff. The former staff sections were amalgamated into one section, Fordham to Barnwell Junction and it was the responsibility of the guard rostered for the Mildenhall branch freight to obtain the staff with the key from the station inspector at Cambridge before departure. The staff with its key were handed to the 'pilot guard' on arrival at Fordham and, if the intermediate sidings required to be shunted, the key was handed over by the 'pilot guard' to the train guard so that the necessary movements could take place. On arrival at Cambridge, the staff and key were handed back to the station inspector by the train guard. The 'pilot guard' method of working proved so time-consuming and expensive with the provision of a second guard that in practice it was rarely operated. More often than not there was no spare man to act as 'pilot guard' and the train ran with the rostered guard carrying the staff and key throughout the entire journey. With the cessation of services beyond the sidings at Barnwell and Burwell and from Isleham and Mildenhall from 13th July 1964, the signalboxes at Bottisham and Burwell were closed, leaving the remaining section from Burwell to Fordham operating on the 'one engine in steam' principle. The signalbox at Barnwell Junction was finally closed on 10th December 1967, leaving the stub end thence to the oil siding operated as a long siding. Fordham Junction signal-

box closed on 28th October 1973 as part of signalling rationalisation on the Chippenham Junction-Ely line. Most of the signalboxes were quickly demolished after closure when the frames were removed for scrap and the timber for use elsewhere or burnt on site.

The maintenance of the signalling equipment on the Mildenhall branch was always the responsibility of the signal-fitting staff based at Cambridge.

It is not always remembered that the railways first brought standard time throughout the country. Before their coming, each town or village varied in time from minutes to hours. The standard scheme finally adopted by the GER before the advent of the telegraph and radio was, like many other companies, that of giving a 10 a.m. time signal via the single needle telegraph to each station and signal box on the system. By the time the headquarters at Liverpool Street had telegraphed down the line and the message had been manually passed on, it was two minutes past the hour before the stations and signalboxes on the Mildenhall line received their time check. The gap in time was generally accepted as this was a far better system of ensuring a standard time throughout the land than was possible by any other system. Once standard time was set, clocks and watches in the villages and towns served by the line were invariably aligned with the station time. The method of passing on the vital information was often amusing, as the inhabitants of Lode were well aware. In the early 1900s, as soon as the 10 a.m. time signal was received, Alfred Mott Ayres, signalman at Bottisham and Lode station, went to the top of the signal box steps and blew a fanfare on an old battered horn. On hearing the sound, local people and farmers put their clocks and watches to the correct time and it was said that the clock on Lode church was so accurate that it was chiming when Ayres was blowing his horn.

This 1960 photo shows two fine examples of GER lower quadrant signals, the down home in the off position and the up starter complete with finial nearer the camera. Note also how the wooden arm has been worn away by the metal stop on the post!
Dr. I. C. Allen

HALF-DAY EXCURSION

TO

BURWELL FORDHAM ISLEHAM MILDENHALL

SUNDAY, 11th JULY

OUTWARD JOURNEY		RETURN FARE—Third Class			
		Burwell	Fordham	Isleham	Mildenhall
	p.m.	s. d.	s. d.	s. d.	s. d.
Cambridge ... dep.	12 30	1 0	1 3	1 6	2 0
Barnwell ... ... ,,	12 40	—	1 3	1 3	1 6
Quy ... ... ,,	12 48	—	1 0	1 3	1 6
Bottisham & Lode ,,	12 53	—	—	1 3	1 3
Swaffhamprior ... ,,	12 58	—	—	1 0	1 3
Burwell ... ... ,,	1 5	—	—	—	1 3
		p.m.	p.m.	p.m.	p.m.
Arrival Times		1 4	1 15	1 25	1 35

RETURN ARRANGEMENTS
(On day of issue)

	p.m.			p.m.
Mildenhall ... ... dep.	8 30	Swaffhamprior ... ... arr.		9 3
Isleham ... ... ,,	8 38	Bottisham & Lode ... ... ,,		9 8
Fordham ... ... ,,	8 47	Quy ... ... ,,		9 15
Burwell ... ... ,,	8 57	Barnwell ... ... ,,		9 25
		Cambridge ... ... ,,		9 35

Tickets can be obtained in advance from the Stations, also at

CAMBRIDGE { L·N·E·R Town Office, 5, Market Hill
{ Pickfords, Ltd., 37, Hills Road and 2, Free School Lane

It will assist the Railway Company in making arrangements
FOR YOUR COMFORT if you TAKE TICKETS IN ADVANCE

For further information apply to the District Goods and Passenger Manager, Cambridge; or the Passenger Manager, Liverpool Street Station, London, E.C.2

GET YOUR HOLIDAY HANDBOOK 6d
From L·N·E·R Stations, Offices and Agencies

CONDITIONS OF ISSUE

London, June, 1937

S.5059.37   Printed in Great Britain at the L·N·E·R Company's Printing Works, Stratford Market   4,000

CHAPTER SIX

TIMETABLES, TRAFFIC AND STAFF

WHATEVER pretentions the GER directors had of the Mildenhall branch forming an alternative through route between Cambridge and Norwich, were nullified when effective repairs against flooding were made on the Ely-Norwich line near Lakenheath. Although the figures Allix produced regarding traffic flows were realistic in respect of local freight, those pertaining to passenger traffic were probably highly optimistic. Once building of the railway from Barnwell Junction to Mildenhall was completed, hopes of attracting a gradual increase in population, as the railway encouraged trade, were quickly dispelled. Like many other GER routes, most of the land served by the Mildenhall branch formed part of large agricultural estates with little industry, the majority of the populace being employed on the land. Local industry was almost non-existent and therefore travel to and from work was minimal. In later years, the branch train was the lifeline for schoolchildren travelling to Cambridge but other than this late influx, the line only carried a sizeable proportion of passengers on Cambridge and Newmarket market days and other traffic was purely long distance and spasmodic. It is thus surprising that this 19-mile branch from Barnwell Junction supported a service of between four and six weekday trains for 78 years when the population of the villages and towns served (excluding Cambridge) was around the 15,000 mark as the figures quoted below show. Even expansion at Mildenhall after World War Two failed to save the line.

The population of the villages served by the line were:

The extension of the line beyond Fordham to Mildenhall produced immediate additional traffic, and the following passenger services were provided in 1886:

		a.m.	a.m.	p.m.	TO p.m.	p.m.	ThO p.m.	p.m.
Cambridge	dep	7.15	9.20	12.25		3.00T		5.53
Barnwell Junction	dep	7.22	9.25	12.30		3.05T		5.58
Quy	dep	7.33	9.32	12.37		3.12T		6.05
Bottisham	dep	7.43	9.36	12.41		3.16T		6.09
Swaffhamprior	dep	7.55	9.41	12.47		3.22T		6.15
Burwell	dep	8.10	9.46	12.52		3.27T		6.20
Fordham	arr	8.20	9.53	12.58		3.33T		6.26
	dep	8.35	10.06	1.08	2.05	4.10	5.10	6.28
Isleham	dep	8.45	10.14	1.16	2.13	4.23	5.18	6.36
Mildenhall	arr	9.00	10.23	1.25	2.22	4.35	5.27	6.45

TO – Tuesdays only   ThO – Thursdays only
T – Thursdays excepted between Cambridge and Fordham

		a.m.	a.m.	p.m.	TO p.m.	p.m.	ThO p.m.	p.m.
Mildenhall	dep	7.43	9.43	12.43	1.35	3.28	4.40	5.54
Isleham	dep	7.52	9.52	12.52	1.44	3.37	4.48	6.10
Fordham	arr	8.00	10.00	1.00	1.52	3.45	4.57	6.20
	dep	8.03	10.30	1.02T		3.47		6.40
Burwell	dep	8.09	10.36	1.08T		3.53		6.50
Swaffhamprior	dep	8.15	10.42	1.14T		3.59		7.00
Bottisham	dep	8.21	10.48	1.20T		4.05		7.10
Quy	dep	8.25	10.52	1.26T		4.09		7.20
Barnwell Junction	dep	8.34	11.01	1.33T		4.18		7.30
Cambridge	arr	8.38	11.05	1.37T		4.22		7.38

TO – Tuesdays only   ThO – Thursdays only
T – Thursdays excepted between Fordham and Cambridge

From the opening of the line to the West Suffolk town, the GER outbased an engine and two sets of men at Mildenhall to work some of the passenger services. The

	1881	1891	1901	1911	1921	1931	1951	1961
Fen Ditton	668	680	680	759	781	1056	632	634
Stow-cum-Quy	351	387	324	327	322	307	527	447
Bottisham	1555	1501	1283	1383	1193	1287	1363	975
Lode	790	793	659	679	569	638	895	607
Swaffham Bulbeck	744	800	706	714	639	601	611	633
Swaffhamprior	1678	1006	950	934	892	866	695	634
Burwell	1949	1998	1974	2144	2108	2257	2289	2734
Fordham	1193	1284	1326	1410	1461	1475	1705	1708
Isleham	1697	1698	1600	1643	1490	1487	1342	1592
Mildenhall	3764	3732	3567	3645	3370	3235	6742	7132
Barton Mills	468	407	444	475	464	466	561	666
TOTAL	14857	14286	13513	14113	13289	13675	17362	17562

The GER initially provided four trains in each direction between Cambridge and Fordham. Later in the year this was increased to five trains Thursdays excepted. Departures from Cambridge were 7.15 a.m., 9.35 a.m., 12.30 p.m., 3.00 p.m. ThX and 5.53 p.m., returning from Fordham at 8.45 a.m., 10.30 a.m., 1.15 p.m. ThX, 3.47 p.m. and 6.40 p.m. On Thursdays only the 12.30 p.m. ex Cambridge continued beyond Fordham to Ely, returning at 3.30 p.m. ex Ely to form the 3.47 p.m. ex Fordham to Cambridge. This arrangement was provided to form an additional service for Ely market day.

remaining passenger service and the goods trains were handled by Cambridge engines and men.

By 1890 the branch was provided with four Thursdays excepted and three Thursdays only passenger trains, one mixed and one goods train in the down direction, weekdays only, with an additional passenger service between Fordham and Mildenhall on Tuesdays and Thursdays only. The mixed train departed Cambridge at 7.15 a.m. and was allowed 1 hour 50 minutes for shunting wagon traffic at sidings on the 20 mile 59 chains journey. General freight was handled by the goods which departed

Cambridge at 12.30 p.m. and called at Coldham Lane siding when required to pick up and set down traffic. On Mondays the final passenger train of the day, 5.53 p.m. ex Cambridge, was permitted to work two trucks of cattle from Cambridge. On Tuesdays only, this train also worked forward from Fordham to Mildenhall cattle traffic, arriving by the 6.15 p.m. ex Newmarket.

In the up direction five passenger trains Thursdays excepted, four Thursdays only, and one goods train, ran through from Mildenhall to Cambridge with an additional train on Tuesday and Thursday only to Fordham. The second up passenger train, 9.43 a.m. ex Mildenhall, was allowed on Mondays, Tuesdays, Wednesdays and Thursdays to convey a maximum four trucks of cattle from the terminus for Cambridge, Newmarket, Bury and Ely markets respectively, all but the first named being dropped off at Fordham, for the forwarding service. The 11.55 a.m. passenger train terminated at Fordham on Thursday only and then ran to Ely, whilst the last up passenger train of the day, 6.08 p.m., was permitted to convey a maximum of two trucks of cattle from Mildenhall. A single goods train departing Mildenhall at 4.50 p.m., considered adequate for agricultural requirements, was allowed 3 hours 35 minutes for the run to Cambridge, which included a 50 minute sojourn at Burwell waiting for the last up passenger train to pass.

The working timetable for 1897 showed minor alterations to the service provided in earlier years. In the down direction were four passenger and one goods train and the first working, the 9.43 a.m. ex Cambridge, was permitted to convey two trucks of important goods from Cambridge to Mildenhall if the vehicles were fitted with brake pipes. This train was also downrated to work as a mixed train from Fordham to Mildenhall. Of the other passenger trains, the 4.25 p.m. ex Cambridge, booked to stand at Fordham from 4.56 p.m. to 5.06 p.m., departed five minutes later on Tuesdays to allow for additional market traffic transferring from the connecting service ex Newmarket. The last down passenger train of the day, 6.48 p.m. ex Cambridge, was allowed to work cattle traffic from Cambridge or Fordham to Mildenhall again if the vehicles were fitted with brake pipes, whilst the solitary goods train left Cambridge at 11.50 a.m., calling at stations with a 2 hours 35 minutes timing to Mildenhall.

In the up direction a similar service of four passenger and one goods train was provided. The first up passenger, the 8.33 a.m. ex Mildenhall, was permitted to work cattle traffic to Fordham or Cambridge only, with fitted vehicles, whilst the return goods working at 5.00 p.m. ex Mildenhall shunted at Fordham for the last up passenger train, the 5.40 p.m. ex Mildenhall, and then worked traffic to and from Francis siding between Bottisham and Quy. An additional goods train also ran at 3.30 p.m. when required from Mildenhall to Fordham, calling at Isleham if required. The engine and brake van returned from Fordham at 4.00 p.m.

During this period the Mildenhall-based engine and men worked all the passenger duties whilst the goods was covered by a Cambridge engine and crew.

A decade later in 1907 the working timetable provided for four passenger and one goods trains in each direction, with an additional passenger train on Tuesdays only from Mildenhall to Fordham and return, to connect with an Ely-Newmarket line service run in connection with the market at the Suffolk town. An additional express fruit train also ran as required Saturdays excepted, between Mildenhall and Fordham, worked by the Cambridge goods engine. Departing from Mildenhall at 3.35 p.m. and returning from the junction at 4.10 p.m., these trains were treated as specials, with the Mildenhall station master making the necessary local arrangements to run them in the paths provided.

Of the down passenger trains, the 9.52 a.m. ex Cambridge was permitted to work with a maximum of two trucks of important goods from Cambridge to Mildenhall, providing the vehicles were fitted with Westinghouse brake pipes. The train was also downclassed to run as a mixed working from Fordham to Mildenhall with two minutes additional running time allowed over normal passenger train times between these points. The first down passenger train, 7.00 a.m. ex Cambridge, also conveyed Westinghouse-piped horse-boxes conveying horses in transit from London to Burwell, or cattle traffic in fitted wagons from Cambridge or Fordham to Mildenhall only. Similarly, the first up passenger train, 8.25 a.m. ex Mildenhall, was permitted to work cattle from Mildenhall to Fordham or Cambridge in trucks fitted with the Westinghouse brake pipes.

The down goods, worked by Cambridge engine and men, departed Cambridge at 10.25 a.m. and took 3 hours 35 minutes for the 20 miles 59 chains journey, although much of this time was spent shunting at intermediate station sidings. Very often, if traffic was light, the train ran early. The goods duly returned from Mildenhall at 3.25 p.m. Saturdays only, or 5.00 p.m. Saturdays excepted, working wagon loads to or from Francis siding and Stephenson's siding, as well as picking up traffic at Barnwell Junction. The SX goods also shunted at Fordham to allow the last up passenger train, 5.35 p.m. ex Mildenhall, to proceed it across the branch to Cambridge.

The basic service of four passenger trains in each direction, with the additional short return trip from Mildenhall to Fordham, remained until shortly after the outbreak of World War One. In the interests of economy from July 1915 all services were worked from the Cambridge end of the line, and in consequence the footplate staff were withdrawn from Mildenhall and transferred to the parent depot at Cambridge. The train services were rearranged with five passenger and one goods train in each direction weekdays only. The passenger services departed Cambridge at 6.55 a.m., 10.21 a.m., 1.46 p.m., 4.25 p.m. and 7.53 p.m., returning from Mildenhall at 7.55 a.m., 11.52 a.m., 3.14 p.m., 5.48 p.m. and 8.57 p.m.

From May 1916 the initial down passenger train departing Cambridge at 6.55 a.m. was permitted to work two trucks of important goods from Cambridge to Mildenhall if the wagons were fitted with Westinghouse brake pipes. Similarly, the afternoon 4.25 p.m. departure from Cambridge conveyed horse-boxes *en route* from London to Burwell or cattle traffic from Cambridge or Fordham to Mildenhall only, provided the trucks were fitted with brake pipes.

As a result of the earlier down working, the first up train departed Mildenhall at the earlier time of 7.55 a.m. and when required was permitted to work cattle from Mildenhall to Fordham and Cambridge only in Westinghouse fitted trucks. This timetable also showed a much later evening departure from Mildenhall at 8.37 p.m.

The down goods train departed Cambridge at 10.30 a.m., with arrival at Mildenhall at 1.50 p.m., whilst the return up service varied its departures at 3.25 p.m. SO and 4.42 p.m. SX. The SO working shunted at Burwell from 5.20 p.m. to 6.19 p.m. to pick up traffic and allow the 5.48 p.m. passenger train ex Mildenhall to precede it across the branch. On Mondays to Fridays this passenger train passed the up goods at Fordham. Both SX and SO trains worked traffic to and from Francis and Stephenson's sidings and attached traffic at Barnwell Junction.

In 1920 the service was almost identical with five passenger and one goods in both directions and slight adjustments in timings. The 4.25 p.m. down passenger departed at 4.32 p.m. whilst in the up direction the 11.32 a.m. started three minutes later. The 3.14 p.m. passenger ex Mildenhall was advanced to 3.07 p.m. whilst the goods now departed at the uniform time of 3.17 p.m. SX and SO. The 5.48 p.m. also advanced 5 minutes to 5.43 p.m., leaving the last up passenger of the day, 8.37 p.m. now MX, to convey goods traffic from Mildenhall to Cambridge and cattle from Fordham to Cambridge if the trucks were fitted with Westinghouse brakes. If this tail traffic was conveyed, the train was downgraded to the status of a mixed train.

Two years later the 1922 working timetable showed a reduction of train services between Cambridge and Mildenhall to three passenger and one goods train in each direction. To achieve economies and give maximum utilization of stock, the first down passenger and last up passenger workings between Cambridge and Mildenhall ran via Newmarket, Warren Hill and Snailwell Junctions and only joined the branch proper at Fordham Junction. The diversion of certain services via Newmarket remained until the branch closed to passenger traffic. The first down train, 6.47 a.m. ex Cambridge, was permitted to convey not exceeding two trucks of important goods from Cambridge to Mildenhall provided the vehicles were fitted with the Westinghouse brake. Horse traffic from London to Burwell or cattle from Cambridge or Fordham to Mildenhall was conveyed in fitted wagons attached to the last down passenger train, 7.36 p.m. ex Cambridge, whilst the 10.30 a.m. and 4.24 p.m. ex Cambridge, were allowed two minutes extra running time between Isleham and the terminus to cater for recovery of time lost by exceptional circumstances.

In the up direction the three passenger trains routed via Burwell and Barnwell Junction departed Mildenhall at 7.55 a.m., 11.36 a.m. and 5.30 p.m. and were allowed three minutes recovery time between Barnwell Junction

GER Working Timetable for 1922

CAMBRIDGE, FORDHAM AND MILDENHALL.

Single Line between Barnwell Junction and Mildenhall.

DOWN WEEK DAYS.

Miles from Camb'dge	Miles from Mildenh'll		1 Pass.	2	3 Pass.	4 Gds.	5	6 Pass.	7	8 Pass.	9	10
0	20 62	Cambridge .... dep.	a.m.	—	a.m. 10 30	a.m. 10 35	—	p.m. 4 21	—	p.m. 7 36	May work not exceeding 2 trucks of important goods from Cambridge to Mildenhall if the trucks are fitted with Westinghouse brake pipes.	
1 46		Barnwell Junction... ⑧ {arr.	—	—	10 33	10 40	—	4 27	—	7 39		
		{dep.	—	—	10 34	10 47	—	4 28	—	7 40		
4 49		Quy.................... ⑧	—	—	10 41	11 0	—	4 35	—	7 47		
6 7		Bottisham and Lode ⑧ {arr.	—	—	10 41	11 5	—	4 38	—	7 50		
		{dep.	—	—	10 45	11 30	—	4 39	—	7 51		
8 3		Swaffhamprior ...... ⑧ {arr.	—	—	10 50	11 45	—	4 44	—	7 56		
9 75		Burwell .... ⑧ {dep.	—	—	10 51	11 50	—	4 48	—	8 0		
		{dep.	—	—	10 55	12 20	—	4 49	—	8 1		
13 39		Fordham .... ⑧ {arr.	7 26	—	11 2	12 30	—	4 56	—	8 10		
		{dep.	7 28	—	11 7	1 0	—	5 2	—	8 10		
16 61		Isleham .... ⑧ {arr.	7 35	—	11 15	1 10	—	5 9	—	8 17		
		{dep.	7 36	—	11 16	1 40	—	5 10	—	8 18		
20 62		Mildenhall .... ⑧ arr.	7 44	—	11 26	1 50	—	5 20	—	8 26		

— 1 From Cambridge, via Newmarket, at 6.47 a.m. See page 22. May work horses London to Burwell, or cattle from Cambridge or Fordham to Mildenhall, if the trucks are fitted with Westinghouse brake pipes.
= 2, 3 & 8 Allowed 2 mts. extra between Isleham and Mildenhall for recovery of time lost by exceptional circumstances.
= 3 & 6 Allowed 2 mts. extra between Isleham and Mildenhall and Mildenhall for recovery of time lost by exceptional circumstances.
= 8 May work horses London to Burwell, or cattle from Cambridge or Fordham to Mildenhall only, if the trucks are fitted with Westinghouse brake pipes.

UP WEEK DAYS.

Miles from Mildenh'll		1	2 Pass.	3 Pass.	4	5	6 Gds.	7	8 Pass.	9	10	11 Pass.
0	Mildenhall .... ⑧ dep.	—	a.m. 7 55	a.m. 11 36	—	—	p.m. 3 20	—	p.m. 5 30	—	—	p.m. 8 40
4 1	Isleham .... ⑧ {arr.	—	8 2	11 43	—	—	3 30	—	5 37	—	—	8 47
	{dep.	—	8 3	11 44	—	—	3 40	—	5 38	—	—	8 48
7 23	Fordham .... ⑧ {arr.	—	8 10	11 51	—	—	3 50	—	5 45	—	—	8 55
	{dep.	—	8 17	11 55	—	—	4 15	—	5 51	—	—	8 57
10 67	Burwell .... ⑧ {dep.	—	8 23	12 1	—	—	4 35	—	5 57	—	—	—
	{dep.	—	8 21	12 2	—	—	5 5	—	5 58	—	—	—
12 59	Swaffhamprior ...... (NB) {arr.	—	8 29	12 7	—	—	5 15	—	6 3	—	—	—
14 55	Bottisham and Lode ⑧ {dep.	—	8 33	12 11	—	—	5 20	—	6 7	—	—	—
16 13	Quy.................... (NB) "	—	8 38	12 16	—	—	5 30	—	6 8	—	—	—
19 16	Barnwell Junction... ⑧ {arr.	—	8 45	12 24	—	—	5 45	—	6 12	—	—	—
	"	—	8 47	12 25	—	—	5 50	—	6 20	—	—	—
20 62	Cambridge .... arr.	—	8 55	12 32	—	—	6 0	—	6 21	—	—	—
							6 5		6 28			

— 2 To work cattle from Mildenhall to Fordham and Cambridge only, if the trucks are fitted with Westinghouse brake pipes.
= 2, 3 & 8 Allowed 3 mts. extra between Barnwell and Cambridge for recovery of time lost by exceptional circumstances.
6 To work traffic to or from Francis siding (between Bottisham and Quy), and Stephenson's siding (between Burwell and Fordham). To attach traffic at Barnwell Junction.
=10 'T. Cambridge, via Newmarket. See page 25.

and Cambridge. In addition, the first train was permitted to work cattle from Mildenhall to Fordham or Cambridge. The last up passenger departing the terminus at 8.40 p.m. left Fordham at 8.57 p.m. *en route* to Cambridge via Newmarket.

Freight traffic on the branch continued to be handled by the solitary goods train in each direction, 10.35 a.m. ex Cambridge, returning each weekday at 3.20 p.m. from Mildenhall. After shunting at all branch stations and picking up or setting down wagons at Francis and Stephenson's sidings and attaching traffic at Barnwell Junction, arrival at Cambridge was timed at 6.05 p.m.

After grouping, the LNER continued the reduced service between Barnwell Junction and Fordham of three trains each way, the first down service and last up service between Cambridge and Mildenhall still being diverted via Newmarket, Warren Hill and Snailwell Junctions, whilst the early afternoon out and return workings via Burwell ran on Mondays and Saturdays only. The fastest down journey between Liverpool Street* and Mildenhall was 2 hours 37 minutes by the 5.05 a.m. which connected with the 6.42 a.m. ex Cambridge. In the up direction an almost incredible 2 hours 5 minutes was possible by catching the 11.56 a.m. ex Mildenhall where the connection from Cambridge arrived in London at 2.01 p.m. Journey times on the branch had increased to 59 or 60 minutes down and 56 to 65 on the up direction because of the additional stops at the recently opened Fen Ditton, Exning Road and Worlington Golf Links Halts.

The full passenger timetable was:

DOWN		N a.m.	MSO a.m. a.m./p.m.	p.m.	p.m.
Liverpool Street	dep	5.05	8.30 11.50	2.34	5.49
Cambridge	dep	6.42	10.30 1.45	4.20	7.36
Mildenhall	arr	7.42	11.29 2.43	5.19	8.35

UP		a.m. a.m./p.m.	MSO p.m.	p.m.	N p.m.
Mildenhall	dep	7.51 11.56	3.07	5.27	8.45
Cambridge	arr	8.55 12.59	4.10	6.32	9.51
Liverpool Street	arr	10.25 2.01	6.10	8.22	

N Via Newmarket   MSO Mondays and Saturdays only

The working timetable for 1924 continued to show the same service, except the first down train in the morning departed Cambridge at the slightly later time of 6.45 a.m., conveying as required two trucks of important goods to Mildenhall. The 7.36 p.m. also retained the authority to convey horse-boxes to Burwell or cattle from Cambridge or Fordham to Mildenhall. On the up road the 7.51 a.m. ex Mildenhall was permitted to work cattle in fitted wagons to Fordham or Cambridge whilst the 8.45 p.m. ex Mildenhall ran via Newmarket to the University city.

The down goods departed from Cambridge at the earlier time of 9.00 a.m. in order to convey traffic from branch stations for Ipswich and district to Fordham, to connect with the 11.35 a.m. ex Whitemoor. The goods also shunted at Burwell for the 10.30 a.m. down passenger ex Cambridge to pass. In the up direction the goods again ran at differing times, 1.45 p.m. ex Mildenhall SO, and

3.00 p.m. SX. The SO working shunted at Burwell for the 3.07 p.m. MSO ex Mildenhall passenger train to pass, whilst on MO the 3.00 SX goods followed the same passenger train ex Mildenhall. Both SX and SO goods continued to shunt Francis siding, Stephenson's siding and attached traffic at Barnwell Junction.

During the coal strike of 1926 the LNER was forced to make economies and, as with all other lines, passenger services were reduced in number. From 31st May the already mediocre Mildenhall services were pruned to two trains in each direction, 6.50 a.m. and 4.20 p.m. Cambridge to Mildenhall and the 7.40 a.m. and 5.27 p.m. Mildenhall to Cambridge.

By 1928 numerous alterations had been made to the Mildenhall branch services. In the down direction four passenger trains traversed the line via Burwell with the first train of the day, 6.50 a.m. ex Cambridge, no longer running via Newmarket. This train covered the 20 miles 59 chains journey to Mildenhall in 45 minutes, omitting the calls at Quy and the three halts, although it continued to work if required not exceeding two trucks of important goods to Mildenhall in fitted wagons. In the up direction three passenger trains ran direct to Cambridge whilst the final service of the day, 8.43 p.m., continued to run via Newmarket. Freight traffic was handled by one goods train in each direction, the down train departing at the earlier time of 7.25 a.m. ex Cambridge with a 3 hours 35 minutes timing to Mildenhall. On Saturdays excepted the up goods departed Mildenhall at 3.00 p.m., calling at all yards as well as Stephenson's siding and Francis siding. All London traffic was required to be attached nearest the engine and worked in one lift from Coldham Lane to Cambridge Up Yard as ordered by the yard supervisor. The Saturdays only goods ran at the earlier time of 1.45 p.m. from the terminus and omitted the calls at Stephenson's and Francis sidings as well as Barnwell Junction.

The increase in horse traffic handled by the branch is evident by the introduction of horse-box special workings on Mondays and Tuesdays only, as and when required. Station masters at the branch stations were requested to wire the Cambridge District Superintendent of expected traffic. In response to such calls, various paths were available in the working timetable. On Mondays only, if traffic required to be moved, an engine and brake van departed Cambridge at 7.00 a.m. for Fordham, placing empty horse-boxes at Burwell and terminating at that station if no traffic was expected at Fordham. The engine then returned with the horse-box special at 8.25 a.m. ex Fordham or 8.35 a.m. ex Burwell. If for any reason Isleham or Mildenhall generated horse traffic on the Monday, the brake van was attached to the 6.50 a.m. passenger train ex Cambridge, which was then double-headed by two locomotives to Mildenhall. In this way, one locomotive departed Mildenhall with the first up passenger train at 7.49 a.m. whilst the second locomotive with brake van worked the 8.00 a.m. horse-box special to Cambridge. On Tuesdays only, if traffic warranted, the down engine and brake departed Cambridge at 7.00 a.m. for Soham via Fordham, returning from Soham at 7.50 a.m. and calling at Fordham, Burwell, Bottisham and the other branch stations as required before arriving at Cambridge at 9.14 a.m.

Two years later few alterations were made to the 1930 timetable, although, after complaints had been raised, the 6.50 a.m. down passenger ex Cambridge again called at Quy, but not the halts. To cater for increased shopping traffic to Cambridge, an additional passenger train ran in each direction on Saturdays only, departing Cambridge at 12.50 p.m. and returning from Mildenhall at 2.00 p.m. The up freight no longer ran at differing times SX and SO, and departed Mildenhall at 3.00 p.m. each weekday.

By 1935 the basic service provided on the branch was four passenger SX, six passenger SO and one goods train in the down direction, and four passenger SX, five passenger SO, and one goods and one empty coaching stock train on the up road. The first down train, 6.50 a.m. ex Cambridge, continued with the provision for not exceeding two piped wagons of important goods from Cambridge to Mildenhall, whilst the 7.29 p.m. ex Cambridge was permitted to work horse traffic to Burwell or cattle from Cambridge to Fordham or Mildenhall. The LNER, in attempting to counteract the menace of local bus routes and attracting traffic, also introduced a late down service on Saturdays departing Cambridge at 11.00 p.m. Omitting the stops at Fen Ditton, Quy, Exning Road and Worlington Golf Links, the service gave inhabitants of the villages and towns a chance to attend late night functions, and deposited them at Mildenhall at 11.43 p.m. On the up road the 7.49 a.m. ex Mildenhall conveyed cattle traffic in piped wagons to Fordham or Cambridge, whilst the 8.40 p.m. was routed via Newmarket. The 'cars' of the late Saturday down passenger train returned from Mildenhall at 11.50 p.m. and departed Fordham at 12.22 a.m. on Sunday, routed via Ely to Cambridge, as the branch signal boxes were closed for the night.

The freight traffic on the branch was handled by the 10.30 a.m. ex Cambridge, which also worked traffic from branch stations for Bury St. Edmunds and beyond to Fordham to connect with the 12 noon ex Whitemoor forwarding service. In the up direction the goods departed Mildenhall at 3.00 p.m., serving all stations and sidings, although on Saturdays it departed Barnwell Junction at 6.35 p.m. instead of 6.48 p.m., arriving Cambridge at 6.40 p.m. The Q path engine and brake van 7.00 a.m. ex Cambridge MTO and the return working of horse-box traffic from Soham, Fordham or Burwell, continued to feature in the timetable. As before, if Mildenhall generated any horse-box traffic, the engine and brake van were attached to the 6.50 a.m. down passenger train ex Cambridge.

With only slight alterations to times, the service remained static for almost four years. By 1939, however, the railway company were seeking economies and the poorly patronised Saturday Only passenger services were withdrawn. The basic working timetable showed four passenger trains and one goods in each direction with the passenger services split to two workings across the branch in the morning and two in the late afternoon/evening, the last up train 8.40 p.m. ex Mildenhall routed via Newmarket to Cambridge. The 6.45 a.m. ex Cambridge down passenger continued to convey not exceeding two piped wagons of important goods to Mildenhall, whilst the 7.26 p.m. was permitted a tail load of horse-boxes conveying horses from London to Burwell, or cattle in fitted wagons from Cambridge to Fordham or

Mildenhall. Conversely, the first up train, 7.53 a.m. ex Mildenhall, conveyed cattle in piped wagons to Fordham and Cambridge only. Goods trains continued to run at 10.30 a.m. down and 3.00 p.m. up, although a Q path was arranged for the up train to permit it to run later between intermediate points when it was required to connect at Fordham with the 3.10 p.m. ex Ipswich goods. The train then conveyed traffic forward to the branch stations as required.

Horse-box traffic on Monday and Tuesdays only continued to be handled as in earlier years.

Following the outbreak of hostilities, minor adjustments were made to the timings of three trains in each direction in 1940, whilst the 7.40 p.m. ex Cambridge via Burwell to Mildenhall and the 8.45 p.m. return via Newmarket, ran on Saturdays only. Two years later the service was reduced to three trains in each direction with the late SO working being withdrawn. Down trains departed Cambridge at 6.40 a.m., 10.28 a.m. and the ubiquitous 4.27 p.m., returning from Mildenhall at 7.49 a.m., 11.50 a.m. and 6.00 p.m.

The fastest down journey from London was possible by the 2.25 p.m. ex Liverpool Street, which connected with the afternoon train to Mildenhall, giving a timing of 3 hours 2 minutes for the overall journey. By returning on the 6.00 p.m. ex Mildenhall, with one change at Cambridge, travellers could arrive at Liverpool Street 2 hours 48 minutes later.

In November 1944 only three passenger trains ran each way between Cambridge and Mildenhall.

		N a.m.	a.m.	p.m.
Cambridge	dep	6.33	10.28	4.27
Mildenhall	arr	7.31	11.27	5.27
		N via Newmarket		
Mildenhall	dep	7.42	11.50	5.48
Cambridge	arr	8.48	12.45	6.43

The fastest down journey between London and Mildenhall was available on the 4.30 a.m. ex Liverpool Street which connected with the first train ex Cambridge via Newmarket, offering a 3 hours 1 minute timing. The two other down trains afforded a slightly slower timing of 3 hours 7 minutes. In the up direction the passengers from Mildenhall were given faster timings of 2 hours 44 minutes on the 11.50 a.m. ex Mildenhall, which connected at Cambridge with the express due at Liverpool Street at 2.34 p.m. The early evening train, 5.48 p.m. ex Mildenhall, although giving the fastest journey on the branch of 55 minutes to Cambridge, connected with a slower service offering only 3 hours 2 minutes timing between the Suffolk town and London, where arrival was at 8.50 p.m.

The increase of farm produce in the war years and petrol rationing brought a welcome increase of freight traffic to the Mildenhall branch. To cater for such traffic, two goods trains were provided in the down direction weekdays only. The 10.35 a.m. ex Cambridge conveyed a parcels van next to the engine and called at Barnwell Junction, Quy (if required), Bottisham, Swaffhamprior and Burwell, to leave London shed traffic only, before continuing to Isleham and Mildenhall. This train also conveyed an additional brake van from Cambridge to

CAMBRIDGE, FORDHAM AND MILDENHALL.
Single line between Barnwell Junction and Mildenhall.

M. C.	DOWN WEEK DAYS			1	2	3 Gds.	4	5	6 Gds.	7	8	9	10
— —	Cambridge .... dep.					a.m. 9 5			a.m. 10 35				
1 56	Barnwell Junction ⑤	arr. dep.				9 40 11 36			10 40 10 50				
4 49	Quy	,,				*			*				
6 5	Bottisham and Lode ⑤	arr. dep.				12 5 12 30			11 10 11 20				
8 2	Swaffhamprior	,,				12 50			11 35				
9 73	Burwell .... ⑤	arr. dep.				12 55 1 20			11 40 11 50				
13 36	Fordham .... ⑤	arr. dep.				1 30			12 0 12 2)				
16 58	Isleham .... ⑤	arr. dep.				—			12 30 12 50				
20 59	Mildenhall .... ⑤	arr.							1 0				

	UP WEEK DAYS			1	2	3 Gds.	4	5	6 Gds.	7	8	9	10	11
M. C.	Mildenhall .... ⑤	dep.				p.m. 3 0			p.m.					
4 1	Isleham .... ⑤	arr. dep.				3 10 3 20								
7 23	Fordham .... ⑤	arr. dep.				3 30			3 30					
10 66	Burwell .... ⑤	arr. dep.							3 50 4 10					
12 57	Swaffhamprior	,,							* 4 35					
14 54	Bottisham and Lode ⑤	arr. dep.							4 55					
16 10	Quy								*					
19 13	Barnwell Junction ⑤	arr. dep.							5 30 5 48					
20 59	Cambridge	arr.							5 53					

3 Ex Coldham Lane. To call at Brick Yard. Engine to return with 3.30 p.m. Fordham to Cambridge.
6 Cambridge to supply Fordham with a brake for use on 5.50 p.m. Fordham to Whitemoor. To call at Barnwell Jct. Quy, Bottisham, Swaffham Prior and Burwell to leave London shed goods only. The road wagon to be attached next engine.

3 To work 5.50 p.m. Fordham to Ely, 8.55 p.m. (SX) Ely to Cambridge and as required from Ely on Saturdays. Traffic for Cambridge and beyond to be worked into Ely on 5 50 p.m. ex Fordham.
6 Fordham to attach road wagon each for Cambridge and Bishopsgate.

LNER Working Timetable (Freight) for 1944

Fordham for use on the 5.50 p.m. Fordham-Whitemoor goods. After the necessary shunting at Mildenhall, the engine and men worked the 3.00 p.m. goods to Fordham before taking the 5.50 p.m. Fordham-Whitemoor as far as Ely. General commodities for stations west of Fordham were worked by the 9.05 a.m. down goods ex Cambridge which, after shunting the Cambridge brick siding and Barnwell Junction yard, continued to Fordham, arriving at 1.30 p.m. The engine and men then worked the 3.30 p.m. up goods from Fordham, calling at all stations except Quy and Swaffhamprior where calls were made only if required.

After the cessation of hostilities in 1945 three passenger trains continued to be provided in each direction between Cambridge and Mildenhall. The first down train of the day, 6.33 a.m. ex Cambridge, omitted calling at the halts, whilst the 5.48 p.m. ex Mildenhall remained the earliest final up departure for some years. Down trains departed Cambridge at 6.33 a.m., 10.28 a.m. and 4.27 p.m. with departures ex Mildenhall at 7.42 a.m., 11.50

CAMBRIDGE, FORDHAM AND MILDENHALL
Single line between Barnwell Jct. and Mildenhall.

M. C.	DOWN WEEK DAYS			1 Pass.	2 Pass.	3 Pass.	4
				a.m.	a.m.	p.m	
	Cambridge .... dep.			6 33	10 28	4 27	....
1 56	Barnwell Jct. ...... ⑤	arr. dep.		6 36 6 37	10 31 10 32	4 30 4 31	— ....
2 31	Fen Ditton Halt	,,		—	10 35	4 34	—
4 49	Quy	,,		6 45	10 41	4 40	—
6 5	Bottisham & Lode ⑤	arr. dep.		6 50 6 51	10 44 10 45	4 43 4 44	— ....
8 2	Swaffhamprior	,,		6 56	10 49	4 49	....
9 73	Burwell .... ⑤	arr. dep.		7 1 7 3	10 54 10 55	4 53 4 54	— ....
10 50	Exning Road Halt	,,		....	10 58	4 57	....
13 36	Fordham .... ⑤	arr. dep.		7 11 7 14	11 5 11 10	5 4 5 10	— ....
16 58	Isleham .... ⑤	arr. dep.		7 21 7 22	11 16 11 17	5 16 5 17	— ....
19 68	Worlington Golf Lks. H.	,,			11 24	5 24	....
20 59	Mildenhall .... ⑤	arr.		7 31	11 27	5 27	....

M. C.	UP WEEK DAYS			5 Pass.	6 Pass.	7 Pass.	8
				a.m.	a.m.	p.m.	
	Mildenhall ...... ⑤ dep.			7 42	11 50	5 48	....
71	Worlington Golf Lks. H.	,,		7 46	11 54	5 52	—
4 1	Isleham .... ⑤	arr dep		7 52 7 53	12 0 12 1	5 58 5 59	— ....
7 23	Fordham .... ⑤	arr. dep.		7 59 8 6	12 7 12 9	6 6 6 7	— ....
10 9	Exning Road Halt	,,		8 13	12 16	6 15	—
10 66	Burwell .... ⑤	arr. dep.		8 15 8 16	12 18 12 19	6 17 6 18	— ....
12 57	Swaffhamprior	,,		8 20	12 23	6 22	....
14 54	Bottisham & Lode ⑤	arr. dep.		8 25 8 26	12 27 12 28	6 26 6 27	— ....
16 10	Quy	,,		8 30	12 32	6 31	—
18 28	Fen Ditton Halt	,,		8 35	12 38	6 36	—
19 13	Barnwell Jct. ...... ⑤	arr. dep.		8 37 8 38	12 40 12 41	6 38 6 39	— ....
20 59	Cambridge .... arr.			8 48	12 45	6 43	....

Passenger trains between Cambridge and Mildenhall are worked on the " Conductor Guard " principle.

LNER Working Timetable (Passenger) for 1945

a.m. and 5.48 p.m. The following year these passenger train times remained unaltered but an additional later train was introduced between Cambridge and Mildenhall via Newmarket, departing Cambridge at 7.40 p.m. and returning from the Suffolk terminus at 9.00 p.m. The goods services again reverted to a single working in each direction, departing Cambridge at 10.35 a.m. and calling at Quy, Bottisham, Swaffhamprior and Burwell to detach and attach as required. After a 1.00 p.m. arrival at the terminus, the necessary shunting was carried out before the up working departed Mildenhall at 3.00 p.m., calling at Swaffhamprior and Quy only if required, with arrival back at Cambridge at 6.05 p.m.

By 1947 the LNER in their last timetable had withdrawn the late train in each direction via Newmarket through lack of patronage and the coal shortage.

After nationalisation British Railways authorities made few alterations to the basic LNER timetable. By 1950 public demand and an improvement in coal supplies enabled the reintroduction of an additional later train in each direction. The new down service, however, ran from Cambridge to Mildenhall via Burwell, but continued to return via Newmarket. Passenger trains departed Cambridge at 6.33 a.m. (not calling at Fen Ditton, Exning Road and Worlington Golf Links Halts), 10.28 a.m., 4.27 p.m. and 7.45 p.m., returning from Mildenhall at 7.45 a.m., 11.50 a.m., 5.48 p.m. and 9.00 p.m., the latter not calling at Worlington Halt. The K class freight services continued to depart Cambridge at 10.35 a.m., calling at all stations yards, except Quy where the call was 'as required'. In the up direction the goods departed Mildenhall at 3.00 p.m., making mandatory stops at all yards except Swaffhamprior and Quy where calls were only made if required.

The service appeared to settle down, but in 1952, because of unsatisfactory patronage, the 7.45 p.m. down and 9.00 p.m. up passenger services were again withdrawn. Other services remained unaltered. The following year minor alterations were again made to timings of the passenger services, with the 6.33 a.m. down retimed to start at 6.25 a.m. and the 10.28 a.m. departing Cambridge five minutes earlier at 10.23 a.m. Up trains departed Mildenhall at 7.35 a.m., 11.49 a.m. and 5.59 a.m., all working via Burwell. By now the fastest down timing for passengers from London to Mildenhall was three hours by the 8.24 a.m. ex Liverpool Street, changing at Cambridge, whilst in the up direction it was possible to reach Liverpool Street in 2 hours 18 minutes by catching the connection off the 7.35 a.m. ex Mildenhall.

In 1955 the loss of traffic to the road competition was reflected in the railway services offered across the branch. In the down direction Mildenhall was served by three trains from Cambridge SX and four SO. The 6.28 a.m. ex Cambridge, however, ran non-stop to Fordham via Burwell and omitted calling at Worlington Golf Links, leaving only the 10.23 a.m. SO and 4.27 p.m. school train to serve all stations. The 6.02 p.m. SX and 6.13 p.m. SO ran to Mildenhall via Newmarket. In the up direction on Mondays-Fridays only, the 7.35 a.m. ex Mildenhall called all stations to Cambridge via Burwell, supplemented on Saturdays by the 11.49 a.m., the later 5.40 p.m. and 7.40 p.m. departures from Mildenhall being routed via Newmarket.

The following year an additional train was provided, departing Ely at 10.25 a.m., involving a reversal at Fordham 10.42 a.m. to 10.48 a.m. before arrival at Mildenhall at 11.06 a.m. The up train departed at 11.12 a.m. but was routed via Newmarket to Cambridge. The final steam only timetable provided on the branch followed the trend of the previous years with only the 6.28 a.m., 10.22 a.m. SO and 4.27 p.m. ex Cambridge being routed via Burwell. Other services provided between Fordham and Mildenhall only were 10.25 a.m. ex Ely and the 6.02 p.m. SX and 6.13 p.m. SO ex Cambridge routed via Newmarket. In the up direction the 7.38 a.m. and 11.49 a.m. SO ex Mildenhall were the only services routed via Burwell, leaving the 11.12 a.m. SX, 7.19 a.m. SX and 7.44 p.m. SO ex Mildenhall, routed via Fordham and Newmarket to Cambridge.

Following the introduction of diesel railbuses and multiple units on the branch, the service followed the same pattern with the service in 1961 divided as follows:

DOWN

6.37 a.m.	ex Cambridge to Mildenhall via Burwell	DMU
10.06 a.m. SO	Cambridge to Fordham	DMU
10.32 a.m.	Ely to Mildenhall via Fordham	DMU
4.21 p.m.	Cambridge to Mildenhall via Burwell	Railbus
5.56 p.m. SO	Cambridge to Mildenhall via Newmarket	Railbus
6.13 p.m. SX	Cambridge to Mildenhall via Newmarket	Railbus

UP

7.34 a.m.	Mildenhall to Cambridge via Burwell	DMU
11.15 a.m.	Mildenhall to Ely via Fordham	DMU
11.36 a.m. SO	Fordham to Cambridge	DMU
5.15 p.m.	Mildenhall to Cambridge via Newmarket	Railbus
7.31 p.m.	Mildenhall to Cambridge via Newmarket	Railbus

The final public timetable showed the following service of passenger trains:

DOWN

		a.m.	SO a.m.	E a.m.	p.m.	SO p.m.	SX p.m.
Cambridge	dep	6.37	10.06		4.21	5.56	6.13
Barnwell Junction	dep		10.09		4.24		
Fen Ditton Halt	dep		10.12		4.27		
Quy	dep		10.17		4.31	N	N
Bottisham and Lode	dep		10.20		4.35		
Swaffhamprior	dep		10.25		4.39		
Burwell	dep		10.29		4.43		
Exning Road Halt	dep		10.32		4.45		
Fordham	arr	7.07	10.38		4.50	6.35	6.53
	dep	7.08		10.47	4.51	6.36	6.54
Isleham	dep	7.15		10.50	4.57	6.42	7.00
Worlington Golf Links Halt	arr			11.02	5.03	6.48	7.06
Mildenhall	arr	7.25		11.05	5.09	6.54	7.12

E   through train from Ely dep 10.32 a.m.   N via Newmarket

UP

		a.m.	EE a.m.	SO a.m./p.m.	p.m.	p.m.
Mildenhall	dep	7.34	11.15		5.15	7.31
Worlington Golf Links Halt	dep	7.37	11.18		5.18	7.34
Isleham	dep	7.43	11.24		5.24	7.40
Fordham	arr	7.49	11.30		5.30	7.46
	dep	7.50	11.38	11.36	5.31	7.47
Exning Road Halt	dep	7.55		11.42		
Burwell	dep	7.58		11.44		
Swaffhamprior	dep	8.01		11.49		
Bottisham and Lode	dep	8.05		11.53	N	N
Quy	dep	8.09		11.57		
Fen Ditton Halt	dep	8.13		12.01		
Barnwell Junction	dep	8.17		12.04		
Cambridge	arr	8.21		12.08	6.24	8.45

EE to Ely arr 11.49 a.m.   N via Newmarket

As explained at the closure enquiry, the stations Barnwell Junction to Burwell inclusive were served by only one train in each direction SX and two each way on Saturdays, a poor reflection of former years.

From 16th June 1962 the line was served by a weekdays only freight service which called at all stations and yards, shunting as required. Latterly, this worked out from Cambridge via Newmarket to Mildenhall, returning via the branch and using the Pilot Guard method of operation Fordham to Barnwell. As traffic declined, the goods often ran early. After closure of the Barnwell Junction-Burwell section and Fordham to Mildenhall, the truncated section between Fordham and Burwell was served by the weekdays only Ely to Newmarket goods train which latterly only ventured along the line if there was traffic to pick up or put down. The short remaining stub of the branch to the Flitwick Oils terminal near Barnwell Junction at one time was served twice a week, but is now only served as required by an oil train trip from Cambridge Yard connecting with a Speedlink service from Fawley Terminal and Eastleigh.

FARES

From the outset, first, second and third class fares were offered to and from all stations. The fares from Liverpool Street to Cambridge and the branch stations in 1884 were:

Liverpool St. to	1st Single	2nd Single	3rd Single	1st Return	2nd Return	3rd Return
Cambridge	8/9	6/9	4/7½	15/10	13/4	9/3
Barnwell Junction	9/1	7/-	4/9	16/3	13/8	9/6
Quy	9/7	7/5	5/-	17/1	14/4	10/-
Bottisham	9/11	7/7	5/1½	17/6	14/8	10/3
Swaffhamprior	10/3	7/11	5/3½	18/1	15/2	10/7
Burwell	10/7	8/2	5/5½	18/7	15/7	10/11
Fordham	11/4	8/9	5/9	19/9	15/9	11/6

These fares, surprisingly, remained the same until World War One. Inflation, however, had increased charges by 1921. Second class was abolished on the branch trains in 1892 and the fare structure in 1911 was as above, with the following additions, reflecting the extension to Mildenhall opened in 1885:

	1st Single	3rd Single	1st Return	3rd Return
Isleham	12/-	6/0½	£1 0s. 7d.	12/1
Mildenhall	12/8	6/4½	£1 1s. 8d.	12/9

Local fares during the same period were:

from Cambridge

Barnwell Junction	4d	1½d	5d.	3d.
Quy	10d	4½d	1/3	9d.
Bottisham and Lode	1/2	6d	1/8	1/-
Swaffhamprior	1/6	8d	2/3	1/4
Burwell	1/10	10d	2/9	1/8
Fordham	2/7	1/1½	3/11	2/3
Isleham	3/2	1/4½	4/9	2/9
Mildenhall	3/11	1/8½	5/10	3/5

By 1935 fares from Liverpool Street to the branch stations were:

	Single		Monthly Return (valid 1 month)		Ordinary Return (valid 3 months)	
	1st	3rd	1st	3rd	1st	3rd
Cambridge	11/11	7/2	14/9	9/9	1 3 10	14/4
Barnwell Junction	12/3	7/4	15/-	10/-	1 4 6	14/8
Quy	12/10	7/9	15/9	10/6	1 5 8	15/6
Bottisham and Lode	13/2	7/11	16/3	10/9	1 6 4	15/10
Swaffhamprior	13/7	8/2	16/6	11/-	1 7 2	16/4
Burwell	13/11	8/4	17/6	11/3	1 7 10	16/8
Fordham	14/9	8/10	18/-	12/-	1 9 6	17/8
Isleham	15/4	9/3	18/9	12/6	1 10 8	18/6
Mildenhall	16/2	9/9	19/6	13/-	1 12 4	19/6

Local fares from Cambridge were:

	1st Single	3rd Single
Barnwell Junction	4d	2d
Quy	11d	7d
Bottisham and Lode	1/3	9d
Swaffhamprior	1/8	1/-
Burwell	2/-	1/2
Fordham	2/10	1/8
Isleham	3/5	2/1
Mildenhall	4/3	2/7

Despite the war years, fares for 1952 showed little increase over those charged seventeen years earlier, but in the following five years the increase was quite pronounced.

from Liverpool St. to	1952		1957	
	1st Single	3rd Single	1st Single	3rd Single
Barnwell Junction	12/9	8/6	14/6	9/8
Fen Ditton Halt	13/-	8/8	14/9	9/10
Quy	13/5	8/11	15/3	10/2
Bottisham and Lode	13/8	9/1	15/6	10/4
Swaffhamprior	14/-	9/4	16/-	10/8
Burwell	14/6	9/8	16/6	11/-
Exning Road Halt	14/9	9/10	16/9	11/2
Fordham	15/5	10/3	17/5	11/7
Isleham	16/-	10/8	18/3	12/2
Mildenhall	16/11	11/3	20/9	13/10

In 1957 return fares were twice the single fare.

EXCURSIONS

As with many branch lines of the GER, the excursion and special traffic offered by the company was slow to materialize and patronage on such excursions varied considerably, according to the season, destination, and, not the least, the weather. When the line opened, agricultural and other manual workers' wages were low and so it was to the middle and upper classes that the railway excursions appealed most. Gradual alterations were made and the introduction of paid holidays and additional leisure periods brought the price of railway excursions within the pockets of most inhabitants served by the line.

Special tickets and excursion fares were issued for local events such as the 50th annual horticultural fete held at Mildenhall on Thursday, 14th July 1887, in the grounds of the Manor House. The GER issued return tickets at single fares, and special trains ran from Newmarket and Cambridge.

Another special excursion ran from Mildenhall on Monday, 5th September 1887, when over 300 members and friends of the Mildenhall and Icklingham Primrose League travelled to Harwich. Their special train departed the terminus at 7.30 a.m., travelling direct to Ipswich, where the excursionists alighted for a special boat trip along the River Orwell to Harwich. After a cold buffet in the GER Hotel at Harwich, the party returned on the special train direct to Mildenhall via Ipswich and Bury St. Edmunds.

For many local people the excursions on the branch provided the first long railway journey in their life. Such was the case for the boys of Quy Parish Church Choir when they journeyed with their senior members and parents to Yarmouth on Tuesday, 16th July 1889. The train arrived at Yarmouth by 11.00 a.m. and, after a pleasant day by the sea, the gathering returned, arriving at Quy at 11 p.m. It is interesting to note that a sub-scription of £5 6s. 0d. paid for the fares, dinner and tea, leaving each member of the choir 3s. 7d. to spend. In later years the Quy Band of Hope regularly used the railway for their annual outings to Hunstanton.

From the turn of the century until the outbreak of World War One the GER offered a comprehensive excursion programme to most town and seaside resorts served by their system. Excursionists were favoured with

the choice of 5, 6 or 8 day third class tickets at Bank Holidays and Christmas. Examples of fares offered for the Easter Holiday 1911 from Liverpool Street to Mildenhall were 5 day 7s. 6d., 7-8 day 9s. 6d. Five-day tickets issued on Thursday, 13th April, were only available for return on the following Monday, whilst 6-8 day returns could be used on Tuesday to Thursday inclusive. On the Coronation Day of George V later in the year, Friday to Tuesday tickets were issued from Liverpool Street to Mildenhall priced at 9s. 5d. first class and 4s. 2d. third class.

The halcyon days of the excursions from Mildenhall and the branch stations to destinations as diverse as London, Clacton, Walton, Felixstowe, Harwich and Dovercourt, Lowestoft, Yarmouth, Aldeburgh, Cromer, Wells and Hunstanton was before World War One, when either cheap fares were offered by normal service trains or special trains ran from stations on the branch.

After the opening of the halts in 1922, the GER and later LNER offered third class 'market tickets', available on Mondays and Saturdays to Cambridge at the following fares:

Fen Ditton	6d.
Exning Road	2s. 0d.
Mildenhall Golf Links	3s. 11d.
(after 1st Jan 1923 renamed Worlington Golf Links)	

Probably the most notable visitor to the Mildenhall branch was LNER class 'B12' No. 8526 which worked a through Sunday excursion from Liverpool Street in June 1932. The excursion was well patronised and the short platforms at the branch stations were crowded with local people meeting relatives off the train. After arrival at the terminus the locomotive crew experienced difficulty in turning the engine, for although the 50ft diameter could accommodate the 48ft 3in wheelbase of the 'B12', there were problems in balancing the engine so that the table could be moved smoothly. The operation took an hour to perform and finished with the rear tender wheels balanced precariously on the end of the rail. The crew were grateful for additional assistance to push the engine round. *Dr. I. C. Allen*

During World War One all excursion traffic had ceased except for cheap day offers to London. By the early 1920s and 1930s the GER and later the LNER reinstated much of the excursion programme including trips to the ever popular Hunstanton, Yarmouth and Skegness.

In 1935 weekday excursions to Hunstanton, departing Mildenhall at 7.49 a.m., were priced at 6/-, but Sunday excursions, leaving at the later time of 10.10 a.m., were 2/- cheaper. Sunday excursions to Skegness, departing the terminus at 11.15 a.m., were priced at 5/6d, whilst Sunday excursions to London were 4/6d.

The LNER issued Holiday Handbooks priced at 6d to encourage rail travel during a time of recession, and examples of the fares offered from stations on the branch in 1937 showed third class half-day excursions on Sundays to Cambridge priced at Mildenhall 2/-, Isleham 1/6, Fordham 1/3 and Burwell 1/-. Similar half-day excursions to London Liverpool Street were priced at 4/6 from all stations, Mildenhall to Quy inclusive. Patrons for these excursions departed Mildenhall at 9.45 a.m. and returned from Liverpool Street at 9.20 p.m., reaching Mildenhall at midnight.

In the same year a half-day excursion to Hunstanton on Sunday, 11th July, was priced at 4/- third class for all stations Barnwell Junction to Mildenhall except Fordham from where the price was 3/6. The special departed Barnwell Junction at 9.50 a.m., calling all stations to Fordham where it joined up with the Mildenhall portion which had departed the terminus at 10.10 a.m. for the combined run to Heacham and Hunstanton, arriving at 12.20 p.m. and 12.25 p.m. respectively. The return journey departed Hunstanton eight hours later with arrival back at Mildenhall at 10.30 p.m. and Barnwell Junction at 10.40 p.m.

Yarmouth Races were another attraction and on Thursday, 16th September 1937, a special day excursion train ran from Barnwell Junction at 6.30 a.m. and Mildenhall at 6.45 a.m., calling all stations. Third class fares ranged from 8/- at Barnwell, Quy, Bottisham and Lode, Swaffhamprior and Mildenhall, to 7/6 at Isleham, Burwell and Fordham. During the 1930s the branch was opened on Sundays for local excursions from Cambridge to Mildenhall and, on certain Sundays in mid summer, half-day excursions were offered between intermediate stations departing from Cambridge at 12.30 p.m. and returning from Mildenhall at 8.30 p.m. To encourage travel by rail in the pre-Christmas period in 1937, the LNER offered cheap evening excursion fares from stations Mildenhall to Burwell into Cambridge on the 5.00 p.m. train, returning from Cambridge at 11.00 p.m. Fares offered included Mildenhall 1/1, Isleham and Fordham 10d and Burwell 7d.

On the outbreak of World War Two, all excursion facilities were withdrawn, a restriction which was not lifted until 1946. The facilities then offered were rather sparse compared with the pre-war years. Even after nationalisation, British Railways offered only a restricted excursion programme to the branch stations. Destinations again offered to passengers using service trains included Cambridge, Ely, Newmarket, Bury St. Edmunds and Ipswich as well as Liverpool Street. Yarmouth, Hunstanton, Clacton and Lowestoft, provided the chief seaside

destinations for excursionists and were usually served by special trains on Sundays. A typical post-war excursion run to Heacham and Hunstanton on Sunday, 25th July 1954, was :

Barnwell Junction	dep 10.25 a.m.
Quy	dep 10.35 a.m.
Bottisham and Lode	dep 10.40 a.m.
Swaffhamprior	dep 10.50 a.m.
Burwell	dep 10.55 a.m.
Mildenhall	dep 10.45 a.m.
Isleham	dep 10.55 a.m.
Fordham	dep 11.10 a.m.

returning from Hunstanton at 8.15 p.m. and Heacham at 8.20 p.m. Compared with seventeen years earlier, fares charged were Barnwell Junction, Quy, Bottisham and Mildenhall 7/3, Swaffhamprior 7/-, Burwell and Isleham 6/9 and Fordham 6/3.

Excursion trains continued to run to the usual seaside destinations until 1961 whilst cheap fares were offered by service trains to London, Cambridge and various resorts in 1962.

TRAFFIC STAFF

Civil Engineering and Motive Power staff have been referred to in their respective sections, but a brief mention must be made of the traffic staff.

When the Mildenhall branch opened to traffic in 1884/5, staff appointed to the various stations were already on the GER establishment. Within months, however, additional manpower was recruited locally and in the nineteenth century and, indeed, the early years of the twentieth century, a position with the railway company meant security in an area where there was little industry except agriculture.

The station masters appointed in 1884/5 were fortunate that each station was provided with living accommodation. Initially, Jonas Chilvers took charge of Barnwell Junction, with George Hillier at Quy, Charles Murfitt at Bottisham and Albert James Bagley at Swaffhamprior. William Howard, appointed station master at Fordham on its opening in 1879, transferred to Burwell when the branch opened to traffic in 1884. His place at Fordham was taken by Edward Warrington who remained at the junction station until 1896. Howard remained even longer at Burwell where he served until retirement in 1919.

When the extension to Mildenhall opened on 1st April 1885, George Frederick Vipan was promoted from Ryston on the Stoke Ferry branch to take charge of Isleham, whilst the terminus was put under the supervision of Henry Charles Sharpe. In 1891 George Hillier resigned from Quy through ill health. As a retirement present, a collection among local villagers realised £10 10s. 0d., whilst the parish magazine recorded him as 'a most kind and obliging Station Master'. Hillier was replaced as SM by G. Potter who had the distinction of being the last station master before the post was withdrawn three years later. Evidently the GER authorities were of the opinion that such a small station barely warranted such an officer. When Potter was transferred away, he was replaced by a Foreman in Charge. The year 1892 saw the transfer of

O

A Buffet Car will run on this Half-day Excursion

(See tariff on reverse side)

TO

CAMBRIDGE AND LONDON

SUNDAY, 12th SEPTEMBER

OUTWARD JOURNEY				RETURN FARE 3rd Class		RETURN JOURNEY (On day of issue)			
				Cambridge	London				
			a.m.	s. d.	s. d.				p.m.
Mildenhall	...	... dep.	9 45	2 0		Liverpool Street	... dep.	9 20
Isleham	...	,,	9 54	1 6		Whittlesford ...	... arr.	10 40
Fordham	...	,,	10 2	1 3		Cambridge	... {arr.	10 55
Burwell	...	,,	10 12	1 0			{dep.	11 0
Swaffhamprior	...	,,	10 18	—	4 6	Barnwell	... arr.	11 5
Bottisham and Lode	...	,,	10 24	—		Quy	... ,,	11 14
Quy	...	,,	10 30	—		Bottisham and Lode...	,,	11 18
Barnwell	...	,,	10 40	—	—	Swaffhamprior	... ,,	11 25
Cambridge	... {arr.	10 45	—	—	Burwell...	... ,,	11 30
	{dep.	10 50	—	—	Fordham	... ,,	11 40
Whittlesford	...	,,	11 5	—	3 6	Isleham...	... ,,	11 50
			p.m.			Mildenhall	... ,,	12 0
Liverpool Street	... arr.	12 20						

TICKETS CAN BE OBTAINED IN ADVANCE AT THE STATION

SUNDAY AFTERNOON CONCERTS IN LONDON

LIVERPOOL STREET TERMINUS (L·N·E·R)
is centrally situated for reaching all parts of the City, the West End and Suburbs, being connected by subways with Metropolitan and Underground Tube Railways, with electric trains every few minutes. Frequent Motor Bus services pass Liverpool Street

It will assist the Railway Company in making arrangements
FOR YOUR COMFORT if you TAKE TICKETS IN ADVANCE

For further information apply to the District Goods and Passenger Manager, Cambridge or the Passenger Manager, Liverpool Street Station, London, E.C.2

CONDITIONS OF ISSUE

Day, Half-day and Evening Tickets are issued subject to the conditions applicable to tickets of these descriptions as shown in the Company's Time Tables
Children under three years of age, Free; three years and under fourteen, Half-fares
For LUGGAGE ALLOWANCES also see Time Tables

London, August, 1937

L·N·E·R

S.5433.37   Printed in Great Britain at the L·N·E·R Company's Printing Works, Stratford Market   3,000

Charles Murfitt from Bottisham where George Fisher took his place. Along the line at Swaffhamprior, A. J. Bagley moved on, his place as station master being taken by William Fordham. After only eight years at Isleham, G. F. Vipan was promoted to Soham, to be replaced by Henry Mallett Butters. In 1900 Butters moved on to become station master at Elsenham on the London-Cambridge main line and was promoted to a higher grade in 1913 when he also took charge of the Thaxted Light Railway. Unfortunately, he died a few years later while still in office. His connection with the Mildenhall branch remained for some years after his departure from Isleham, as his son was employed as a booking clerk at Burwell.

At Barnwell Junction, station master Jonas Chilvers moved on in 1895 and was replaced for a short period by Henry Woodcock before the station came under the supervision of Henry Leeds during the decade 1898 to 1908. Two years earlier, in 1896, Francis Hopkins took over from George Fisher as station master at Bottisham, but he only stayed for four years before being promoted. Bottisham station then came under the supervision of Jonathan Rice who remained in charge until the post was abolished in the 1920s.

Along the branch at Swaffhamprior Robert Arnold became station master in 1896 and was obviously satisfied with the post and the locality for he remained there until his retirement in 1916. Further changes took place within a short period at Barnwell Junction. In 1908 Henry Leeds was succeeded as station master by Henry Fuller Read, but the latter was obviously eager to seek early promotion for he remained at the junction station for a mere three years before being promoted a few miles up the Cambridge main line to Shelford. The replacement appointment was William George Nunn, who transferred on promotion from the post of station master at Burnt Mill. Nunn, however, suffered from ill health and when H. M. Butters died in office at Elsenham, it was thought the move to a station situated on higher land than Barnwell would be beneficial to his health. Unfortunately, soon after taking office at Elsenham in 1922, Nunn passed away. During his time at Barnwell Junction he had been a member of the Church Council and Sidesman at Fen Ditton Church.

Edward Warrington was succeeded at Fordham in 1896 by Joseph Burton who remained in charge at the junction station until 1908. John Goddard was then appointed as station master and during his time in office became renowned for his picturesque garden which, attached to the station master's house, contained over one hundred standard roses. How the standard roses in full bloom survived the gale force winds which blew across the fens remained a secret with Goddard. The second longest serving station master on the branch, William Howard of Burwell, finally retired after 33 years at the station, to be replaced by William G. Wybrew.

After World War One the GER authorities were concerned with the poor traffic returns from many of their branch lines. The Mildenhall branch was included in subsequent investigations and, as the rural line had never shown healthy receipts, it was considered ripe for economies. As part of this cost-cutting exercise, in 1921

rationalisation of station masters' posts was implemented. Under these new arrangements Jonathan Rose, on promotion from Bottisham and Lode to Barnwell Junction, also took over the supervision of Quy, Bottisham and Lode, and Swaffhamprior stations, and William G. Wybrew, station master at Burwell, was transferred to take charge of Mildenhall on the retirement of Henry Sharpe who had been in charge of the terminus for 36 years since the opening of the line. Burwell station from 1922 was under the supervision of station master D. H. L. Davies, who transferred from Warboys on the Somersham to Ramsey High Street line. In the spring of 1921 D. Webb, a divisional relief signalman at Cambridge, was appointed station master at Isleham, but his stay was short, for in June 1922 he was promoted to Trimley on the Felixstowe branch. Isleham then came under the supervision of station master Charles Sparrow who was promoted from a similar position at Holme Hale. In 1927 Sparrow took charge of both Isleham and Mildenhall before deafness forced early retirement after 42½ years' railway service on 14th August 1933. At a presentation, local staff gave him a smoker's companion set in recognition of his services. Davies remained at Burwell until he was promoted in 1926 and replaced by Bernard Arthur Green. In 1930 the last stage in the rationalisation took effect when the Fordham station master also took control of Burwell. Samuel Thomas Beales, who had taken charge at the junction in 1926, was promoted to Hunstanton in October 1930. The following month G. Button, station master at Soham, took charge of Fordham including Soham and Burwell.

Subsequent station master appointments were:

Barnwell Junction including Quy, Bottisham and Lode and Swaffhamprior
1924	Frederick Thomas Poole
1928	William Barratt
1936	Stanley Porter
1948	Frederick Hammond
1950	Edwin Theobald

Fordham including Burwell and Soham
1935	Arthur Grantham
1937	Geoffrey Read
1956	Raymond Pollard
1962	Robert Jardine

Mildenhall including Isleham
1933	Stanley Porter
1940	Leslie Turner
1942	Leonard Eady
1959	Michael Goddard
1962	Nathan Sykes

Throughout the life of the Mildenhall branch, station masters and other grades played important roles in the life of the local community as well as furthering the good relationships between the GER and its customers. Many sat on parish councils or as chairmen of the local parish groups. Some were church wardens at their parish church.

Contrary to popular belief, station masters were required to pay rent for their accommodation. Typical annual rentals of station masters' houses at the branch station were:

	1913	1924
Mildenhall	£19 0 0	£18 0 0
Isleham	£16 0 0	£16 0 0
Fordham	£20 0 0	£23 0 0
Burwell	£18 0 0	£18 0 0
Swaffhamprior	£ 5 4 0	£ 7 16 0
Bottisham	£18 0 0	£18 4 0
Quy	£ 5 4 0	£ 5 4 0
Barnwell Junction	£18 0 0	£16 0 0

By 1924 Quy was actually rent free to John Richard Gray who as foreman-in-charge opened and closed the level crossing gates at the station.

OTHER TRAFFIC STAFF

Two of the longest serving staff on the branch spent considerable time at Quy. When Mr. Potter, the last station master was transferred away in 1894 Richard Gray was appointed as foreman-in-charge and stayed for 32 years. When he retired in 1926, Mr. T. Musgrave Francis presented him with a wallet containing £10 and a framed illuminated list of the subscribers. Gray's place was taken by Charles 'Snifter' Dye who transferred from Saffron Walden. Except for a number of years during World War Two when he was sent to cover the position at Barnwell Junction, Dye remained at Quy until he retired after spending 33 years on the branch. During his absence Mrs. Dye took over the running of Quy station. From 1959 until closure to passenger traffic, the station was manned only on a part-time basis by relief staff from Cambridge.

At Swaffhamprior Robert Arnold was Foreman-in-Charge from 1913, being succeeded by Edward Arnold as leading porter for 17 years from 1922 until 1939 when Herbert K. Betts took over. Betts remained in charge at the station until the withdrawal of both passenger and freight traffic. Similarly, Reg Gates took over as leading porter at Burwell in the same year and stayed at the station until 1962.

The public level crossings on the branch were usually staffed by wives of permanent way staff and mention must be made of their loyalty to duty. They were required to open and shut the gates for the passage of every train booked in the timetable as well as specials. This often involved very early rises in the morning and sometimes getting out of bed during the small hours. On one occasion in the 1890s, a relief crossing keeper forgot the passage of a train when manning No. 3 gatehouse, with the result that the down goods demolished the gates. The crossing keeper was warned for his misdemeanour and fined a day's pay. The driver on this occasion was also reminded of his duties for failing to notice the gates across the line and failing to have his train under proper control. On another occasion at No. 2 gatehouse, Mrs. Day completely forgot to open the gates, but fortunately the driver of the approaching train was more observant and blew the locomotive whistle to attract her attention to come and open the gates. However, there were otherwise few accidents involving the branch train

demolishing the gates; the crossing keepers rarely forgot to open and shut them.

Of the other female crossing keepers employed, Mrs. Cornwell manned No. 3 gatehouse for many years after the First World War, whilst Mrs. Nora Start, whose husband Arthur was a platelayer on the Swaffhamprior-Fordham PW gang, was crossing keeper at No. 4 gatehouse. Mrs. Atkin, whose husband was also a platelayer, controlled No. 1 gate crossing. All crossing cottages were rent free to the tenants.

Of the signalmen employed on the line, Nelson Saunders spent many years at Burwell where he helped care for the station gardens between trains. He rented one of the station cottages, paying £9 19s 4d annual rent in 1924/5. His colleague on the opposite shift was Elliot Wells who acted as porter signalman. Probably the most colourful character, however, was Alfred Mott Ayres who, as mentioned earlier, was signalman at Bottisham and Lode in the early 1900s and blew his battered horn from the signalbox steps when the 10 o'clock time signal was received on the single needle telegraph instrument. Ayres subsequently completed his railway career as Goods Porter at Bottisham. Other signalmen employed on the branch included William Bowers, Bertie Bowers and John Finch at Fordham, George Nicholas initially at Burwell then at Mildenhall, and George Leverington at Mildenhall.

GOODS TRAFFIC

Before the advent of the railway, local carriers' carts were a common sight on the roads, linking the villages and towns of the area with market centres. In 1875 Thomas Reeve journeyed from Bottisham to Cambridge on Wednesdays and Saturdays whilst from Lode, Robert Cornwell travelled to Cambridge on Saturdays only. Swaffham Prior was fortunate in having three regular carriers linking with Cambridge, George Lane and Thomas Chapman both travelled on Wednesdays and Saturdays, with Mrs. Sarah Wells making the trip on Saturdays only. Burwell enjoyed the services of George Peachy and John Shaw to Cambridge on Wednesdays and Saturdays, Shaw also taking his waggon to Newmarket on Tuesdays. William Howard provided the necessary link from Fordham to Cambridge on Saturdays whilst Isleham boasted a far greater variety of destinations than other villages in the area. Edward Fletcher travelled to Newmarket on Tuesdays and Bury St. Edmunds on Wednesdays and Saturdays. John Wells went to Ely on Thursdays and Cambridge on Saturdays, leaving John Dilly to serve Newmarket on Tuesdays only.

By 1883 the various routes had changed hands and in some cases additional services were introduced to take local produce to market. From Bottisham William Aves operated to Cambridge on Saturdays only with John Goult travelling to the University City from Lode on Wednesdays and Saturdays. At Swaffhamprior James Chapman went to Cambridge on Wednesdays and Saturdays with Alfred Peachey on Saturdays only. Burwell enjoyed the services of William Bridgeman and Henry Martin to Cambridge on Wednesdays and Saturdays, but showed greater affinity to Newmarket where a daily

'J15' class 0–6–0 No. 5350 passing Bottisham & Lode with the 10.35 a.m. Cambridge–Mildenhall freight on 15th October 1949.

LCGB/Ken Nunn Collection

service was operated by George Hunt and Stephen Blackwell. There had been no change of carrier from Fordham but Isleham and Mildenhall showed considerable increase with a greater service to the Suffolk towns than to Cambridgeshire.

From Isleham

Edward Fletcher	Newmarket	Tuesday
John B. Wells	Ely	Thursday
	Cambridge	Saturday
James Dilly	Newmarket	Tuesday and Saturday
	Soham	Friday
John Taylor	Newmarket	Tuesday
	Cambridge	Saturday
John Cullen	Newmarket	Tuesday
	Ely	Thursday
James Bowd	Bury St. Edmunds	Wednesday
William Diver	Bury St. Edmunds	Wednesday and Saturday

From Mildenhall

William Morley	Bury St. Edmunds	Wednesday and Saturday
James Cliff	Bury St. Edmunds	Wednesday
James Newman	Kennett Station	Daily
Walter Jude	Mildenhall Road Station	Daily

The Mildenhall branch, conceived and built initially as part of a through route to Thetford, soon assumed the role of a farmers' line, providing an effective outlet for growers in the area. The initial freight traffic handled quickly confirmed the optimistic forecast of Charles Allix and his fellow promoters as well as the GER board. Barley, wheat, hay, straw, vegetable traffic and coal were quickly transferred from the River Lark lighters' fen barges and the carriers' carts to the railway for rapid transport to and from Bury St. Edmunds, Cambridge, Newmarket and Ely markets. Water-borne traffic succumbed to the railway and the local riverside wharfs and warehouses at the 'Lode ports' and at Mildenhall were

gradually converted to alternative uses. With the competitive service offered by the GER, many of the direct carrier services were withdrawn and the operators concentrated their efforts in providing a feeder service to the railway from outlying villages.

In addition to the root vegetable crops conveyed, including potatoes, carrots, swedes and turnips, from the early 1920s sugar beet was grown increasingly in the fens. Considerable loads were transferred from fen tumbrels and horse-drawn waggons to railway wagons at the station yards, for conveyance to the British Sugar Corporation sugar-processing factories at Ely, Bury St. Edmunds and Wissington. By the late 1950s much of this traffic had transferred to road haulage for direct delivery from farm to factory, but until closure in 1964 sugar beet was still loaded at Quy in reasonable quantities.

Milk was regularly despatched from all stations on the branch and conveyed to dairies at Bury St. Edmunds, Cambridge, Newmarket and Ely in the familiar 17-gallon churns. Two loads were despatched daily during the summer months by the early morning train and then again in the late afternoon. During winter months the milk was forwarded by the early morning train only. Smaller quantities of milk were also sent further afield including consignments from Hall Farm, Bottisham, to Manor Farm Dairy at East Finchley. This area of Cambridgeshire and Suffolk was not noted for its dairy farming and the relatively small amounts of traffic were quickly lost to road transport in the late 1930s when milk churns were collected from the farms and delivered direct to the dairies.

From the outset livestock handled at the branch stations was two-way traffic. The potential of the railway for the speedy transit of animals was quickly realised and horses were regularly conveyed in wagons or horseboxes attached to passenger trains. Until World War Two, hunting horses were conveyed to and from local hunt meetings on 24 hours notice being given to the forwarding stations. Although on many GE branches horse traffic declined after World War One, on the Mildenhall branch the opposite occurred. The proximity of the branch to Newmarket and its famous heath renowned to the horse-racing fraternity, found the establishment of various stables in the area of Burwell, Fordham, Soham and Mildenhall. To cater for the movement of livestock, from 1910 the GER arranged for the late afternoon down passenger train from Cambridge to convey horse-boxes *en route* from London to Burwell. After the Great War this traffic increased and the working timetables showed paths for horse-box trains to run from Burwell, Fordham, Soham and Mildenhall as required on Mondays and Tuesdays. Such provisions remained in the timetable for over a decade but by the late 1930s the traffic had fluctuated and on many occasions the working was cancelled as the horses were despatched by road.

Cattle wagons were a common feature until the early 1950s and the branch was utilized for the conveyance of livestock to Cambridge, Ely, Newmarket and Bury St. Edmunds markets held on Saturday, Thursday, Tuesday and Wednesday respectively. Outgoing cattle was also regularly despatched to Saffron Walden, Bishops Stortford, King's Lynn and Huntingdon markets and, as already mentioned, certain passenger trains were permitted to convey cattle wagons. Pigs and sheep also formed an important commodity for markets but trade declined with the relaxation of petrol rationing after World War Two when nearly all livestock traffic was lost to road transport.

Coal traffic was handled at all stations with coal received from Sherwood, Newstead Kirkley, Bestwood, Hucknowle, Sheepbridge, Stanton, Shirebrook, Clipstone, Worksop and Blidworth collieries. The wagons usually travelled via Peterborough where the Stanground sidings acted as a clearing house for empty wagons to collieries and loaded ones returning to the branch. Other coal traffic was routed via the GN and GE Joint Railway via Spalding and March.

In the 1920s and 30s coke was conveyed for horticultural purposes, but after World War Two this commodity was taken by road. When the branch closed to freight traffic, local fuel merchants were required to travel to Cambridge, Newmarket or Bury St. Edmunds for their supplies.

Another feature of the diverse traffic was eggs. Local poultrymen delivered to the various stations on the branch where they were despatched by passenger train to destinations as far afield as London and the north of England. In 1916 the GER, eager to promote agricultural ideas to boost the supply of foodstuffs lost by the lack of imports in the war years, sponsored an Egg and Poultry Exhibition Train. During its tour of the GE system, the train visited Mildenhall where it was visited by 653 people (381 adults and 272 children).

Of the specific commodities carried by the branch goods, Coprolite, excavated at the adjacent Quy Fen Coprolite Works owned by Mr. Musgrave Francis, was loaded at Francis Siding near Quy. After a few years the works were exhausted, and from 1922 the siding, worked by a 4-lever ground frame, was taken over by Mr. Bendall and Mr. Brown and used for loading of vegetables, notably

potatoes and sugar beet from local farms. Incoming traffic to the siding included fertilizers and manure/London sewerage. If the west wind was blowing, Mrs. Day, the crossing keeper at the adjacent No. 2 gatehouse, and her successors, had to keep their windows firmly shut.

At Barnwell Junction the Commercial Brewery Sidings, installed in 1898, received regular consignments of malt and coal. Later, after H. & D. Taylor had taken over the premises and renewed the siding agreement in 1920, the imports of barley and despatch of malt gradually increased, mostly consigned to local breweries. A second siding was installed in 1923 and from 6th September an agreement was signed between the British Petroleum Co. and the LNER. The siding was later owned by Shell Mex and BP but has since changed to Flitwick Oils and is still served as an oil terminal by rail traffic, but on an 'as and when required' basis.

Stephenson's siding between Burwell and Fordham, worked by a 6-lever ground frame, was installed in 1901 and served brick and cement works, the clay being extracted from adjacent pits and conveyed by a narrow tramway up an incline to the kilns. The works were some half a mile north of the Mildenhall branch and the single connection from the main single line led to a number of sidings. At one time a small industrial locomotive was utilized to shunt wagons within the siding complex, the engine being stabled in a small engine shed near the works. GER and LNER locomotives were not permitted beyond the gates at the entrance to the siding. Brick and tile traffic gradually declined and the work was later taken over by British Portland Cement Manufacturing Ltd. who continued to send cement by rail until the late 1950s. From about the early 1920s the siding was also used for agricultural purposes for loading vegetables and fruit traffic and unloading fertilizer. In 1925 W. Hitch used the siding for such purposes and later Henry Coleman. In the latter years of the branch, the siding became disused, its traffic removed by road transport.

One of the most unusual items of goods conveyed on the branch passenger services was domestic washing. Baskets of soiled linen were sent from London to Quy where for many years a Mrs. Wolfe, who lived opposite the Swan public house, would wash and iron the items and return them to London. It appears that on one occasion cockroaches were discovered in the clunch walls of the row of houses where Mrs. Wolfe resided and it was always supposed that the beetles came down from the metropolis in the washing baskets.

In the late 1920s and early 1930s many of the fenland roads remained unmetalled — dust tracks in summer or muddy morasses in wet weather. County councils undertook a rolling programme of road improvement which involved levelling the surface before covering with granite chippings and tarmacadam. Much of this material was delivered by rail to the branch stations from where the material was offloaded and taken to site by horse and waggon. The granite and tarmacadam was levelled by steam roller. One of the roads included in the programme was that from Quy station to Six Mile Bottom where the local carrier William Flack was employed to cart the material from the station, leaving heaps of granite on the grass verges up Albert Road and along the Wilbraham Road.

Although not situated in such a prolific fruit-growing area as the fenland centres of Cottenham and Wisbech, the branch regularly conveyed fruit by both the branch passenger and goods trains, especially after World War One. Considerable tonnages of gooseberries, currants, strawberries, raspberries, plums and apples, were loaded at Burwell, Fordham, Isleham and Mildenhall for despatch to the north of England, or Spitalfields and Covent Garden markets in London. The season commenced in May and loadings continued unabated until September, after which only apples were despatched. Initially, in May and June, fen drays, carriers' and farmers' wagons brought gooseberries loaded in 28 or 56 lb bags if unripe or 6 lb baskets if ripe. This fruit was also sent away in 12-24 lb sieves. By mid June and through July strawberries were loaded into wagons, 4 lb chips being tiered one above the other in the fruit vans. July was by far the busiest month in the station yards as currants in 10 lb chips, 12 lb trays and 24 lb sieves were loaded alongside tubs or chips of raspberries. As the small soft fruit season waned, so plums and apples were delivered to the railway for transit to market. By early September the plum traffic was finished, leaving the 21 lb or 42 lb flats and 21 lb baskets of apples the only fruit to be despatched, which lasted until Christmas. Unfortunately, after World War Two, nearly all fruit traffic quickly transferred to road transport for conveyance to markets, thus saving the double handling into and out of railway wagons.

Small quantities of flower traffic were sent from various stations to destinations countrywide, for example, Fordham despatched between 300 and 400 boxes in season, together with decorative trees, bushes and shrubs.

Freight statistics at Fordham for the years 1957 and 1958 showed:

		1957	1958
Forwarded	Merchandise	6,997 tons	1,587 tons
	Minerals		5,357 tons
Received	Merchandise	18,925 tons	1,267 tons
	Minerals		16,783 tons
Coal and Coke		14,415 tons	13,983 tons
Livestock		38 heads	123 heads

which make an interesting comparison with the 11,128 total tonnage of goods and coal traffic handled at Mildenhall in 1892.

During GER days an appointed agent carted goods and parcels at Mildenhall, whilst local carriers served other stations.

Freight facilities were finally withdrawn from Quy, Bottisham and Lode, Swaffhamprior, Isleham and Mildenhall on and from 13th July 1964, from Burwell on 19th April 1965, and Fordham, except for a local private siding, on 12th September 1966. The goods yard at Barnwell Junction was closed on 31st October 1966, leaving only the short spur to the oil terminal siding available for traffic.

The only mechanical aids available to goods staff at branch stations were two 1 ton 10 cwt fixed cranes at Fordham and a 1 ton 10 cwt capacity fixed crane at Mildenhall. In addition the use of a tow rope was authorised for shunting vehicles in adjacent sidings from the main single line at Quy, Bottisham and Lode, Swaffhamprior and Isleham.

The following facilities were available for goods and livestock traffic at the branch stations:

Barnwell Junction	1 5-ton capacity cart weighbridge 2 11-cwt weighing machines (later 10-cwt) 1 lock-up for small parcels 1 loading gauge
Quy	1 loading gauge 1 loading dock 1 10-cwt weighing machine 1 lock-up for small parcels
Bottisham and Lode	2 paved cattle pens with water supply 1 loading dock 1 loading gauge 1 lock-up for small parcels 1 5-ton cart weighbridge 1 11-cwt weighing machine (later 10-cwt)
Swaffhamprior	2 paved cattle pens with water supply 1 loading dock 1 loading gauge 1 lock-up for small parcels 1 5-ton cart weighbridge 1 11-cwt weighing machine
Burwell	2 paved cattle pens with water supply 1 loading dock 1 loading gauge 1 lock-up for small parcels 1 5-ton cart weighbridge 1 11-cwt weighing machine
Fordham	3 paved cattle pens with water supply 2 1-ton 10-cwt capacity fixed crane 1 goods shed with storage for 350 qtrs of grain 1 loading dock 1 loading gauge 1 lock-up for small parcels 1 10-ton cart weighbridge 1 1-ton 12-cwt weighing machine
Isleham	3 paved cattle pens with water supply 1 loading gauge 1 lock-up for small parcels 1 5-ton cart weighbridge 1 6-cwt weighing machine
Mildenhall	3 paved cattle pens with water supply 1 1-ton 10-cwt capacity fixed crane 1 goods shed with storage for 500 qtrs of grain 1 loading dock 1 loading gauge 1 wagon turntable 1 lock-up for small parcels 1 5-ton cart weighbridge 1 1-ton 2-cwt weighing machine

In GER days the latest time for receipt of animals or goods for forwarding the same day was as follows: Mildenhall 5.00 p.m. SX, 3.00 p.m. SO; Isleham 5.30 p.m. SX, 3.00 p.m. SO; Fordham 6.00 p.m.; Burwell 5.00 p.m.; Swaffhamprior, Bottisham and Lode, Quy and Barnwell Junction 6.00 p.m. These times were later revised to Mildenhall 2.00 p.m. (stations to Barnwell Junction other than perishables); Isleham 2.30 p.m.; Fordham and Burwell 4.00 p.m.; Swaffhamprior, Bottisham and Lode, Quy and Barnwell Junction 4.30 p.m.

The loads of freight authorised to be hauled by locomotives between Cambridge and Mildenhall in GER days were as follows:

	Number of Wagons			
	Goods		Coal	
	Down	Up	Down	Up
First Class Engines	30	30	25	25
Second Class Engines	25	25	20	20
Third Class Engines	20	20	15	15

The Y class 2—4—0 tender locomotives were first class engines whilst the 417 and 477 class 0—6—0s were second class locomotives and the Little Sharpies 2—4—0s, third class engines.

Around the turn of the century the loads for goods engines were revised as under:

Class of Locomotive	Minerals Down and Up	Goods Down and Up
A	38	40
B	27	38
C	25	35
D	20	28
E	18	26
F	18	26
G	15	21
H	14	20

The following locomotives regularly allocated to the branch were classified as follows:

GE Class (LNER Class)		Classified
Y14	J15	C
M15	F4	D
M15R	F5	D
G69	F6	D
Y65	F7	E
417	—	F
477	—	F
T26	E4	G
Little Sharpie	—	H

Under the LNER the freight train loads on the Mildenhall branch were not to exceed 60 wagons in the down direction and 52 wagons in length on the up road with individual loadings as follows:

	DOWN			UP		
Engine	Mineral	Goods	Empties	Mineral	Goods	Empties
Class 1	26	39	52	27	40	52
Class 2	29	43	58	30	45	52
Class 3	32	48	60	33	49	52
Class 4	36	52	60	37	52	52
Class 5	39	58	60	41	52	52
Class 6	44	60	60	46	52	52

A Class 3 goods engine was a J15 and a Class 4 a J17.

After dieselisation of freight services, Class 31 diesel electric locomotives were limited to loads of 30 wagons on the down road and 52 wagons in the up direction.

'J17' class 0—6—0 No. 65582 passing Worlington Golf Links Halt with an up freight. The portable steps on the short low platform were introduced after the last ex-GER bogie thirds fitted with side steps were condemned, to enable passengers to gain access to some of the Gresley brake third corridor coaches and later the diesel railbus and DMUs.

Dr. I. C. Allen

'417' class 0—6—0s, introduced by Samuel Johnson, worked the initial freight services on the Mildenhall branch after displacement from main line duties. No. 446, built by the Worcester Engine Company, is typical of the class.

Johnson 'T7' class 0—4—2T No. 84 was used with others of the class in the initial years on passenger and freight work between Cambridge and Mildenhall. It was scrapped in 1892.

LCGB/Ken Nunn Collection

CHAPTER SEVEN

LOCOMOTIVES AND STOCK

DESPITE through route pretentions, the light construction of the permanent way on the branch effectively precluded, except in special circumstances, the use of the heavier GER classes of locomotive from working across the line. The rural nature of the area and the relatively small loads conveyed were well within the capabilities of the smaller classes of tank and tender locomotives which, with their low axle loading, were ideal

other members of the class also worked to Mildenhall, Nos. 12 and 16. Nos. 12, 83 and 84 were condemned in 1892, No. 11 in 1893, and 16 in 1894. In addition to the T7s, some K9 class 0—4—2 tank locomotives designed by William Adams were also drafted to work the line. Ironically, they were the only locomotives built at Stratford Works while Adams was in office. At first only a hand brake was supplied but the class was later fitted

Alongside the 'T7' class, Adams 'K9' 0—4—2Ts were utilized on the branch services in the first decade. 'K9' No. 23, shown here at Stratford in 1905, was often outbased at Mildenhall when allocated to Cambridge.   *LCGB/Ken Nunn Collection*

for the route, and the GER had ample locomotives of low route availability.

Initially the LNER only permitted the following classes between Barnwell Junction and Mildenhall, E4 and J15 tender engines, F4, F7, J62, J63, J65, J67, J70, Y1, Y3, Y5, Y6 and Y10 tank engines. Later the Mildenhall branch was classified as route availability RA3, which continued into the British Railways era, but with additional allowance for the following classes of higher route availability: J17 (RA4) across the whole route and D16 and D16/3 for occasional excursion trains between Barnwell Junction and Fordham only. Later, NB1 Type 1 800 hp (RA4), BTH Type 1 800 hp BR Class 15 (RA4), BR Sulzer Type 2 (RA7), Brush Type 2 Class 31 (RA6) were also permitted. The main line diesel locomotives were, however, restricted to a speed of 30 mph.

Initially, passenger and mixed train services on the line were hauled by the T7 class 0—4—2 tank locomotives specially built for light branch traffic and designed by Samuel W. Johnson, who was later to gain greater fame on the Midland Railway. Fifteen were built between 1871 and 1875; the first three, Nos. 81-3, were actually prototypes of the T7s but were included in the total class. One of the trio, No. 83, was regularly employed on the branch in the first five years, together with Nos. 11 and 84. Two

with the Westinghouse brake. A half cab was originally provided when the locomotives were built, but after a few years, back weather plates were fitted and later the roof was extended to completely cover the footplate. Nos. 7, 22 and 24 were known to have worked the branch in the late 1880s and early 1890s and the class was withdrawn from service between 1903 and 1907.

From the opening of the line until the mid 1890s, the freight services on the Mildenhall line were hauled by Samuel Johnson's 417 and 477 class 0—6—0 tender locomotives. The 417 class were introduced between 1867 and 1869 by Neilson and Company and the Worcester Engine Company. The sixty built were numbered 417-476 and had 5ft 4in driving wheels, 16½in x 24in cylinders, a total heating surface of 1072.66 sq ft and a grate area of 13.27 sq ft. The locomotive weighed 30 tons 14 cwt and the four-wheel tender 21 tons 17 cwts. On the introduction of the 477 class and Y14 class 0—6—0s, the 417s were displaced from main line goods work and took up duties on pick-up freights and branch line work. Various members of the class allocated to Cambridge depot worked out their last years on the Mildenhall branch freight. They were also called upon to haul excursion trains which were too heavy for the 0—4—2Ts. In such a capacity No. 435 was recorded working a Cambridge

In the early years Sinclair's 'Y' class 2—4—0 tender locomotives were regularly utilised on branch passenger and freight services. Originally built between July 1859 and August 1866 for goods traffic, 71 of these engines were later rebuilt and used extensively on passenger duties. Six of the class worked college boat specials from Mildenhall to Barnwell Junction in 1888. No. 0396, shown here at Norwich in 1895, is typical of the class.
LCGB/Ken Nunn Collection

College Boat Race excursion from Mildenhall to Barnwell Junction on 8th June 1888. By the following year, the last of the class had been condemned.

The larger 477 class came from a variety of builders, Beyer Peacock, Robert Stephenson, Dübs, Nasmyth Wilson and the Yorkshire Engine Company, between 1871 and 1875 and were numbered 477-526. They were originally introduced to cope with the rapidly increasing goods traffic and the need for a locomotive which could provide a greater hauling capacity and more efficient brake power than the 417 class. After the introduction of the Y14 class 0—6—0 tender locomotives, the 477 class were relegated to more menial tasks and, like their smaller sisters, those allocated to Cambridge subsequently worked pick-up freights and branch goods traffic including the Mildenhall line. As with the 417s, the 477s appeared on excursion traffic, often working as far as Hunstanton.

Nos. 486 and 506 were recorded working Cambridge College Boat Race excursion trains from Mildenhall to Barnwell Junction on 13th and 16th June 1887 respectively. Members of the class were withdrawn between 1897 and 1902.

Another class regularly seen in the early years on branch passenger and freight services was Sinclair's Y class 2—4—0 tender locomotives. Originally built for working goods traffic, 110 engines were introduced between July 1859 and August 1866. Later, 71 were rebuilt and used extensively on passenger work. Six manufacturers were responsible for their construction, Neilson and Company building 307-320, R. Stephenson & Co. 327-341, R. & W. Hawthorn 342-356, Kitson & Company 357-381, Vulcan Foundry 382-406, and the last ten, Nos. 407-416 by Schneider et Cie of Creusot. Twenty locomotives were also altered by William Adams with the leading pair of

Samuel Johnson's No. 1 class 'Little Sharpie' No. 27 along with others of the class allocated to Cambridge shed, worked regularly on the Mildenhall line.

wheels replaced by a four-wheel bogie to make them into 4—4—0s. From 1878 sixty-three of the rebuilt locomotives were fitted with the Westinghouse brake and worked mostly on secondary branch and excursion passenger duties. From the late 1880s most of the locomotives allocated to Cambridge took over the Mildenhall branch passenger services complementing the ageing and by now underpowered 0—4—2 tank locomotives. They were also popular on excursion trains and Nos. 385, 362 and 415 worked College Boat Specials from Mildenhall to Barnwell Junction on 9th, 11th and 12th June 1888 respectively. From the same year most were put on the duplicate list and given a '0' prefix to their numbers. Other locomotives known to have worked on the line included 0360, 0389 and 0408. It is interesting to note that on 10th February 1881 the firebox of No. 385 exploded whilst it was shunting the 6.00 a.m. Cambridge to Ipswich goods train into the sidings at Bury St. Edmunds. Condemnation of the unrebuilt locomotives began the following year and all were withdrawn by 1894.

The next class to be associated with the Mildenhall branch were representatives of Samuel Johnson's No. 1 class, nicknamed 'Little Sharpies', thirty of the forty locomotives being built by Sharp Stewart and Company. These 2—4—0 tender engines were built between October 1867 and August 1872 but during the years 1889-1893 the whole class was rebuilt and mostly allocated to cross-country and branch line duties. The 'Little Sharpies' allocated to the Cambridge district included Nos. 1, 3, 27, 32, 36, 47, 48, 104, 106, 118, 160 and 161. As well as being outbased at Ely, St. Ives, Ramsey High Street and Saffron Walden, one of the class was also allocated to Mildenhall for branch duties. Their association with the branch remained until the turn of the century. In their final years they were drafted away to branch lines in Norfolk, from where they were withdrawn from service. The class was scrapped between 1901 and 1913, the last to go being the first built, by then on the duplicate list, and numbered 01.

The most celebrated of all the classes of locomotives to work on the Mildenhall branch was the GER T26 class 2—4—0s nicknamed 'Intermediates'. A total of 100 were built to the design of J. Holden between 1891 and 1902. Most were assigned for mixed traffic duties, long cross-country routes and slower traffic on the main line. From about the turn of the century the class took over some of the Mildenhall branch duties from the 'Little Sharpies' and from thereon for over half a century they formed the mainstay of motive power on the line. The LNER classified them E4, but in the 1920s and '30s many were scrapped. By 1936 Cambridge only had an allocation of two, one of which was allocated to the Mildenhall branch services. In 1942 the class was reduced to eighteen locomotives of which eleven were at Cambridge. From then until their final demise, representatives of the E4 class were responsible for passenger services on the line, although from the late 1920s Worsdell's Y14 (LNER J15) class 0—6—0 tender locomotives had taken over some of the duties as well as hauling all freight trains. The following locomotives are known to have worked on the line when allocated to Cambridge.

GER No.	LNER 1924 No.	LNER 1946 No.	BR No.	Condemned
407	7407	2792	62792	June 1956
408	7408	2793	62793	February 1955
409	7409	2794	62794	August 1955
410	7410	–	–	January 1935
411	7411	2795	62795	March 1955
414	7414	2796	62796	May 1957
416	7416	2797	62797	March 1958
427	7427	2780	62780	September 1955
460	7460	–	–	April 1929
463	7463	2781	62781	January 1956
466	7466	2782	62782	November 1954
467	7467	–	–	April 1937
474	7474	–	–	April 1929
477	7477	2783	62783	December 1954
478	7478	2784	62784	May 1956
490	7490	2785	62785	December 1959
492	7492	2786	62786	July 1956
494	7494	2787	62787	November 1956
496	7496	2788	62788	March 1958
497	7497	2789	62789	December 1957
503	7503	2790	62790	January 1956
504	7504	–	–	November 1938
506	7506	2791	62791	May 1955

The final locomotive in service, No. 62785, made its last run in steam on 28th November 1959 from Cambridge to Mildenhall and return, hauling a two-coach special organised by the Cambridge University Railway Club. After withdrawal the following month, it was restored at Stratford Works to its former GE livery as No. 490 and now resides in the National Railway Museum at York.

In 1909-10 S. D. Holden introduced into traffic his Y65 class 2—4—2 tank locomotives which were built for light branch passenger traffic. The twelve engines, Nos. 1300-11, were constructed at Stratford Works, and their small boiler and enormous cab soon earned them the nickname of 'Crystal Palaces'. Cambridge received an allocation of five locomotives Nos. 1302, 1306, 1307, 1308 and 1310 and these were soon drafted to the Mildenhall branch passenger trains. Others based at the University City were also outbased at Saffron Walden and Ramsey High Street. Unfortunately they proved to be the least successful of Holden's 2—4—2Ts and found difficulty handling anything above a four-coach train. They appear to have been unpopular with Cambridge and Mildenhall men and were soon displaced to autotrain working and other menial tasks. In this capacity No. 1311 was fitted for auto working and was initially tried out on the Mildenhall branch with a two-coach formation for a few weeks from 5th October 1914. It later worked for an experimental period on the Ramsey High Street branch before finding regular duties on the White Hart Lane-Cheshunt shuttle on the reopened Churchbury loop line in 1915.

The LNER later designated the Y65s 'Class F7', renumbering them 8300-11, and the locomotives known to have worked on the Mildenhall services were disposed of as follows: No. 8306 was condemned in April 1931,

'Y65' class 2–4–2T No. 1311, designed by Holden and introduced into traffic in 1910, was the locomotive selected for
auto-train trials on the Mildenhall branch in 1914. She is shown
here at Ipswich in 1910.   *LCGB/Ken Nunn Collection*

and 8302 a month later, 8311 went for scrap in September
1931, No. 8307 (renumbered to 7596 in October 1942)
was condemned in June 1943, whilst 8308 and 8310 were
sent to Scotland in 1931 for working the Gifford, Lauder
and Selkirk branches and the Galashiels-Peebles line.
Renumbered 7597 and 7598 in 1942, and 7093 and 7094
in 1946, they finally went for scrap in November 1948.

Occasional use was made of M15 and M15R class
2–4–2 tank locomotives initially designed by T. W.
Worsdell and introduced into service in 1884. Between
1903 and 1909 another 120 locomotives were built, and
from June 1911 to 1920 the GER rebuilt a total of 32
locomotives with higher boiler pressure and designated
them 'M15R'. The earliest built locomotives were all
condemned by 1929 whilst the LNER classified the
M15s 'Class F4' and the rebuilt locomotives 'Class F5'.
Known as the 'Gobblers' because the original locomotives
suffered from excessive fuel consumption, partly caused
by the incorrect setting of the Joy's valve gear, they only
worked across the branch in the event of the non-
availability of a Y65 or T26 class engine. Few of the class
were ever allocated to the Cambridge district and most
were employed in the London Suburban area. Those
which are known to have worked from Cambridge across
to Mildenhall included:

Class	LNER 1924 No.	LNER 1946 No.	BR No.	Condemned
F4	7174	7170	–	April 1948
F5	7790*	7219	67219	November 1956
F4	7079	7187	67187	August 1955
F4	7573	7153	–	July 1951

* classified F6 until December 1948

The GER G69 class (LNER F6) represented the final
development of the 2–4–2 tank locomotives designed by
S. D. Holden. Built at Stratford Works in 1911/12, the

class were readily distinguishable from the M15 and M15R
classes by the side windows in the cab side sheets. Like
the M15R (F5), they were officially barred from using the
Mildenhall branch, but in an emergency such restrictions
were lifted. Most of the class worked on the London
suburban traffic and their visits to the branch were
infrequent. The following were known to have worked on
Cambridge-Mildenhall passenger services from around
1937 until the withdrawal of steam when Cambridge shed
had an allocation of two or three of the class.

GER No.	LNER 1924 No.	LNER 1946 No.	BR No.	Scrapped
8	7008	7237	67237	August 1955
62	7062	7221	67221	October 1957
63	7063	7222	67222	August 1955
68	7068	7227	67227	May 1958

Together with No. 67230, No. 67227 was the last of
the class to be withdrawn.

Other locomotives which occasionally worked across
the branch, notably on excursion traffic in LNER days,
were Holden's D13, D15 and Gresley rebuilt D16/3 class
4–4–0 tender engines although they were only permitted
between Barnwell Junction and Fordham.

An example of the use of a 'Claud' D16/3 working
across the branch occurred on Sunday, 25th July 1954,
when an excursion ran from all stations on the Mildenhall
line to Hunstanton. No. 62549 hauled the train from
Cambridge to Fordham where the four coaches from
Mildenhall, which had been worked to the junction by
LM Class 2 No. 46465, were attached to the main train.
The D16/3 then worked the combined train forward to
the Norfolk resort.

A notable visitor to Mildenhall in June 1932 was B12
class 4–6–0 tender locomotive No. 8526, which was
within the RA3 availability permitted. The engine worked
a through Sunday excursion from Liverpool Street across
the branch. The trip was well patronised and the string of
eight bogie coaches extended well beyond the relatively
short station platforms on the line. The 50ft long turntable
at Mildenhall could just accommodate No. 8526 with its
48ft 3in wheelbase. Balancing was a lengthy business and
it took an hour to turn the locomotive ready for its return
working.

After the withdrawal of the 417 and 477 classes, the
majority of freight traffic on the Mildenhall line was
handled by members of the GER Y14 class 0–6–0s
designed by T. W. Worsdell. Introduced in 1883, these
diminutive machines were later classified J15 by the
LNER. Such was the success of the design that building
continued until 1913. All except nineteen of the class of
289 were built at Stratford Works, the others being constructed by Sharp Stewart and Company. Because of their
low route availability, this ubiquitous class was responsible
for handling most of the branch freight services until
replaced by diesel traction. Locomotives fitted with
Westinghouse and vacuum brakes also deputised for the
T26 (E4) 2–4–0s on passenger services, especially from
the early 1920s when the Cambridge shed allocation of
E4s was reduced. Their RA1 availability and sturdiness
enabled them to handle all traffic on the branch with

ease. Locomotives known to have worked on the line included:

GER No.	LNER 1924 No.	LNER 1946 No.	BR No.	Condemned
523	7523	5438	65438	June 1958
532	7532	5356	65356	April 1957
546	7546	5474	65474	February 1960
547	7547	5475	65475	September 1959
549	7549	5477	65477	February 1960
553	7553	5451	65451	September 1959
559	7559	5457	65457	February 1962
562	7562	5460	65460	September 1962
563	7563	5461	65461	April 1960
571	7571	5469	65469	August 1962
642	7642	5442	65442	May 1958
813	7813	5350	—	February 1951
887	7887	5390	65390	December 1958
888	7888	5391	65391	December 1958
911	7911	5405	65405	August 1958
913	7913	5406	—	April 1951
924	7924	5413	—	November 1950
942	7942	5425	65425	October 1956

Nos. 65391, 65405 and 65438 were fitted with side window cabs, vacuum ejector, steam heating, balanced wheels and tender backplates in 1934/5 for tender-first working on the Colne Valley line, but they often saw use on the Mildenhall branch. Before withdrawal, No. 65405 was allocated to Aylesbury in 1957 to work the ex-Great Western Railway branch from Princes Risborough to Watlington.

No. 65460 is remembered for working Cambridge University Railway Club Specials across the branch on 9th and 13th June 1962 during which time members took turns at driving the locomotive under supervision. No. 65460, allocated to Stratford, had replaced failed No. 65469 at short notice, and was painted in black livery with plain red lining. This lined livery had been applied the previous year when the locomotive appeared in the film *Postman's Knock* on location at West Mill on the Buntingford branch.

The advent of eight-coupled heavy goods locomotives on the Whitemoor-Temple Mills and other GE main line freights, from the 1930s, gradually released the J17 class (GER G58) 0—6—0 tender locomotives for cross-country and branch line freight working. The J17s, built to the

'J15' class 0—6—0 No. 7571 waiting to depart from Cambridge with the Mildenhall branch train in the late 1920s. The leading vehicle is a former GER bogie coach.

Mildenhall turntable at right-angles to the table road as 'J15' class No. 65438, fitted with side window cab and tender backplate, is turned in readiness for the return trip to Cambridge in May 1957. When not in use on the Colne Valley line, the 'J15s', fitted with side window cab, were popular with Cambridge crews on the Mildenhall branch and were used in preference to other 'J15s' or 'E4s'.

Another 'E4' which regularly worked across the Mildenhall branch, No. 62795, ex-GER 411 and LNER 7411.

Steam-braked 'J17' class 0—6—0 No. 65532 about to be turned at Mildenhall after working the branch goods from Cambridge. The cab of 65532 sustained damage while the engine was unfortunately positioned under a coaling plant, hence the stoved-in effect at the back.
Dr. I. C. Allen

design of J. Holden and introduced between 1900 and 1911, were of Class 4 Route Availability and were only officially permitted on the Mildenhall branch after World War Two. Occasional forays were, however, noted in the mid and late 1930s when a J15 class 0—6—0 was not available for the goods working. After the war their visits to the branch were more frequent and they often deputised for the usual J15 on goods or ballast workings.

J17s known to have worked across the Mildenhall branch in later years were:

65501, 65502, 65503, 65505, 65506, 65512, 65517,
65518, 65520, 65525, 65528, 65529, 65532, 65534,
65535, 65537, 65538, 65546, 65547, 65548, 65561,
65562, 65563, 65565, 65568, 65573, 65575, 65580,
65582, 65584, 65585, 65587, 65588, 65589

H. A. Ivatt designed his 2MT 2—6—0 tender locomotives for cross-country and light branch duties on the London Midland and Scottish Railway. They were introduced in 1946 and building continued after nationalisation. In 1951 five of the class commenced their working life at ex-GER depots on the Eastern Region, Nos. 46465, 46466 and 46467 being allocated to Cambridge, whilst Nos. 46468 and 46469 were allocated to Colchester. Except for No. 46466, these particular locomotives had very narrow chimneys and were the first of the class to carry this modification.

Introduced as replacements for older engines, the class 2s were immediately put to work on the Stour and Colne Valley lines as well as Mildenhall branch in place of the ageing E4 2—4—0s and J15 0—6—0s. Being slightly superior in power to the ex-GE locomotives, the class 2s easily coped with the light loads and at weekends the locomotives were called upon to haul excursions and holiday specials of eight coaches from Cambridge to Clacton and Hunstanton. They also worked excursions from Mildenhall, often double-heading as far as Ely where a B1 4—6—0 replaced the lighter locomotives.

LMR class '2MT' No. 46465 approaching Swaffhamprior with a Cambridge-Mildenhall train. *Dr. I. C. Allen*

With enclosed cab and tender design, self-cleaning smokebox and rocking grate, which aided preparation and disposal of the engines on shed, the locomotives were popular with the Cambridge crews. In January 1961 Nos. 46468 and 46469 joined their sister locomotives at Cambridge, but unlike their predecessors, were never called upon to haul the Mildenhall branch passenger services and had to be content working the branch freight or excursion traffic. Nos. 46468 and 46469's reign at Cambridge was short-lived for they were soon transferred to Parkeston to be replaced by No. 46400 and 46494 from the London Midland Region for the final few months before the demise of steam in the area and the closure of Cambridge shed in June 1962.

Another ex-LMS class associated with the Mildenhall branch was the larger Ivatt 4MT 2—6—0 locomotives.

Getting to grips with her lengthy train, LMR 4MT 2–6–0 No. 43149 is shown approaching Worlington Golf Links Halt with the
M & GN Preservation Society tour train on 26th May 1962.   *Dr. I. C. Allen*

Cambridge only received an allocation of three engines, Nos. 43086, 43105 and 43109 and, although they frequently worked on the Cambridge-Colchester line, especially with the Sudbury goods, their forays on the Mildenhall branch were rare. On one notable occasion, however, another of the class, No. 43149, handled the Midland and Great Northern Railway Society Special to Mildenhall, hauling ex-LNE and BR Mark I bogie vehicles. Like the smaller 2MTs, the enclosed cab was popular with locomotive crews.

With the withdrawal of steam traction in East Anglia BR utilised Sulzer Type 2 (classes 24 and 25) and Brush Type 2 (classes 31/0 and 31/3) diesel electric locomotives on freight services. The 31s quickly gained the monopoly and it was usual for a March depot-based locomotive to work on the Mildenhall goods. The class continued until the withdrawal of freight traffic, No. D5662 hauling the

last through freight between Mildenhall and Cambridge on 10th July 1964.

In 1957 British Railways placed orders with five manufacturers for the delivery of 22 lightweight railbuses with a view to carrying out extensive trials on selected rural services. Five 150 hp four-wheel diesel railbuses were built by Waggon und Maschinenbau GmbH at Donauworth, Germany, to Lot No. 50482 for use on Eastern Region routes. The first two, Nos. E79960 and E79961, travelled via the Zeebrugge-Harwich train ferry and were delivered to Stratford diesel depot on 31st March 1958. The remaining three, Nos. E79962/3/4, quickly followed and, after trials on the Witham-Maldon East and Witham-Braintree branches, were sent to Cambridge on 19th April to commence work on the Saffron Walden, Haverhill and Mildenhall lines. They subsequently replaced steam traction on the Witham-Maldon, Witham-Braintree,

Saffron Walden and Mildenhall branches from 7th July 1958.

The bodies of these buses were designed to meet British Railways' requirements whilst the underframe power equipment, transmission and brake gear were similar to the Uerdinger type of railbuses then running on the German Federal Railway. The underframe consisted of channel-shaped cross beams welded to longitudinal girders whilst the body framing was of light steel structure. The side and roof panels were of light alloy sheets riveted to the body framing, the body being suspended elastically and swung from four points of the running bogie frame. The floor body, sides and roof were fitted with insulation materials against heat and sound. The interiors were finished with polished plywood panels while ceilings were painted ivory. The upper parts of the side windows were hinged to give limited ventilation, whilst curtains were also provided.

The centrally situated doors on each side of the body were power operated and under the control of the driver. Push button operation for the guard or passengers was also used. In cases of emergency the doors were opened and closed by hand and once in service, this appeared to be the main method adopted by train crews to open doors at stations. Seating was arranged for 56 passengers in rows of two seats on one side of the car and three seats on the other in two saloons.

When the railbuses were initially transferred for use on the branch, they were worked turn and turn about with a DMU, or E4 2—4—0 No. 62785 or the J15 on station pilot duty at Cambridge. Part of this diagram involved a return working to Mildenhall.

At first the railbuses were unpopular on the Mildenhall branch as the riding on four wheels was uncomfortable, and swaying and bouncing at speeds in excess of 30 mph was alarming.

In the first months their failure rate was high and a J15 class locomotive hauling two coaches or a two-car diesel railcar (Wickham, Craven or Metro-Cammell units) substituted for the casualty. After modification, the railbuses settled down to work the branch, each working for four days before returning to Coldham Lane Diesel Depot, Cambridge for maintenance. The initial cyclic working of the diesel railbuses called for a total of four working and one available for maintenance or repairs. Unfortunately, the availability was not always up to requirements and often a 2-car railcar was called on to deputise on the five branch lines operated by these vehicles.

The diagrams were:

Day 1   6.22 a.m. Cambridge to Mildenhall, 7.36 a.m. Mildenhall-Cambridge, then to Chappel & Wakes Colne via the Colne Valley line, before working the Witham-Braintree branch. Stabled overnight at Braintree.

Day 2   Worked the Braintree branch in the morning, then to the Witham-Maldon branch. Stabled overnight at Maldon East.

Day 3   Worked the Maldon East branch in the morning, then empty railbus to Marks Tey to work 1.22 p.m. to Cambridge via the Colne Valley line. From Cambridge worked 4.27 p.m. Cambridge to Mildenhall, 5.46 p.m.

Mildenhall to Newmarket, 6.35 p.m. Newmarket-Mildenhall, 7.21 p.m. Mildenhall to Cambridge. Thence light diesel to Audley End and Saffron Walden. Stabled overnight at Saffron Walden.

Day 4   Worked Saffron Walden branch, then light diesel to Cambridge for maintenance.

Day 5   Maintenance at Cambridge.

The principal dimensions of the railbuses were:

Type	2—2 (1—A)
Weight in working order	18 tons
Wheelbase	19 ft 8¼ in
Wheel diameter	3 ft 3½ in
Length over buffers	45 ft 9¼ in
Length over body	41 ft 10 in
Width over body	8 ft 8½ in
Inside width	8 ft 4 in
Overall height from rail	11 ft 9 in
Floor height from rail	4 ft 0 in
Interior height floor to ceiling	7 ft 8¼ in
Power weight ratio	10 hp/ton
Maximum speed, equivalent engine speed and ratio gear	1st gear 8 mph 1800 rpm 5.54
	2nd gear 14 mph 1800 rpm 2.99
	3rd gear 24 mph 1850 rpm 1.85
	4th gear 33 mph 1800 rpm 1.34
	5th gear 45 mph 1850 rpm 1.00
	6th gear 55 mph 1600 rpm 0.72
Fuel oil capacity	44 galls
Fuel oil capacity for pre-heating unit	5½ galls
Cooling water capacity	22 galls
Control system	Pneumatic and electro pneumatic
Brake	Compressed air-disc brakes
Engine	One horizontal 6 cylinder diesel four stroke engine underfloor Bussing Braunscheig 150 hp at 1900 rpm
Fluid coupling	Bussing type FK 9.2 Oil capacity 17½ to 18½ pints
Heating equipment	Dreiha hot water heating type W60A connected 6 diesel engine cooling water system

Three of the railbuses, Nos. E79961/3/4, were later fitted with AEC A220X type engines which proved more reliable in service.

The closure of the Mildenhall line and the later withdrawal of services on the Saffron Walden and Maldon East branches rendered the German-built railbuses surplus to requirements. Their use on the Witham-Braintree line was short-lived and they were soon replaced by 2-car diesel multiple units. All five were placed in store at Cambridge diesel depot until June 1965 when No. E79964 was sent north for trials on the Haltwhistle-Alston branch. After failing dismally, it joined No. 79961, then prefixed 'M', at Buxton where they both worked the branch. Nos. E79960/2/3 were withdrawn from Cambridge in November 1966 and Nos. M79961 and M79964 were condemned from Buxton depot on 29th October 1966 and April 1967 respectively. Four of the five railbuses survived for further service on preserved lines, Nos. 79960/3 going to the North Norfolk Railway at Sheringham and Nos. 79962/4 to the Keighley and Worth Valley Railway.

One type of 2-car diesel multiple unit which worked alongside the German railbuses was supplied by D. Wickham and Co. Ltd. of Ware. Originally built for British Railways under their modernisation programme, the five units with power cars numbered in the range E50415-9 and trailer cars E56170-4 spent part of their 'running in' period on the St. Margarets-Buntingford branch in Hertfordshire. Trailer car E56170, when new, was also exhibited with other modern BR rolling stock at Battersea. After acceptance trials, the five units were allocated to Cambridge, working with other 'blue square' coupling code multiple units on most branch lines in East Anglia. No. E50416/E56171 worked the last passenger train from Mildenhall on Saturday, 16th June 1962.

The other regular type of diesel multiple unit involved were Craven 2-car sets consisting of driving motor brake second and driving trailer composite with combined seating for 103 second class and 12 first class passengers. Introduced initially in 1956, these units worked turn and turn about with the Wickham cars and railbuses and were numbered in the series E50359-50389, E51254-51301 and E51471/1 driving motor brake second, and E56114-56144, E56412-56461 driving trailer composite.

The principal dimensions of these units were:

	DMBS	DTC
Engine	BUT (AEC)	—
	BUT (Leyland)	—
	2 x 150 hp	
Weight	29 tons	23 tons
Length over body	57 ft 6 in	57 ft 6 in
Height	12 ft 7 in	12 ft 7 in
Width	9 ft 3 in	9 ft 3 in
Max speed	70 mph	70 mph
Coupling Code	Blue square	Blue square
Seating 1st	—	12
2nd	52	51

A third type of DMU utilised on the branch were BR Derby Works 2-car sets formed of motor brake second and driving trailer composite with combined seating for 109 second class and 16 first class passengers. The vehicles were numbered in the series E79021-E79046 for motor brake seconds and E79250-E79262, E79613-E79625 for the driving trailer composites.

The principal dimensions of these units were:

	DMBS	DTC
Engine	BUT (AEC)	—
	2 x 150 hp	
Weight	27 tons	21 tons
Length over body	57 ft 6 in	57 ft 6 in
Width	9 ft 2 in	9 ft 2 in
Height	12 ft 7 in	12 ft 7 in
Max Speed	70 mph	70 mph
Coupling Code	Yellow diamond	Yellow diamond
Seating 1st	—	16
2nd	56	53

Motive power for the Mildenhall branch was supplied from Cambridge shed (later coded 31A by British Railways). Initially the locomotive outbased at Mildenhall was stabled in the open on the turntable road at the terminus between the last down service in the evening and the first up trip of the morning. In 1915, as a war economy measure, the locomotive crews were withdrawn from the terminus and the locomotives used on branch services worked out and back from Cambridge.

Strangely enough, no water supply was available for locomotive use at Mildenhall and, if engines were not replenished during their visit to Cambridge, the tender and side tanks had to be topped up at Fordham Junction where water columns were located at the north end of the down platform and south end of the up platform. Around the turn of the century the GE employed pumping enginemen at Fordham including John Haddow in 1913 and Robert Sparrow ten years later. Because of this no locomotive was regularly outbased at Mildenhall and engines were changed over from day to day. The GER and later the LNER preferred to work the branch services with tender locomotives which had greater tank capacity for the overnight stop at the terminus. No coaling was carried out at Mildenhall and locomotives working the branch were fully coaled before leaving Cambridge shed.

When the line beyond Fordham opened to traffic in 1885, two sets of footplate crews were outbased at Mildenhall covering the full fifteen hours of working. The senior of the two drivers was designated locomotive foreman or driver in charge and received a half day's extra pay per week for administrative duties which included the submission of drivers' tickets and coal and oil returns to the locomotive shedmaster at Cambridge. The two drivers 'signed the road' for the branch and to Cambridge via Newmarket, they also later signed for the route to Ely. The footplate staff at Mildenhall were not provided with accommodation and lived away from the railway. By 1903, however, housing was difficult to find and the crews requested the company to rectify the position. James Holden subsequently authorised the building of two cottages for the driver in charge and acting driver, and these were completed in October 1905 at a cost of £508.

Soon after the outbreak of World War One the GER were seeking operating economies and after investigation it was decided the branch could be worked effectively by out and back diagrams from Cambridge. As a result of these findings, the four men were withdrawn from Mildenhall in July 1915 after which the line was worked entirely by Cambridge men. Cambridge footplate crews were already fully conversant with the branch as they worked the initial services to Fordham in 1884 and the remaining services not covered by the Mildenhall set of men from 1885. In reality Cambridge men were outbased, lodging at Mildenhall for several months before the revised working arrangements, as the last two Mildenhall drivers were transferred away prior to July 1915. Driver D. Thorne departed in October 1913 and his colleague Driver B. Coe a year later. Both paid an annual rental of £10 8s 0d for the railway cottages they occupied.

By the late 1920s two sets of Cambridge men were involved working trains to Mildenhall, either direct or via

Newmarket, and few changes were made until the withdrawal of steam traction from the branch passenger services in 1958. Typically in 1925 the first set, working with Cambridge diagram 23 engine, signed on at 5.50 a.m. and worked two round trips to Mildenhall before returning to shed at about 1 p.m. The second set signed on at 3.5 p.m. and prepared the engine for two further round trips across the branch. On Mondays and Saturdays only a third set, working with Cambridge diagram 22 engine,

CAMBRIDGE DEPOT—*Continued.*

WEEK DAYS.

No. 22.

arr. a.m.		dep. a.m.
	On Duty	10 15 M S O
	Loco'	11 0 M S O
	Cambridge	11 15 M S O
		p.m.
11 45	St. Ives	12 12 M S O
p.m.		
12 45	Cambridge	1 45 M S O
2 43	Mildenhall	3 7 M S O
4 10	Cambridge	6 18
6 48	St. Ives	6 50
7 2	Huntingdon	7 33
7 45	St. Ives	7 51 A
8 25	Cambridge	

Men change at Cambridge at 4.40 p.m.

No. 23.

arr. a.m.		dep. a.m.
	On Duty	5 50
	Loco'	6 35 L
	Cambridge	6 50
7 36	Mildenhall	*7 49
8 53	Cambridge	10 30
11 29	Mildenhall	11 36
p.m.		
12 39	Cambridge	L
		p.m.
	Loco	3 50 L
	Cambridge	4 20
5 19	Mildenhall	5 27
6 32	Cambridge	7 36
8 35	Mildenhall	8 45*
9 51	Cambridge	L
	Loco'	

* Via Newmarket.

Second set on duty 3.5 p.m.

worked the 1.45 p.m. Cambridge to Mildenhall and return.

In addition to Cambridge men, some Ely and Bury St. Edmunds drivers signed the route knowledge sheet from Cambridge to Mildenhall via Fordham to enable them to work special traffic across the branch, especially in the two World Wars and after for excursion trains.

Amusing incidents between footplate and traffic staff were a feature of every branch line over the years and the Mildenhall branch had its fair share. On one occasion in the late 1920s the last up passenger train pulled into Swaffhamprior where the guard alighted to chat to the porter and pick up a consignment of eggs from the staff room. Being a November evening, the meagre illumination from the platform oil lamps hardly penetrated the damp and misty conditions. The engine crew, huddling near the

fire in the cab, took only cursory glances back along the train to see if the guard had returned. The conversation in the porters room took longer than usual; the engine crew, eager to get back to Cambridge and home, 'whistled up' to attract the guard's attention. Unbeknown to all parties, however, some boys from the village, meeting a friend off the train, had taken an interest in the porter's oil lamp placed on the platform and started playing with the coloured slides, first red, then green. At just the right moment when the green was being displayed, the fireman looked back from the cab and suspecting the guard was back on the train and giving 'right away', told the driver to start the train. As the two-coach train disappeared into the mist and inky blackness of the night, the guard and porter rushed from the room aghast to see the tail lamp receding into the gloom. The boys made a hasty retreat and although they were known and suspected by the porter, their admonition was for the future; the main concern of both men on the platform was to get the guard to his train and home. A hurried call to Bottisham advised the station staff of the situation but, as no bicycle was available at Swaffhamprior for the guard to use and it was considered too dark for him to walk along the line, it was arranged to propel the train the two miles back down the line. This reversal was carried out without incident, and, once the guard was aboard, the train made a speedy journey back to Bottisham and on to Cambridge, often exceeding the line limit. Few passengers were on the train to witness such goings on and the subsequent late arrival at Cambridge was attributed to 'Cattle on the Line'.

The local goods working across the branch was allowed excessive running time between Cambridge and Mildenhall, partly to allow for shunting at station yards and also to allow for crossing with passenger trains. A favourite place for the goods to be 'locked in' was Burwell for this allowed the crew ample time to visit the local hostelry when shunting was completed. On one such occasion, the driver, known for his ale consumption, returned a little worse for wear after partaking in a drinking competition. He insisted that he was on an up working when in fact he was in charge of the down train, and only after considerable argument with guard, fireman and not the least the signalman, did he accept the fact that for the present he did not know which way he was booked to go. Without wishing to attract the attention of officialdom in the form of the station master who was away at Swaffhamprior, the guard, fireman and signalman decided to arrange matters to their mutual benefit until the driver had improved. A hot black strong mug of coffee was hastily obtained and handed to the driver who was then forced to sit in the brake van. The signalman set the road for Fordham and the train set forth for the junction with the fireman in charge of the locomotive. By the time the train reached Fordham, the driver showed little improvement so the fireman and guard decided their colleague required further remedial treatment. Arrangements were made for the locomotive to take water and for this exercise the driver was guided from the brakevan to operate the stopcock for the watercrane while the fireman placed the bag in the tender tank. Standing well back, the guard watched the operation with unusual interest, for just as the tank was overflowing the fireman swung the bag, still gushing with

'E4' 2—4—0 No. 7479 approaching Barnwell Junction with a Mildenhall-Cambridge train in 1932. The brewery siding is on the right.

Dr. I. C. Allen

water, towards the driver. The cold sobering action had the desired effect — much more potent than black coffee. Despite the rough deal given to his mate, the driver later forgave both the fireman and the guard. Clothes were quickly dried in front of the open firebox door on the run to Mildenhall and it was a more sober driver who worked the return freight to Cambridge.

Motive power facilities at the terminus included a 50ft diameter turntable, later reduced to 49ft 6in, and an inspection pit for locomotive examination. As Mildenhall was devoid of any maintenance facilities, all tube cleaning, boiler washing, running repairs and maintenance of locomotives was carried out at Cambridge shed. Coincidentally, Cambridge Motive Power Depot finally closed for steam working on 18th June 1962, the same day as the withdrawal of the passenger services on the Mildenhall branch.

Breakdown facilities for the branch were initially covered by Cambridge Motive Power Depot using tool vans and later 45-ton steam breakdown crane No. 133, subsequently renumbered No. 330133.

The first headcode carried by locomotives working the Mildenhall branch was one green disc with white outer rim over the centre of the buffer beam for ordinary services, and a green disc with white outer rim over the centre of the buffer beam and white disc over the left-hand buffer for special trains. At night or during the hours of darkness, the headcode carried by locomotives was one red light under the chimney at the top of the smokebox and one green light in the middle of the buffer beam. Special trains carried the same headcode with an additional white light over the left-hand buffer. As the red light was normally used as headcode on branch services only, the red headlamp was removed from or placed on the engine at Barnwell Junction so that the red light was not conveyed between the Junction and Cambridge.

Later the ordinary and special train headcode on the branch was standardised with a green disc with white outer rim or green light at night carried in the centre of the buffer beam. A red disc with white outer rim and red light at night was also carried at the foot of the chimney between Barnwell Junction and Mildenhall.

After grouping the LNER phased out red and green lights and discs as a possible source of danger and introduced the standard stopping passenger train code of one white light or white disc under the chimney. This code remained in use on the Cambridge-Mildenhall passenger services until the demise of steam traction, whilst freight trains carried the appropriate class of headcode.

Local whistle codes under the GER were as follows:

Barnwell Junction:
Main Line	1 distinct sound
To or from Mildenhall branch	5 distinct sounds

Fordham Junction:
Ely and Newmarket Line	1 distinct sound
To or from Cambridge line	3 distinct sounds
To or from Mildenhall line	4 distinct sounds

By 1919 the codes had the following amendment:

Barnwell Junction:
To or from Mildenhall branch	3 distinct sounds

The initial coaching stock allocated to the line was composed of four-wheel vehicles 27ft in length, originally built for main line services during the late 1870s. Trains were usually formed of 4-6 vehicles, two of these being third class, one second, one composite and a brake third. The *Cambridge Chronicle*, reporting the opening of the railway, recorded that 'all trains run over the line contain first, second and third class accommodation. The carriages which have been placed upon the track are not new ones, but are coaches of good quality. The third class carriages have cushioned seats attached to them.' In common with the majority of GER branches and less important cross-country lines, these vehicles served on the Mildenhall branch regularly until the turn of the century.

Principal dimensions of the four-wheel vehicles were:

Diagram	217	302	402	504
Type	Composite	Second	Third	Brake/Third
Length over body	27ft 0in	27ft 0¾in	27ft 0in	27ft 0in
Max height	10ft 11in	10ft 11in †	11ft 2in	10ft 11in
Body height	6ft 8in	6ft 8¼in	6ft 11in	6ft 8in
Max width	8ft 0in	8ft 0in	8ft 0in	9ft 3½in
Wheelbase	15ft 3in	15ft 3in	15ft 3in	15ft 3in
Seating 1st	16	–	–	–
2nd	20	30	–	–
3rd	*	–	30	20
Total weight empty	8 tons 15 cwt	9 tons 18 cwt	9 tons 8 cwt	9 tons 12 cwt

*also 16 x 1st, 20 x 3rd
†also 11ft 2in

With the introduction of bogie stock on the principal GER trains from the late 1890s, the use of four-wheel coaching stock outside the London Suburban area became less common as six-wheel vehicles were cascaded down for use on country branch services. The replacement stock on the Mildenhall branch dated from 1879 onwards and varied in length from 32ft for a full brake to 34ft 6in for a six-compartment third. The branch train then comprised a composite, one third and a brake third, strengthened at busy periods by an additional full third. Before the abolition of second class travel outside the London area, the composite vehicle possessed first and second class accommodation, but later the vehicle contained first and third class seating. During the early years of the twentieth century, trains were formed of mixed 4- and 6-wheel vehicles.

Principal dimensions of the 6-wheel coaching stock used on the branch were:

Diagram	219	404	422	514
Type	Composite	Third	Third	Brake/Third
Length over buffers	35ft 1½in	37ft 4½in	37ft 7½in	37ft 7½in
Length over body	32ft 0in	34ft 6in	34ft 6in	34ft 6in
Max height	11ft 2in	11ft 3in	11ft 7in	11ft 3in
Body height	6ft 11in	7ft 0in	7ft 4in	7ft 0in
Max width	8ft 0in	8ft 0in	8ft 0in	–
Width over guard's lookout	–	–	–	9ft 3½in
Wheelbase	20ft 0in	21ft 0in	22ft 6in	21ft 0in
	–	–	–	22ft 6in
Seating 1st	12	–	–	–
3rd	20	60	60	30
Luggage	–	–	–	2 tons
Total weight empty	12 tons 16 cwt	13 tons 3 cwt	18 tons 3 cwt	12 tons 16 cwt
				16 tons 14 cwt

The coaching vehicles provided with Y65 class 2–4–2T No. 1311 for the auto train trials in 1914 consisted of bogie driving compartment third GE No. 522, originally built in 1906 as an internal corridor lavatory third to diagram 417. On being converted in 1914 to diagram 433, the lavatory was removed and the compartment became part of the corridor. The second vehicle of the set, trailer composite first/third GER No. 633, converted to diagram 240 in 1914, was originally a lavatory/luggage composite built in 1904 to diagram 212.

Auto-train driving trailer third No. 522 (to Diagram 433) leads composite trailer 633 (to Diagram 240) forming the 2.48 p.m. Lower Edmonton–Cheshunt train approaching Theobalds Grove on 20th March 1915. 'Y65' No. 1311 is pushing.
LCGB/Ken Nunn Collection

The LNER later renumbered 522 to 61328 and 633 to 63521.

Principal dimensions of the vehicles were:

Diagram	240	433
GER No.	633	522
LNER No.	63521	61328
Type	Composite trailer	Driving trailer
Length over buffers	51ft 4½in	53ft 1½in
Length over body	48ft 3in	50ft 0in
Max height	12ft 8in	12ft 8in
Body height	8ft 5in	8ft 5in
Max width	8ft 6in	9ft 0in
Wheelbase to bogie centres	33ft 3in	35ft 0in
Bogie wheelbase	8ft 0in	8ft 0in
Seating 1st class	9	–
3rd class	30	46
Total weight empty	25 tons 8 cwt	26 tons 10 cwt

As already mentioned, the Cambridge-Mildenhall branch was provided with three unstaffed rail level halts at Fen Ditton, Exning Road and Worlington Golf Links. Consequently, conductor-guard working was introduced from December 1922 when the existing rolling stock was replaced by specially adapted 3-coach sets comprising a brake third, full third and first/third composite. Each coach had a centre gangway and connecting doors at each end of the vehicle, intended for the guard's use only, to enable him to gain access to the whole train to collect fares.

The brake third was equipped with retractable steps on each side of the vehicle, although the halts on the Mildenhall branch were all located on the up side of the line. The guard operated the steps by pulling a lever in the brake van to extend them, and returning it to bring the steps back within the loading gauge. Passengers joining or leaving the train at the halts therefore had to use the brake third which bore the following notice inside: 'Passengers for Fen Ditton, Exning Road and Worlington Golf Link Halts must not attempt to alight until the steps have been fixed and the guard has opened the door'. The

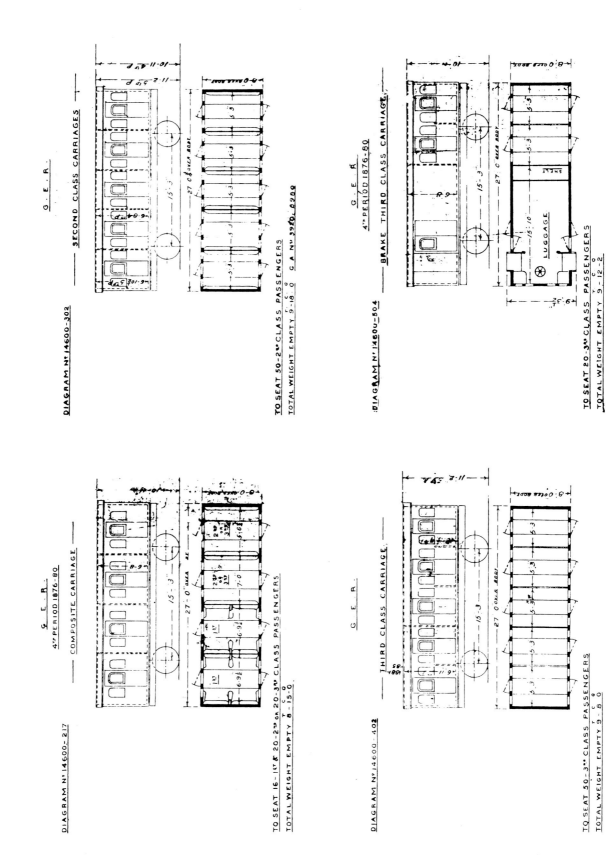

Taken from official coach diagrams.

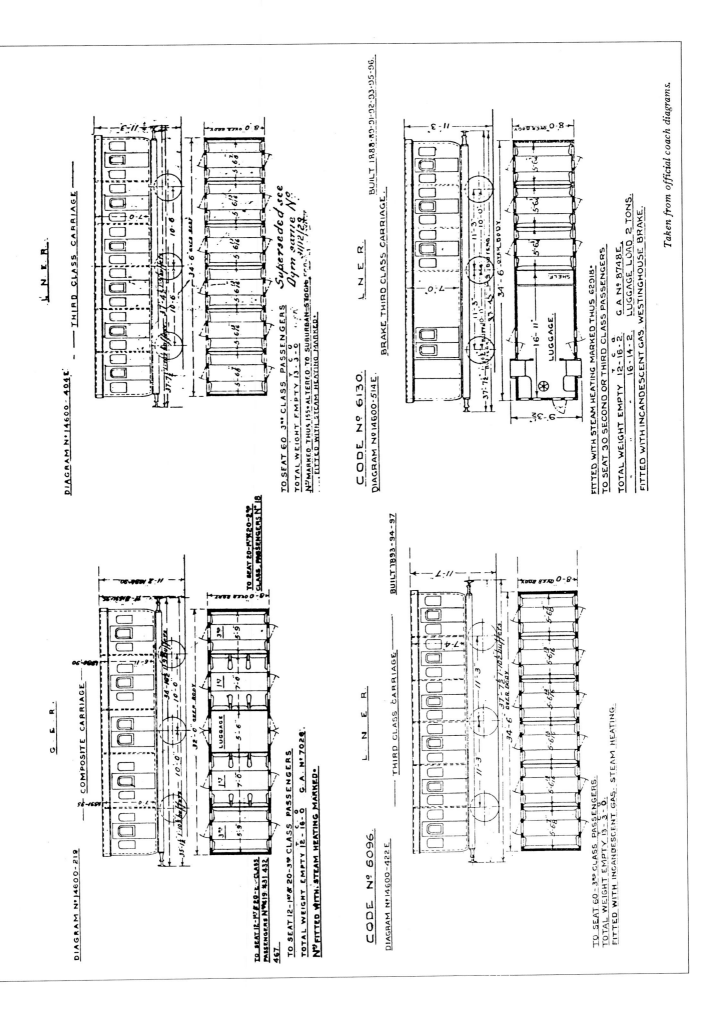

L N E R
THIRD CLASS CARRIAGE

DIAGRAM Nº 14600 - 404 E

TO SEAT 60 3ᴿᴰ CLASS PASSENGERS
TOTAL WEIGHT EMPTY 13 - 3 - 0
Nº MARKED THUS 155 ● ALTERED TO SUBURBAN STOCK
FITTED WITH STEAM HEATING MARKED ●

*Superseded see
Dym series Nº*

G. E. R.
COMPOSITE CARRIAGE

DIAGRAM Nº 14600 - 219

TO SEAT 12 - 1ˢᵗ & 20 - 3ᴿᴰ CLASS PASSENGERS
TO SEAT 12 - 1ˢᵗ CLASS
PASSENGERS Nºˢ 419 431 432
467
TOTAL WEIGHT EMPTY 12 - 16 - 0   G. A. Nº 7028
Nºˢ FITTED WITH STEAM HEATING MARKED ●

CODE Nº 6096
DIAGRAM Nº 14600 - 422 E

L N E R
THIRD CLASS CARRIAGE

BUILT 1893 - 94 - 97

TO SEAT 60 - 3ᴿᴰ CLASS PASSENGERS
TOTAL WEIGHT EMPTY 13 - 3 - 0
FITTED WITH INCANDESCENT GAS, STEAM HEATING

L N E R
BRAKE THIRD CLASS CARRIAGE

BUILT 1888 · 89 · 90 · 91 · 92 · 93 · 95 · 96

CODE Nº 6130
DIAGRAM Nº 14600 - 514 E

FITTED WITH STEAM HEATING MARKED THUS 6291ª •
TO SEAT 30 SECOND OR THIRD CLASS PASSENGERS
TOTAL WEIGHT EMPTY 12 - 16 - 2   G. A. Nº 8748 E
16 - 14 - 2   LUGGAGE LOAD 2 TONS.
FITTED WITH INCANDESCENT GAS, WESTINGHOUSE BRAKE.

Taken from official coach diagrams.

G·E·R·

DIAGRAM Nº 14600-240 — COMPOSITE CARRIAGE — AUTO-TRAIN

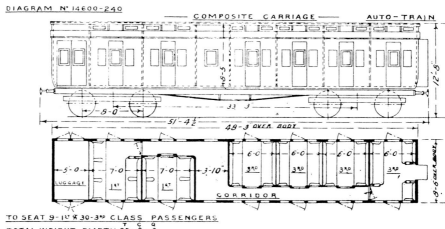

TO SEAT 9-1ˢᵗ & 30-3ᴿᴰ CLASS PASSENGERS
TOTAL WEIGHT EMPTY 25-8-3
FITTED WITH ELECTRIC LIGHT & STEAM HEATING
Nº 633

CODE Nº 6105.   L N E R

DIAGRAM Nº 14600-433E — THIRD CLASS CARRIAGE — BUILT 1906 AUTO-TRAIN

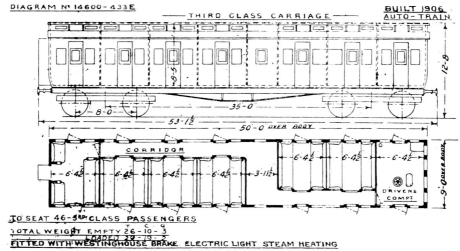

TO SEAT 46-3ᴿᴰ CLASS PASSENGERS
TOTAL WEIGHT EMPTY 26-10-3
LOADED 29-19-3
FITTED WITH WESTINGHOUSE BRAKE ELECTRIC LIGHT STEAM HEATING
Nº 61228

Taken from official coach diagrams.

Interior view of a 6-wheel third converted for conductor-guard working as used on the Mildenhall branch. Note gas mantles and through end doors to enable the guard to gain access between vehicles.
Cambridgeshire Collection

Side door of first/third composite 6-wheel vehicle GER Dia. 248 converted for conductor-guard working, showing Mildenhall destination board and 3rd class door lettered as entrance to first class. *Collection J. Watling*

brake third also carried a notice on the exterior side panel of the vehicle: 'This car for Fen Ditton, Exning Road and Worlington Golf Links Halts'.

The carriage sets used for conductor-guard working were converted from ordinary main line stock and appeared in the crimson livery adopted by the GER in 1919. In due course the LNER repainted the stock in the familiar teak and brown livery. The three types used on the Mildenhall branch services were third class, GER diagram 440 converted from former main line stock diagrams 404 and 422, brake thirds to diagram 552 converted from main line stock diagram 514, and first/third composites to diagram 246 and 248 converted from main line vehicles diagrams 219, 404 and 422.

The typical formation of each set was full third, composite and brake third, although specific numbers of carriages used on the branch are unknown. Brief details of conversions are given below.

Full third diagram 440	Converted from main line thirds, built 1889-92 (diagram 404) and 1893-4 (diagram 422). 22 vehicles converted — 10 in 1922, 12 in 1923. 6 withdrawn in 1932-3, 16 in 1940.
Brake third diagram 552	Converted from main line brake thirds built 1888-96 (diagram 514). 18 vehicles converted — 4 in 1922, 14 in 1923. 5 withdrawn in 1932-3, 1 in 1937 and 12 in 1940.
First/third composite diagrams 246-248	2 converted from composites built in 1890 and 1891 (diagram 219). Converted 1922 and withdrawn 1933 and 1935. 18 converted from main line thirds built in 1892 (diagram 404) and 1893-4 (diagram 422). 9 converted in 1922, 9 in 1923. 2 vehicles withdrawn in 1932, 1 in 1934 and the remaining 15 in 1940.

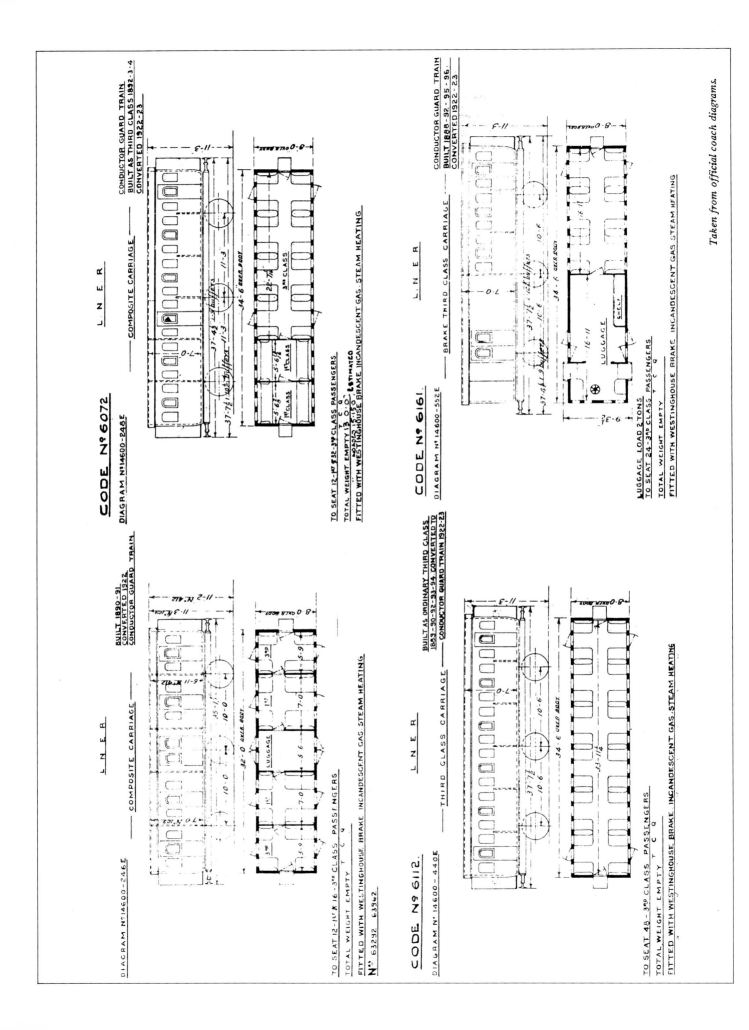

L N E R

— COMPOSITE CARRIAGE —

CODE Nº 6072

DIAGRAM Nº 14600-248E

CONDUCTOR GUARD TRAIN
BUILT AS THIRD CLASS 1892-3-4
CONVERTED 1922-23

TO SEAT 12-1ST & 32-3RD CLASS PASSENGERS
T C Q
TOTAL WEIGHT EMPTY 13-0-0 ESTIMATED
FITTED WITH WESTINGHOUSE BRAKE INCANDESCENT GAS STEAM HEATING

L N E R

— COMPOSITE CARRIAGE —

DIAGRAM Nº 14600-246E

BUILT 1890-91
CONVERTED 1922
CONDUCTOR GUARD TRAIN

CODE Nº 6112.

DIAGRAM Nº 14600-440E

TO SEAT 12-1ST & 16-3RD CLASS PASSENGERS
T C Q
TOTAL WEIGHT EMPTY
FITTED WITH WESTINGHOUSE BRAKE INCANDESCENT GAS STEAM HEATING
Nº 63292 63962

L N E R

— THIRD CLASS CARRIAGE —

BUILT AS ORDINARY THIRD CLASS
1893-90-92-93-94 CONVERTED TO
CONDUCTOR GUARD TRAIN 1922-23

TO SEAT 48-3RD CLASS PASSENGERS
T C Q
TOTAL WEIGHT EMPTY
FITTED WITH WESTINGHOUSE BRAKE INCANDESCENT GAS STEAM HEATING

L N E R

— BRAKE THIRD CLASS CARRIAGE —

CODE Nº 6161.

DIAGRAM Nº 14600-552E

CONDUCTOR GUARD TRAIN
BUILT 1888-92-95-96.
CONVERTED 1922-23

LUGGAGE LOAD 2 TONS
TO SEAT 24-3RD CLASS PASSENGERS
T C Q
TOTAL WEIGHT EMPTY
FITTED WITH WESTINGHOUSE BRAKE INCANDESCENT GAS STEAM HEATING

Taken from official coach diagrams.

'E4' 2-4-0 No. 62789 negotiating the 40 chain radius curve on the approach to Barnwell Junction with a two-coach Mildenhall-Cambridge train formed of GER bogie brake third, fitted with side steps for use at halts, and ex North Eastern Railway corridor composite.
Cambridgeshire Collection

Following the withdrawal of the 6-wheel conductor-guard stock, GER bogie main line vehicles were converted for conductor-guard operation and remained on the branch until 1957, although by that time many were withdrawn and often ordinary coaching stock was used, with a pair of portable steps for the halts. Again no specific numbers of converted vehicles are known but the following types appeared, usually formed of a two-coach formation composite and brake third, although an additional full third was attached when trains required strengthening as on Cambridge market day.

Composite diagram 227/1	Converted from main line stock built 1907/8 including four vehicles for the Norfolk Coast Express (diagram 227). Withdrawn 1954-7.
Full third diagram 419/1	Converted from main line stock built 1906/7 (diagram 419). Withdrawn between 1951-58.
Brake third diagrams 527/529	Diagram 527 built for the 'Norfolk Coast Express' and diagram 529 built for main line services. All built 1907. A total of 9 vehicles converted and equipped with retractable steps. All withdrawn 1954-57.

After withdrawal of the conductor-guard stock and before the advent of the diesel railbuses in 1958, the coaching stock regularly utilised on the Mildenhall branch services was formed of Set 106 CKBS, BSK and SKBS seating 12 first class and 118 second class passengers. The three-vehicle set weighed 94 tons and was equipped for conductor-guard working. The BSK employed was a Gresley vehicle with portable steps.

The passenger rolling stock required for branch or special traffic came under the control of Cambridge. Before the advent of steam heating on passenger trains, the foot warmer storage and supply points were Cambridge and Mildenhall. Conversion of passenger stock from oil to gas lighting was almost complete by the early 1900s and recharging of gas cylinders was carried out on the branch stock at Cambridge where repairs and routine maintenance were also undertaken.

A variety of non-passenger-carrying stock was used on the branch ranging from fitted vans for perishable produce, fruit and flowers, cattle wagons for the conveyance of livestock to neighbouring markets, horse-boxes, carriage wagons and milk vans. As with passenger vehicles, there was no restriction in force to limit GER wagon types although the great majority consisted of five plank or high-sided opens for general merchandise and covered vans for grain and flowers. Coal traffic was usually handled in local merchants' wagons or private owner colliery wagons for domestic use.

Side steps on Gresley corridor brake third in extended position as used by passengers alighting or joining the train at Fen Ditton, Exning Road or Worlington Golf Links Halts. *M. Brooks*

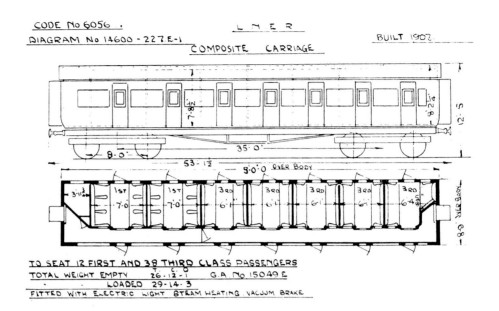

CODE No 6056 .

DIAGRAM No 14600 - 227.E-1

L N E R

COMPOSITE CARRIAGE

BUILT 1907

TO SEAT 12 FIRST AND 38 THIRD CLASS PASSENGERS

TOTAL WEIGHT EMPTY   26·12·1   G.A. No 15049 E

LOADED   29·14·3

FITTED WITH ELECTRIC LIGHT STEAM HEATING VACUUM BRAKE

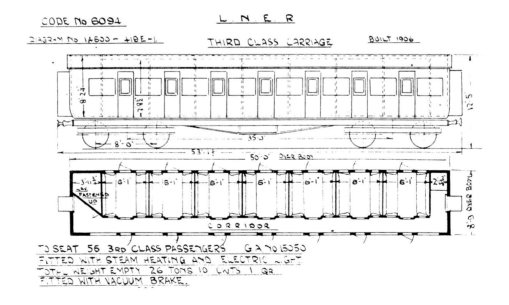

CODE No 6094

DIAGRAM No 14600 - 418 E-1

L N E R

THIRD CLASS CARRIAGE   BUILT 1906

TO SEAT 56 3RD CLASS PASSENGERS   G.A. No 15050

FITTED WITH STEAM HEATING AND ELECTRIC LIGHT

TOTAL WEIGHT EMPTY 26 TONS 10 CWTS 1 QR

FITTED WITH VACUUM BRAKE.

Taken from official coach diagrams.

CODE Nº 6138.

DIAGRAM Nº 14600-527E.

L N E R

BRAKE THIRD CLASS CARRIAGE.

BUILT 1907

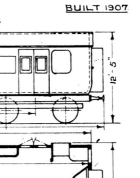

TO SEAT 24 THIRD CLASS PASSENGERS.

TOTAL WEIGHT EMPTY 25-16-1.   G.A. Nº 15071E.

LOADED 30-17-3.   LUGGAGE LOAD 3½ TONS.

FITTED WITH ELECTRIC LIGHT. STEAM HEATING. VACUUM BRAKE.

CODE Nº 6140.

DIAGRAM Nº 14600-529 E.

L N E R

BRAKE THIRD CLASS CARRIAGE.

BUILT 1907

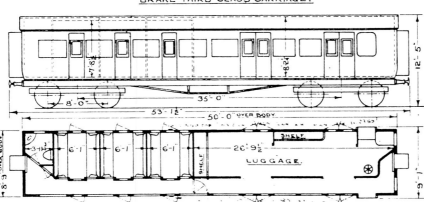

TO SEAT 24 THIRD CLASS PASSENGERS.

TOTAL WEIGHT EMPTY 25-11-3.   G A Nº 15071E.

LOADED 30-13-1.   LUGGAGE LOAD 3½ TONS.

FITTED WITH ELECTRIC LIGHT. STEAM HEATING VACUUM BRAKE.

Taken from official coach diagrams.

CAMBRIDGE, FORDHAM AND MILDENHALL

Single Line between Barnwell Junction and Mildenhall

DOWN WEEKDAYS

M. C.	No.	1	2	3	4	5	6	7	8	9	10	11	12	13	14	15
	Class			B				B		K			B		B	
	Description															
				am				am		am			PM		PM	
	Cambridge			6 33				10 28		10 35			4 27		7 45	
1 56	Barnwell Junction (S)			6 36				10 31					4 30		7 48	
	Barnwell Junction			6 37				10 32		10 45			4 31		7 49	
2 31	Fen Ditton Halt							10 35					4 34		7 52	
4 49	Quy			6 45				10 41		✳			4 40		7 58	
6 5	Bottisham & Lode (S)			6 50				10 44		11 10			4 43		8 1	
	Bottisham & Lode			6 51				10 45		11 20			4 44		8 2	
8 2	Swaffhamprior			6 56				10 50		11 35			4 49		8 7	
	Burwell (S)			7 1				10 54		11 40			4 53		8 11	
9 75	Burwell			7 3				10 55		11 50			4 54		8 12	
10 50	Exning Road Halt							10 58					4 57		8 15	
13 36	Fordham (S)			7 11				11 5		12 0			5 4		8 22	
	Fordham			7 14				11 10		12 20			5 10		8 24	
16 58	Isleham (S)			7 21				11 16		12 30			5 16		8 30	
	Isleham			7 22				11 17		12 50			5 17		8 31	
19 68	Worlington Golf Links H.							11 24					5 24		8 38	
20 59	Mildenhall (S)			7 31				11 27		1 0			5 27		8 41	

Passenger trains between Cambridge and Mildenhall are worked on the " Conductor-Guard " principle.

MILDENHALL, FORDHAM AND CAMBRIDGE

Single Line between Mildenhall and Barnwell Junction

UP WEEKDAYS

M. C.	No.	1	2	3	4	5	6	7	8	9	10	11	12	13	14	15
	Class		B		B				K			B		B		
	Description															
			am		am				PM			PM		PM		
	Mildenhall (S)		7 45		11 50				3 0			5 48		9 0		
71	Worlington Golf Links H.		7 49		11 54							5 52				
4 1	Isleham (S)		7 55		12 0				3 10			5 58		9 8		
	Isleham		7 56		12 1				3 20			5 59		9 9		
7 23	Fordham (S)		8 2		12 7				3 30			6 6		9 15		
	Fordham		8 7		12 9				4 15			6 7		9 17		
10 9	Exning Road Halt		8 14		12 16							6 15				
10 66	Burwell (S)		8 16		12 18				4 35			6 17				
	Burwell		8 17		12 19				4 55			6 18				
12 57	Swaffhamprior		8 21		12 23				✳			6 22				
14 54	Bottisham & Lode (S)		8 26		12 27				5 15			6 26				
	Bottisham & Lode		8 27		12 28				5 30			6 27				
16 10	Quy		8 31		12 32				✳			6 31				
18 28	Fen Ditton Halt		8 36		12 37							6 36				
19 13	Barnwell Junction (S)		8 38		12 39				5 55			6 38				
	Barnwell Junction		8 39		12 41				6 0			6 39				
20 59	Cambridge		8 44		12 45				6 5			6 43				

13 To Cambridge, via Newmarket.

Passenger trains between Mildenhall and Cambridge are worked on the " Conductor-Guard " principle.

CHAPTER EIGHT

NATIONALISATION AND CLOSURE

THE nationalisation of the railways from 1st January 1948 brought few changes to the Mildenhall line which retained its GER/LNER atmosphere until the withdrawal of steam traction from the branch. Most stocks of LNER tickets remained in use until the line closed although a few in constant demand were replaced by tickets bearing the legend 'Railway Executive' or 'British Railways'. Locomotives working the line soon lost the NE or LNER identity from their side tanks or tenders, although varnished teak or brown paint remained the livery on branch coaching stock until the introduction of diesel traction.

British Railways made few alterations to the timetable in which trains were inconveniently timed for people wishing to work in Cambridge or Mildenhall and travelling from other stations on the branch. Even market day traffic to Cambridge, Newmarket and Bury St. Edmunds was a shadow of pre-war numbers, and takings at stations and by the conductor-guard were minimal. Several days went by without passengers joining or alighting at the halts, with Exning Road the least used. Needless to say, the finances of the passenger service on the line came in for serious investigation by the new management. Freight traffic also showed a decline in the late 'forties and early 'fifties as fuel rationing ended and farmers and traders preferred to despatch or receive their produce and goods by motor lorry. Livestock traffic also declined rapidly as cattle and sheep for markets in the surrounding area were sent by road, a method which obviated the double handling of animals at both forwarding and receiving stations.

In 1950 public demand and the easing of coal supplies enabled the later evening services, withdrawn three years earlier, to be reintroduced, departing Cambridge at 7.45 p.m. and returning from Mildenhall via Newmarket at 9.00 p.m. Unfortunately, after two years, lack of patronage forced BR to again withdraw these late trains.

The increase in car ownership and decrease in passengers using the railway services brought about the closure of two near neighbours, the Elsenham-Thaxted branch, which opened as late as 1st April 1913, closed to passenger traffic on 15th September 1952 and completely on 1st June 1953, and the Bury St. Edmunds-Thetford line which closed to passenger traffic on and from 8th June 1953.

Fortunately, not all traffic declined and the daily and Sunday excursions offered became very popular. Passen-

'E4' class 2-4-0 No. 62781 waits to depart from Mildenhall with the 5.48 p.m. train to Cambridge on 18th April 1949. No. 62781 received the side window cab when allocated to work the Darlington—Tebay/Penrith services in the 1930s. *W. A. Camwell*

In the early 1950s the engine working the afternoon Cambridge–Mildenhall train also worked a short round trip to Newmarket which involved tender-first running in one direction. Here 'E4' 2–4–0 No. 62785 is shown at Newmarket with the Mildenhall train. Newmarket station signalbox was later blown down by a mini-tornado.
Dr. I. C. Allen

Worlington overbridge No. 2257 and site of former halt, after the removal of the track. The bridge was subsequently demolished.

P. Turner

trailing connection from the 'up' main line led past the former station to an oil company terminal on the site of the former brewery company's siding. The oil terminal is now rail served on an 'as and when required' basis by freight trip from Cambridge yard. Barnwell Junction station buildings are almost intact with additions, and are used by Kindrum Boarding Kennels Ltd. Beyond the oil terminal the former trackbed can be traced to Howard Road but beyond this point a housing estate has obliterated the route. No trace exists of Fen Ditton bridge or halt but the trackbed thence to Quy is recognisable except where the new Cambridge by-pass road has intersected the railway at right-angles.

Quy station building still stands and since 1980 has been used by the Land and Water Resource Consultants Ltd. who carry out geological and hydrological consultancy work. Beyond the station and almost as far as Bottisham and Lode the trackbed can only be traced for short sections as much has been ploughed in as extension of fields by farmers. Bottisham and Lode station has been restored by its present owners whilst the former goods yard and trackbed are used for storage of timber and coal. From Bottisham the line of route has been ploughed up and obliterated, the only section extant being some quarter mile on either side of No. 3 Gate House on

Swaffham Bulbeck Fen. The bridge No. 2239 still spans Swaffham Bulbeck Lode as evidence of the former railway.

Swaffhamprior station has been converted into a private residence but beyond the former station the line has been obliterated, ploughed up as far as the former Reach road bridge. Beyond this site the gap provided for the route of the railway through the Devils Dyke can be seen. The site of Burwell station is now used as a car park by Tillotson's Corrugated Cases Ltd. whilst from there to Exning Road Halt is ploughed in as additional arable land by local farmers. Exning road bridge survives and the route beyond the structure can be easily traced to the junction at Fordham where only the station house remains. From Fordham the curve of the line has mostly been obliterated although Cambridge road overbridge stands gaunt and stark in the middle of arable land. The Soham road bridge has been demolished and the trackbed in the vicinity cultivated, whilst a farm track occupies the trackbed between Fordham Moor road overbridge and Fordham road bridge. The station at Isleham has been converted into industrial premises by Tenrich Tyres Ltd. who also use the former goods yard for storage. From Isleham to Worlington the line of route can be traced in places but the overbridge No. 2257 by the site of the former halt has been demolished.

APPENDICES

Appendix 1
MILDENHALL BRANCH
LENGTH OF PLATFORMS, SIDINGS, ETC.

Location	Miles & chains ex Liverpool St.	Platforms Up ft in length	Platforms Down	Loop ft	Sidings ft in length
Barnwell Junction	57 m 28 ch	370	380		440
					440
					510 Back Road
Fen Ditton Halt	58 m 3 ch	30			
Quy	60 m 21 ch	380		920	240 Refuge Road
					220 Dock Road
					50 Headshunt
Bottisham and Lode	61 m 57 ch	350	360	600	250 Dock Road
					250 Refuge Road
					60 Headshunt
Swaffhamprior	63 m 54 ch	360		850	100 Refuge Road
					200 Dock Road
					180 Coal Road
					50 Headshunt
Burwell	65 m 45 ch	345	350	680	150 Dock Road
					330 Down Refuge
					370 Yard Loop
Exning Road Halt	66 m 22 ch	30			
Fordham	69 m 8 ch	375	370	700*	500 Straight Road
					480 Shed Road
					340 Coal Road
					710 Back Road
					640 Headshunt
Isleham	72 m 30 ch	380	360	850	580 Refuge Road
					180 Dock Road
Worlington Golf Links Halt	75 m 40 ch	30			
Mildenhall	76 m 31 ch		365	650	290 Turntable Road
					610 Shedside Road
					220 Spur
					620 Shed Road
					210 Dock Road
					650 Back Road

* original length of loop — later replaced by double track

Appendix 2
BARNWELL JUNCTION – MILDENHALL LEVEL CROSSINGS

No.	Location	Mileage M ch ex Liverpool St.		Local Name	Status
1	Barnwell Junc and Quy	57	72	Fisons	Public Footpath
2	,,	58	20	Fisons	Occupation
3	,,	58	26	Fisons	,,
4	,,	58	36		Public Footpath
5	,,	58	59	Fisons	Occupation
6	,,	59	03	Fisons	,,
7	,,	59	44	Fisons	,,
8	,,	59	66	No. 1 Gatehouse	Public Road
9	,,	59	77	Francis	Occupation
10	,,	60	16	Quy Station	Public Road
11	Quy and Bottisham	60	54	No. 2 Gatehouse	,,
12	,,	60	69	Francis	Occupation
13	,,	61	05	Francis	,,
14	,,	61	06	Francis	,,
15	,,	61	16		Public Footpath
16	,,	61	29	Francis	Occupation
17	,,	61	52	Bottisham Station	Public Road
18	Bottisham and Swaffhamprior	62	07	Grawny Drove	Public Footpath
19	,,	62	19	Webbs	Occupation
20	,,	62	35	Webbs	,,
21	,,	62	42	Docking Drove	Public Footpath
22	,,	62	69	Hundred Acre Drove	,,
23	,,	63	02	No. 3 Gatehouse	Public Road
No number	,,	63	03		Public Footpath
24	,,	63	17	Babcocks	Occupation
25	,,	63	21	Butters	,,
26	,,	63	41	Woollards	,,
27	Swaffhamprior and Burwell	63	59	Swaffhamprior Station	Public Road
28	,,	63	76	Ambrose	Occupation
29	,,	63	77	Ambrose	,,
30	,,	64	01	Clarks	,,
31	,,	64	19	Woollard	,,
32	,,	64	52		Public Footpath
33	,,	64	62		,,
34	,,	65	09	Clarks	Occupation
35	,,	65	25	Drivers	,,
36	,,	65	27	Masons	,,
37	Burwell and Fordham	65	55		,,
38	,,	65	64	Bonnetts	,,
39	,,	66	01	Masons	,,
40	,,	66	21	Jeffreys	,,
41	,,	67	14	No. 4 Gatehouse	Public Road
42	,,	67	41	Meachers	Occupation
43	,,	67	60	Meachers	,,
44	,,	67	67	Meachers	,,
45	,,	68	01	Glanilly	,,
46	,,	68	24	Glanilly	,,
47	,,	68	29	Glanilly	,,
48	,,	68	34	Howletts	,,
49	,,	68	61	Howletts	,,
50	,,	68	77	Howletts	,,
51	Fordham and Isleham	69	66	Townsend	,,
52	,,	70	08	Bockings	,,
53	,,	70	36	Collis	,,
54	,,	70	63	Webbs	,,
55	,,	71	04	Webbs	,,
56	,,	71	14	Robins	,,
57	,,	71	45	Robins	,,
58	,,	71	60	Robins	,,
59	Isleham and Mildenhall	73	25	Robins	,,
60	,,	73	43	Abrays	,,
61	,,	74	22	Smiths	,,
62	,,	74	51	Smiths	,,
63	,,	74	54	Sawden	,,
64	,,	74	67	Sawden	,,
65	,,	75	12	Matlocks	,,
66	,,	75	30	Kants	,,
67	,,	75	70	Kants	,,
68	,,	76	09	Parkers	,,
69	,,	76	21	Parkers	,,

APPENDIX 3   BARNWELL JUNCTION — MILDENHALL BRIDGES

No.	Location	Mileage M ch	Local Name	Under or over	Type	Spans	Square span between abutments or supports ft in	Skew span between abutments or supports ft in	Width ft in	Depth of construction ft in	Distance from road or surface of water to rail ft in	Construction	Remarks
2236	Barnwell Junction and Quy	58 06	Fen Ditton Road	Over	Public	1	25 0	27 9	25 1	3 6	19 6	Brick abutments. Brick arch and parapets	Maintenance to Cambridge CC 17.4.1934.
2237	"	58 43	High Ditch Road	Over	Public	1	25 0	34 11	20 3	3 6	19 6	Brick abutments. Brick arch and parapets	Maintenance to Cambridge CC 17.4.1934.
2238	Quy and Bottisham	61 52	Bottisham Lode	Under	Canal	1	12 0	14 7	14 0	1 6	7 6	Brick abutments. Longitudinal trough girders. Longitudinal running timbers	Sold to Lord Fairhaven 19.5.1969.
2238 A	"	61 52	Drove Bridge (down side)	Over	Occupation	1	12 0	14 7	15 0	2 6	8 6	Brick abutments. Brick arch and parapets	Carries drove over Lode adjacent to bridge No. 2238.
2239	Bottisham and Swaffhamprior	63 0	Swaffham Lode	Under	Canal & Public Towpath	1	20 0		14 6	2 0	10 6	Brick abutments. Side girder. Cross girder. Brick jack arches. Plate parapets, Ballast LR	Cambridge CC maintenance from 17.4.1934.
2240	Swaffhamprior and Burwell	64 39	Reach Road	Over	Public	1	25 0	25 11	20 5	3 6	18 6	Brick abutments. Brick arch and parapets	Cambridge CC maintenance from 17.4.1934.
2241	Burwell and Fordham	65 48	Burwell Road	Over	Public	1	25 0		25 5	3 3	18 0	Brick abutments. Brick arch and low brick parapets. Iron fence above.	Cambridge CC maintenance from 17.4.1934.
2242	"	66 23	Exning Road	Over	Public	1	25 0	35 9	20 5	3 6	18 6	Brick abutments. Brick arch and parapets	Cambridge CC maintenance from 17.4.1934.
2243	"	68 20	Stream	Under	Stream	1	6 0	6 4	16 6	1 9	5 9	Brick abutments, arch and invert 6 ft deep	
2244	Fordham and Isleham	69 41	Cambridge Road	Over	Public	1	25 1	31 3	15 3	3 6	18 3	Brick abutments. Brick arch and parapets	Cambridge CC maintenance from 17.4.1934
2245	"	69 71	Lark Hall	Over	Public	1	25 0		15 3	3 6	18 3	Brick abutments. Brick arch and parapets	Cambridge CC maintenance from 17.4.1934.
2246	"	70 13	Soham Road and Carter Street	Over	Public	1	25 0	25 6	20 3	3 9	18 9	Brick abutments. Brick arch and parapets	Cambridge CC maintenance from 17.4.1934.
2247	"	70 66	River Snail	Under		1	13 8	14 8	14 9	1 9	5 9	Brick abutments, longitudinal trough girders, longitudinal running timbers TR	Cambridge CC maintenance from 17.4.1934.
2248	"	71 02	Fordham Moor Road	Over	Public	1	24 9	26 2	15 2	3 7	18 2	Brick abutments, brick jack arches and parapet girders	Cambridge CC maintenance from 17.4.1934
2249	"	71 72	Fordham Road	Over	Public	1	25 0	34 9	20 6	3 6	18 9	Brick abutments. Brick arch and parapets	Cambridge CC maintenance from 17.4.1934.
2250	Isleham and Mildenhall	72 35	Isleham Station Road	Over	Public	1	25 0		25 4	2 9	17 9	Brick abutments. Brick arch and parapets	Cambridge CC maintenance from 17.4.1934.
2251	"	73 02	Beck Row	Over	Public	1	25 0	38 0	20 6	3 3	18 0	Brick abutments. Brick arch and parapets	Cambridge CC maintenance from 17.4.1934.
2252	"	73 24		Under	Occupation	1	9 3		14 9	2 9	10 9	Brick abutments. Brick arch and parapets	Cambridge CC maintenance from 17.4.1934.
2253	"	73 29	Lee Brook	Under	Stream	1	14 7	15 3	14 0	3 0	14 0	Brick abutments. Brick parapets, Brick arch with concrete lining	
2254	"	73 78	Four Cross Ways	Over	Public	1	25 0	26 3	25 4	4 0	18 6	Brick abutments. Brick arch and parapets	West Suffolk CC maintenance from 21.5.1931.
2255	"	74 75	Freckenham Road	Over	Public	1	24 10	36 0	25 3	4 0	18 6	Brick abutments. Brick arch and parapets	West Suffolk CC maintenance from 1.5.1923.
2256	"	75 33	Manor Farm	Over	Occupation	1	25 0		15 3	4 0	18 6	Brick abutments. Brick arch and parapets	West Suffolk CC maintenance from 1.5.1923.
2257	"	75 42	Worlington Halt	Over	Public	1	25 0	25 9	25 9	4 6	19 0	Brick abutments. Brick arch and parapets	West Suffolk CC maintenance from 1.5.1923.

Appendix 4

EXTRACT FROM INSTRUCTIONS INCLUDED IN
GER 1919 APPENDIX TO THE WORKING TIMETABLE

256

Goods Sidings—*contd.*

Commercial Brewery Company's Sidings on Mildenhall Branch, near Barnwell Junction,
with Points facing Down trains.

The Points are controlled by "Annett's" Patent Lock, the key of which is attached to the "Barnwell Junction and Bottisham" Train Staff; the same key also being used to release the Lock at Francis' Siding between Quy and Bottisham.

Trucks for the above Sidings must be worked by Pilot engine from Cambridge into the Barnwell Junction Sidings, with Break attached in front (a Shunter, provided with the necessary signals, riding on the last Truck), or out of the Barnwell Junction Sidings, between 1.0 p.m. and 1.50 p.m., or between 3.50 p.m. and 4.20 p.m. The Pilot engine must be shunted on to the rear of the Trucks in the Barnwell Junction Sidings, and after departure of the Up Branch Passenger train and on his receiving the Signalman's authority to do so, the Engine-driver must draw the Trucks out on to the Up Main Line at Barnwell Junction, and set them back into the **Up Loop Line**; after the Train Staff has been handed to him, he must carefully back the Trucks to the Sidings, where the necessary shunting operations are to be carried out, after which the engine and Trucks, with the Break in rear, must return to Barnwell Junction Sidings, or Cambridge, as may be required.

The Pilot engine must always be accompanied by a competent Shunter, who must obtain the key of the Siding Gate from the Station Master, and the Train Staff from the Driver. The Shunter must unlock and open the Siding Gate, and unlock the Points, and after the shunting operations are completed he must see for himself that the Trucks are placed inside the Catch Points and Gate, that the Gate is locked, and that the Points are replaced and locked in their proper position; he must then hand the Train Staff back to the Engine-driver, and, on his return, give up the key of the Siding Gate to the Station Master.

These Sidings are under the supervision of the Barnwell Junction Station Master, who must see that the Train Staff is handed to, and obtained from, the Engine-driver in all cases of the Sidings being used and the Single Line fouled.

Francis' Siding, about 550 yards on Bottisham side of Quy Station,
with Points facing Down trains.

The Points are controlled by "Annett's" Patent Lock; the key of which is attached to the "Barnwell Junction and Bottisham" Train Staff; the same key also being used to release the Lock at Commercial Brewery Company's Sidings at Barnwell Junction.

All Trucks for the Siding are to be taken through to Bottisham Station.

When the Engine-driver of the train appointed to work the Siding is in possession of a Train Staff Ticket on leaving Bottisham for Cambridge, the Station Master at Bottisham, must, when the train is required to call at the Siding, after handing the Train Staff Ticket to the Engine-driver, deliver the "Barnwell Junction and Bottisham" Train Staff to a competent man of his Station Staff, who must accompany the train to the Siding. After the work is done, the man from Bottisham must see for himself that the Trucks are placed inside the Catch Points, and that the Points are replaced and locked in their proper position before allowing the train to proceed on its journey. When this has been done, he must at once return on foot to Bottisham Station and deliver up the Staff to the Station Master.

When the Engine-driver of the train appointed to work the Siding is in possession of the "Barnwell Junction and Bottisham" Train Staff, the Station Master at Bottisham must send a competent man of the Station Staff to the Siding, who must see for himself that the Trucks are placed inside the Catch Points, and that the Points are replaced and locked in their proper position before handing the Train Staff back to the Engine-driver.

This Siding is under the supervision of the Bottisham Station Master.

Stephenson's Siding between Burwell and Fordham,
with Points facing Down trains.

The Points are controlled by "Annett's" Patent Lock, the key of which is attached to the "Burwell and Fordham" Train Staff.

All Trucks for the Siding are to be taken through to Fordham Station.

When the Engine-driver of the train appointed to work the Siding is in possession of a Train Staff Ticket on leaving Fordham for Cambridge, the Station Master at Fordham, must, when the train is required to call at the Siding, after handing the Train Staff Ticket to the Engine-driver, deliver the "Burwell and Fordham" Train Staff to a competent man of his Station Staff, who must accompany the train to the Siding. After the work is done, this man must see for himself that the Trucks are placed inside the Catch Points, and that the Points are replaced and locked in their proper position before allowing the train to proceed on its journey. When this has been done, he must at once return on foot to Fordham Station and deliver up the Staff to the Station Master.

When the Engine-driver of the train appointed to work the Siding is in possession of the "Burwell and Fordham" Train Staff, the Station Master at Fordham must send a competent man of the Station Staff to the Siding, who must see for himself that the Trucks are placed inside the Catch Points, and that the Points are replaced and locked in their proper position before handing the Train Staff back to the Engine-driver.

This Siding is under the supervision of the Fordham Station Master.

ACKNOWLEDGEMENTS

The publication of this history would not have been possible without the help of many people who have been kind enough to assist. In particular I should like to thank Peter Turner who has made a great study of the line and originally published his findings in a small booklet and has since put all his records at my disposal. Also many thanks to the following: the late A. R. Cox, the late W. Fenton, the late J. Mott, the late G. Woodcock, R. Debenham, G. O'Dell, G. Parslew, W. Suddaby, C. Richardson, B. Witt, J. Watling, D. Taylor, H. C. Casserley, Dr. I. C. Allen, P. Webber, M. Brooks, B. D. J. Walsh, G. Pember, P. Proud, Canon C. Bayes, R. C. Riley, R. Powell and the many other active and retired railway staff, some of whom worked on the line, also members of the Great Eastern Railway Society.

Thanks are also due to The Public Record Office, British Rail Eastern Region, The House of Lords Record Office, The British Museum Newspaper Library, Cambridgeshire County Record Office, Suffolk County Record Office and County of Cambridge Library.

Special thanks go to my mother who typed some of the manuscript before her death and to Mavis Herbert who at short notice so ably completed the typing, also to my wife Madge for checking some of the text and for suffering the Mildenhall Branch for many months.

BIBLIOGRAPHY

GENERAL WORKS

Allen, C. J.	*The Great Eastern Railway*	Ian Allan
Gordon, D. I.	*Regional History of Railways of Great Britain Vol. 5 — Eastern Counties*	David and Charles
Gordon, W. J.	*Our Home Railways Vol. 1*	
Joby, R.S.	*Forgotten Railways of East Anglia*	David and Charles
Tatford, B.	*Story of British Railways*	
RCTS	*Locomotives of the LNER (various volumes)*	RCTS
Aldrich, C. L.	*GER Locomotives*	
Turner, Peter	*By Rail to Mildenhall*	Mildenhall Museum Publications

PERIODICALS

Bradshaw's Railway Guide
Bradshaw's Railway Manual
British Railways (Eastern Region) Magazine
Buses
Great Eastern Railway Magazine
Herepath's Journal
Locomotive Carriage and Wagon Review
Locomotive Magazine
LNER Magazine
Railway Magazine
Railway Times
Railway World
Railway Year Book
Trains Illustrated

NEWSPAPERS

Cambridge Chronicle
Cambridge Independent Press
Cambridge Observer and County Guardian
Eastern Daily Press
Suffolk Chronicle and Mercury
also Minute Books of the
Eastern Counties Railway
Great Eastern Railway
London and North Eastern Railway
London and North Western Railway

Working and Public Timetables: GER, LNER and BR (ER)

Appendices to Working Timetables: GER, LNER and BR (ER)